ORPHAN BLACK

TEMPLE STREET PRODUCTIONS

IDW

Facebook: **facebook.com/idwpublishing**
Twitter: **@idwpublishing**
YouTube: **youtube.com/idwpublishing**
Tumblr: **tumblr.idwpublishing.com**
Instagram: **instagram.com/idwpublishing**

COVER ART BY
NICK RUNGE

COLLECTION EDITS BY
JUSTIN EISINGER
AND ALONZO SIMON

COLLECTION DESIGN BY
JEFF POWELL

978-1-63140-410-8   18 17 16 15   1 2 3 4

Originally published as ORPHAN BLACK issues #1–5.

Ted Adams, CEO & Publisher
Greg Goldstein, President & COO
Robbie Robbins, EVP/Sr. Graphic Artist
Chris Ryall, Chief Creative Officer/Editor-in-Chief
Matthew Ruzicka, CPA, Chief Financial Officer
Alan Payne, VP of Sales
Dirk Wood, VP of Marketing
Lorelei Bunjes, VP of Digital Services
Jeff Webber, VP of Digital Publishing & Business Development

IDW founded by Ted Adams, Alex Garner,
Kris Oprisko, and Robbie Robbins

Special thanks to Mackenzie Donaldson for
her invaluable assistance.

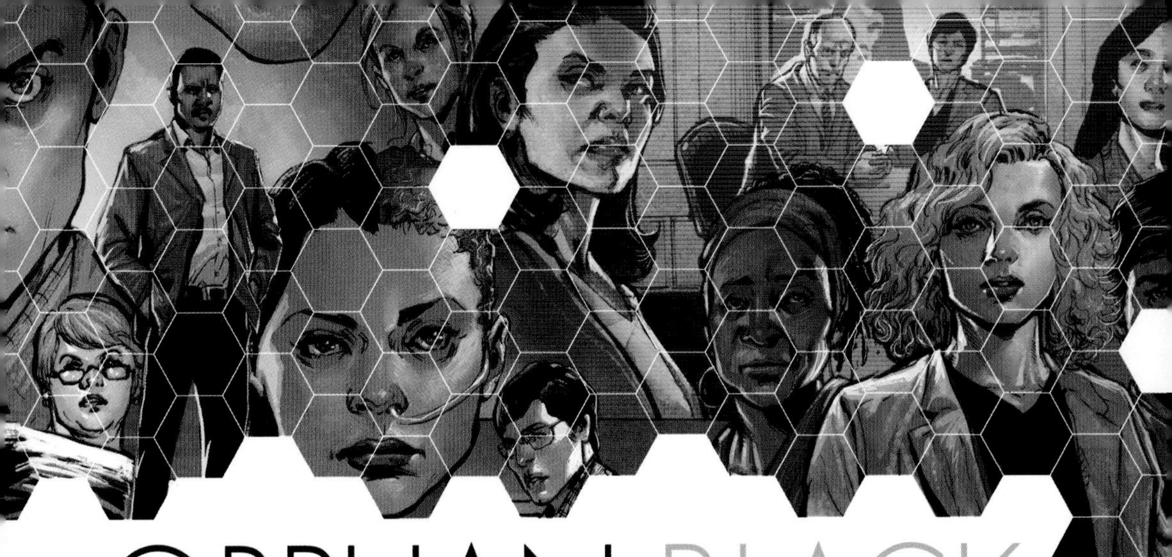

ORPHAN BLACK

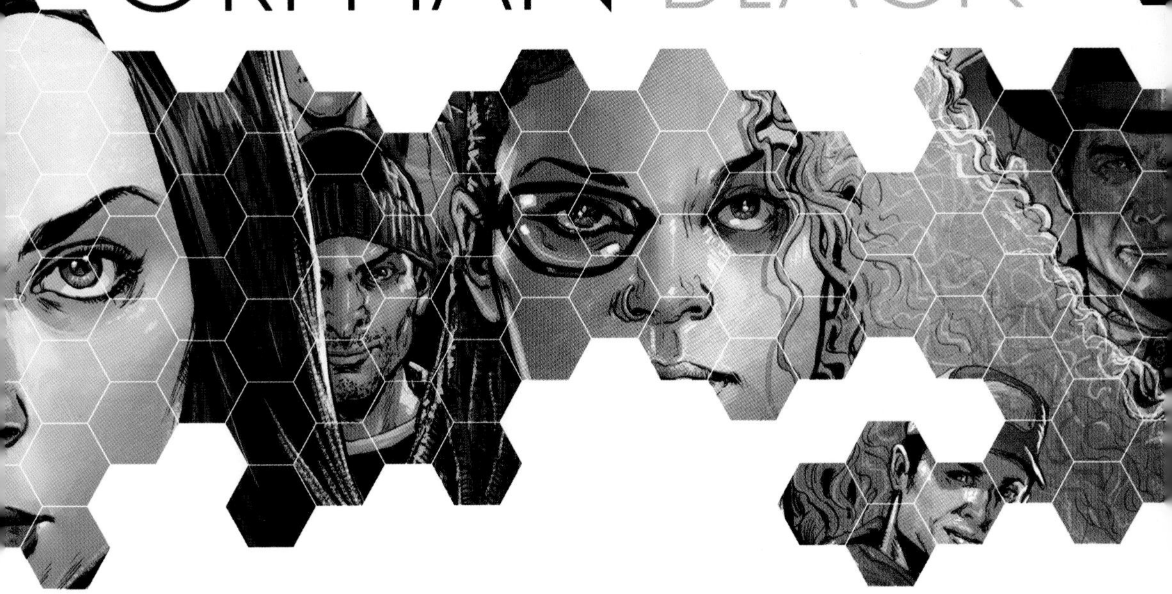

WRITTEN BY
GRAEME MANSON AND JOHN FAWCETT WITH JODY HOUSER

SARAH & HELENA

ART BY
SZYMON KUDRANSKI
COLORS BY
MAT LOPES

ALISON, COSIMA & RACHEL

ART BY
ALAN QUAH WITH CAT STAGGS
& WAYNE NICHOLS
COLORS BY
CHRIS FENOGLIO

LETTERS BY
NEIL UYETAKE

SERIES EDITS BY
DENTON J. TIPTON

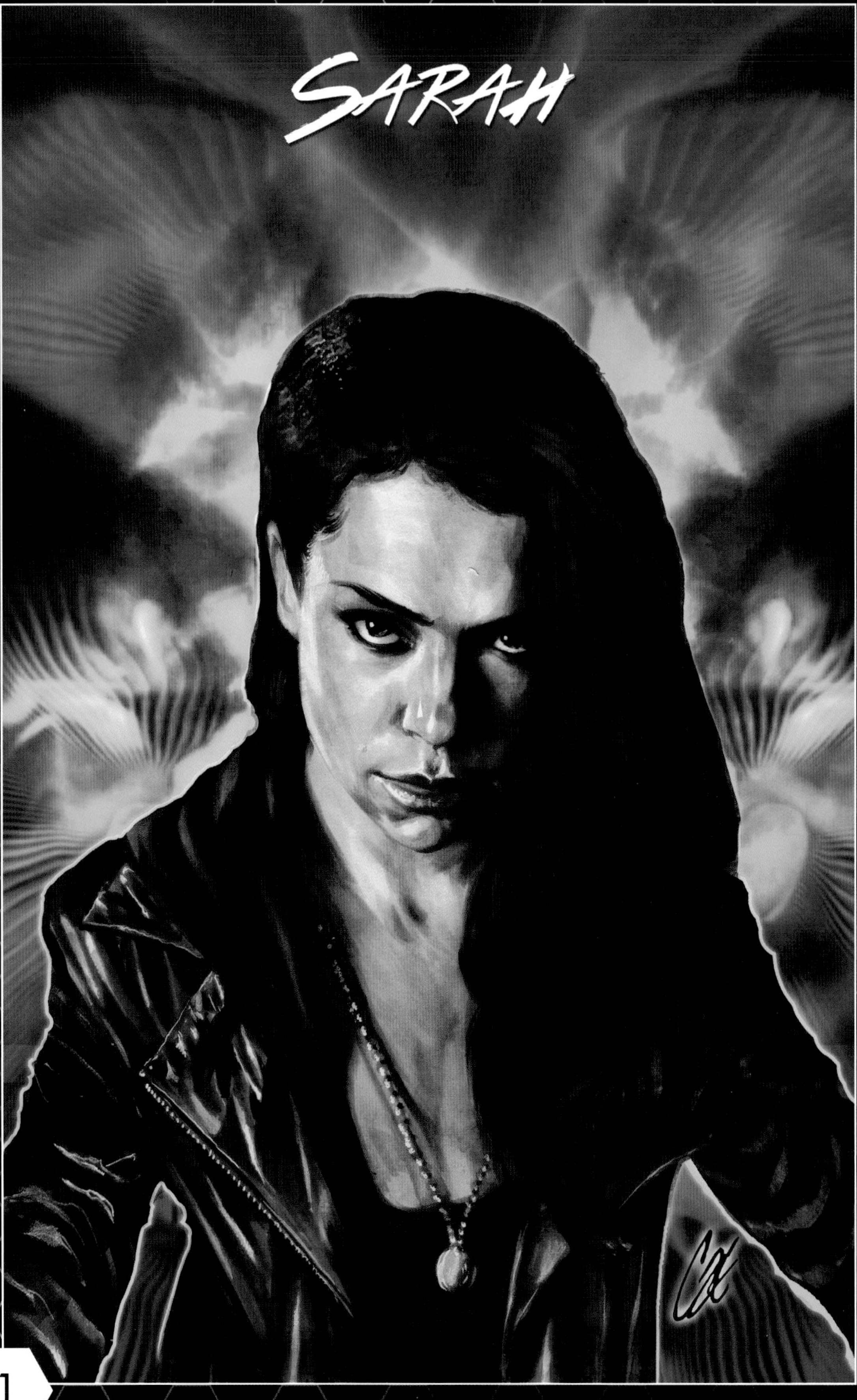
SARAH

BY **CAT STAGGS**

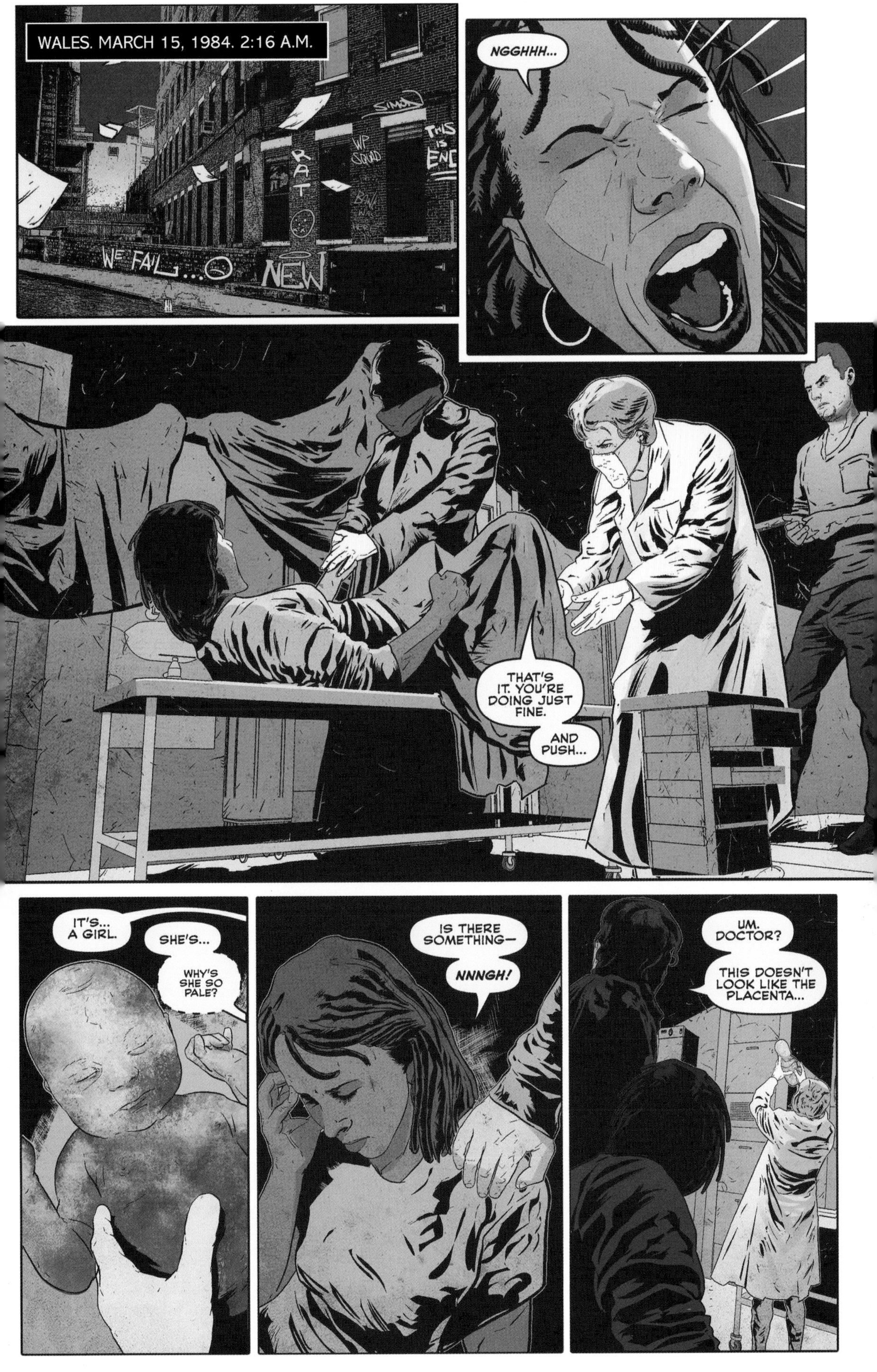
WALES. MARCH 15, 1984. 2:16 A.M.
WP SQUAD
RAT
THIS IS END
WE FAIL...
NEW
NGGHHH...
THAT'S IT. YOU'RE DOING JUST FINE.
AND PUSH...
IT'S... A GIRL.
SHE'S...
WHY'S SHE SO PALE?
IS THERE SOMETHING—
NNNGH!
UM. DOCTOR?
THIS DOESN'T LOOK LIKE THE PLACENTA...

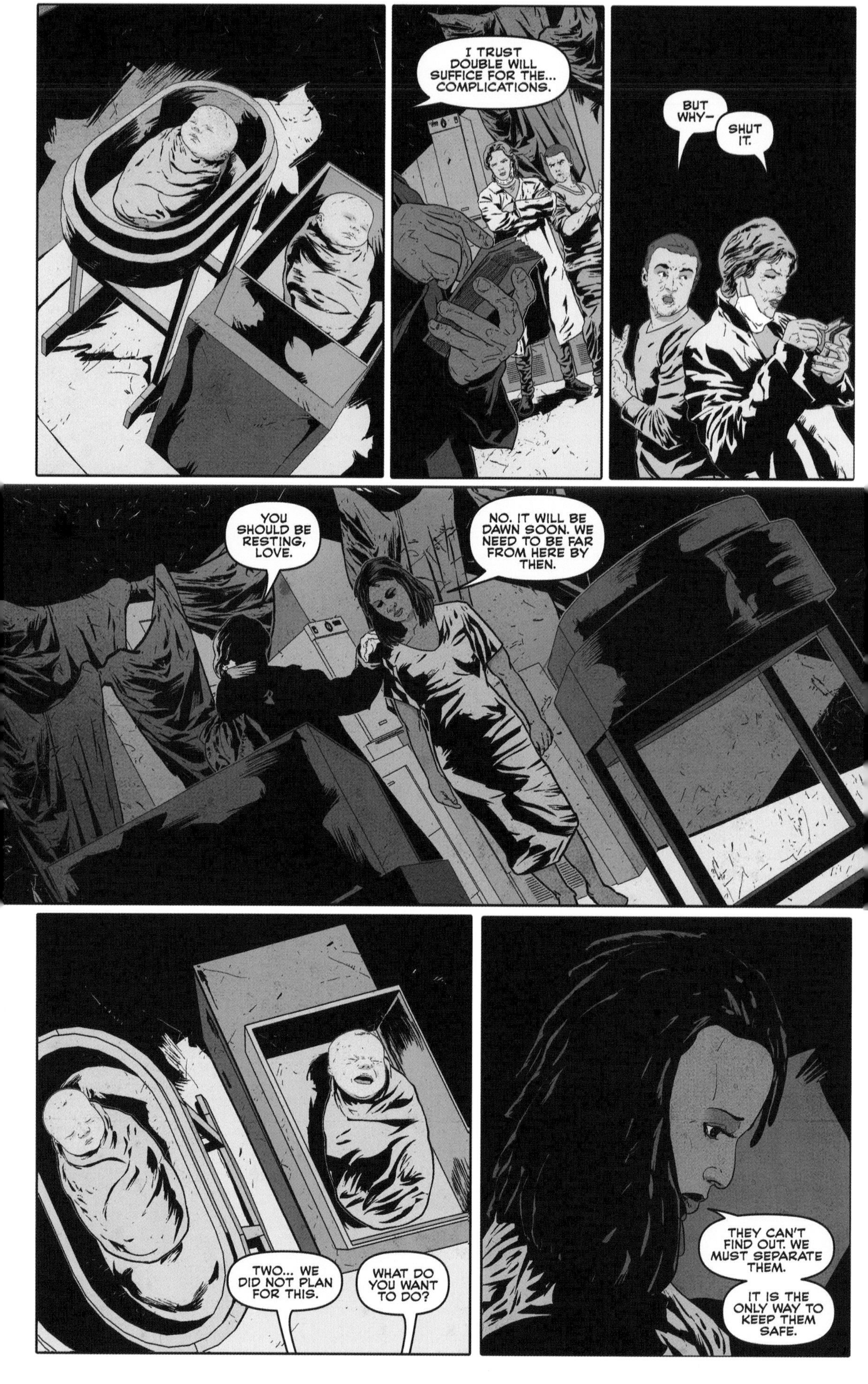
I TRUST DOUBLE WILL SUFFICE FOR THE... COMPLICATIONS.
BUT WHY–
SHUT IT.
YOU SHOULD BE RESTING, LOVE.
NO. IT WILL BE DAWN SOON. WE NEED TO BE FAR FROM HERE BY THEN.
TWO... WE DID NOT PLAN FOR THIS.
WHAT DO YOU WANT TO DO?
THEY CAN'T FIND OUT. WE MUST SEPARATE THEM.
IT IS THE ONLY WAY TO KEEP THEM SAFE.

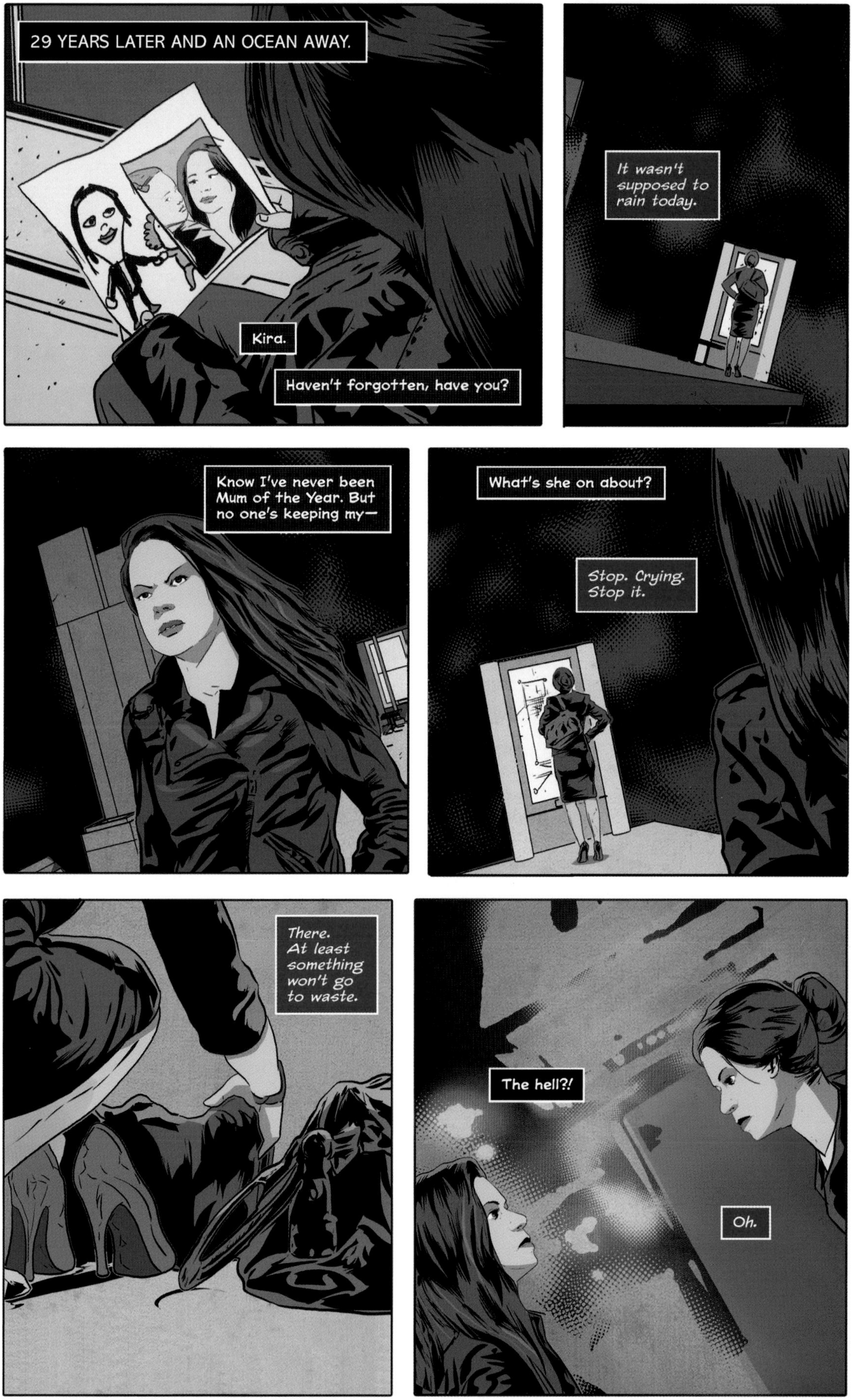
29 YEARS LATER AND AN OCEAN AWAY.
Kira.
Haven't forgotten, have you?
It wasn't supposed to rain today.
Know I've never been Mum of the Year. But no one's keeping my—
What's she on about?
Stop. Crying. Stop it.
There. At least something won't go to waste.
The hell?!
Oh.

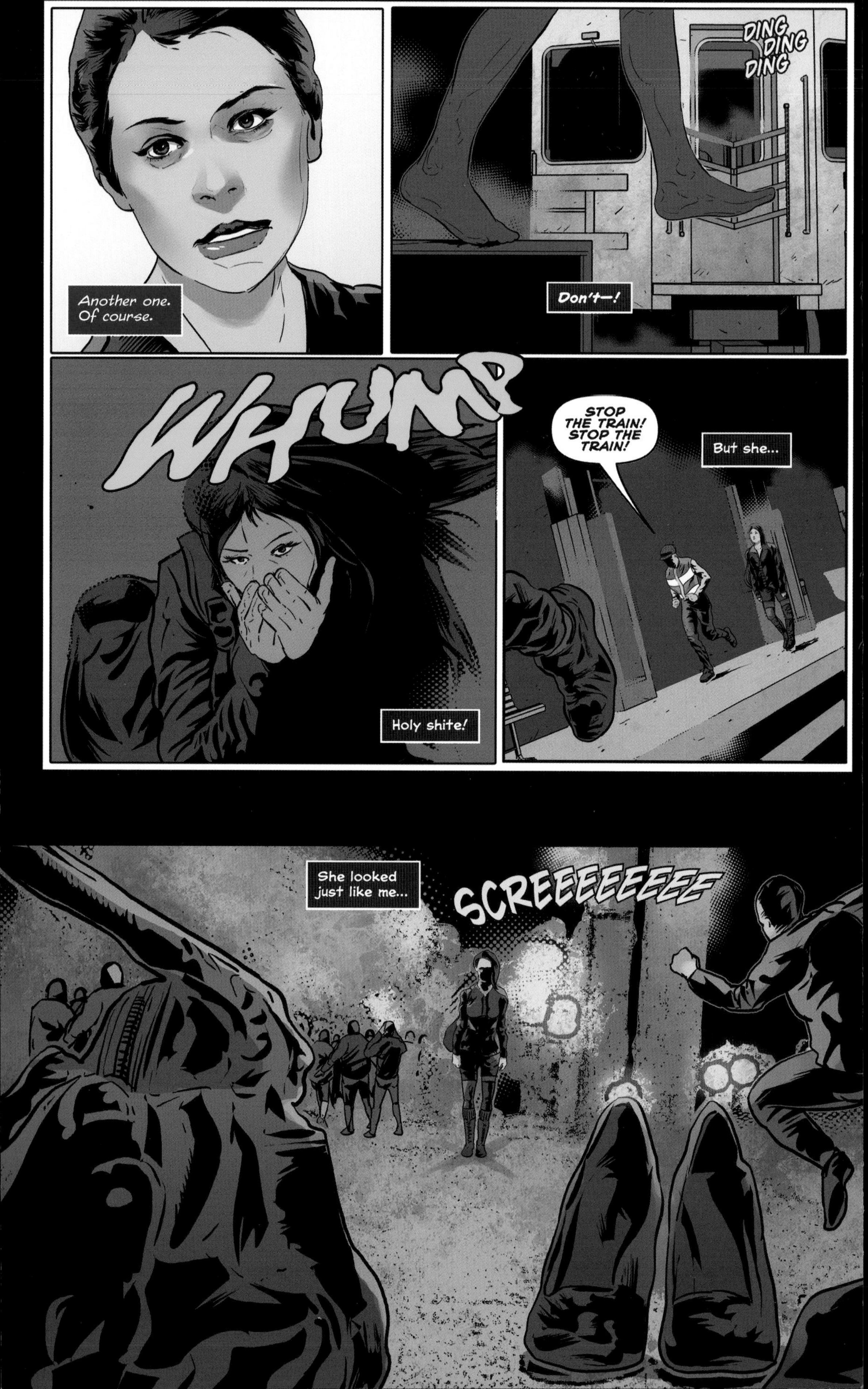
Another one. Of course.
DING DING DING
Don't—!
WHUMP
Holy shite!
STOP THE TRAIN! STOP THE TRAIN!
But she...
She looked just like me...
SCREEEEEEEEE

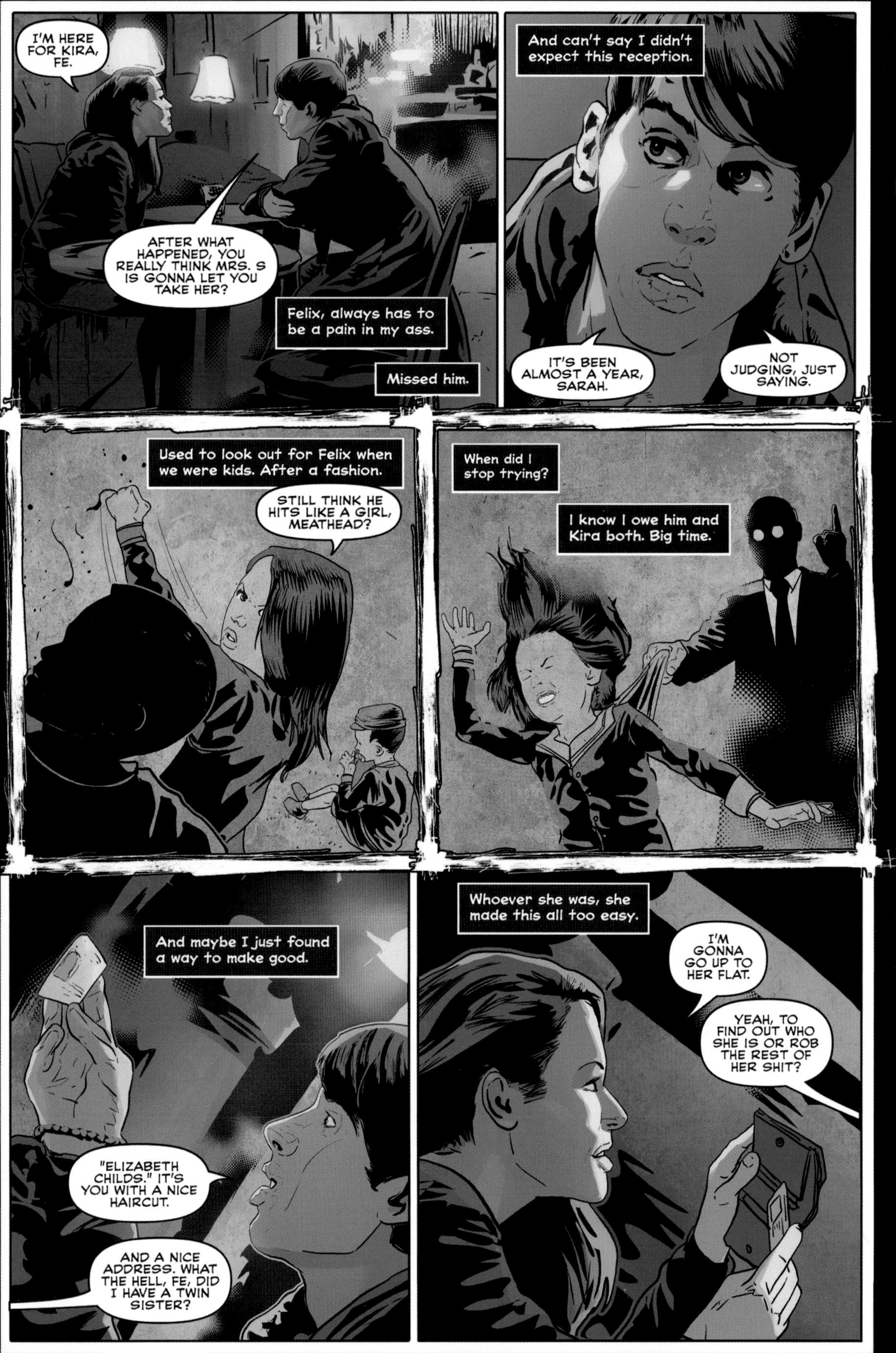
I'M HERE FOR KIRA, FE.
AFTER WHAT HAPPENED, YOU REALLY THINK MRS. S IS GONNA LET YOU TAKE HER?
Felix, always has to be a pain in my ass.
Missed him.
And can't say I didn't expect this reception.
IT'S BEEN ALMOST A YEAR, SARAH.
NOT JUDGING, JUST SAYING.
Used to look out for Felix when we were kids. After a fashion.
STILL THINK HE HITS LIKE A GIRL, MEATHEAD?
When did I stop trying?
I know I owe him and Kira both. Big time.
And maybe I just found a way to make good.
"ELIZABETH CHILDS." IT'S YOU WITH A NICE HAIRCUT.
AND A NICE ADDRESS. WHAT THE HELL, FE, DID I HAVE A TWIN SISTER?
Whoever she was, she made this all too easy.
I'M GONNA GO UP TO HER FLAT.
YEAH, TO FIND OUT WHO SHE IS OR ROB THE REST OF HER SHIT?

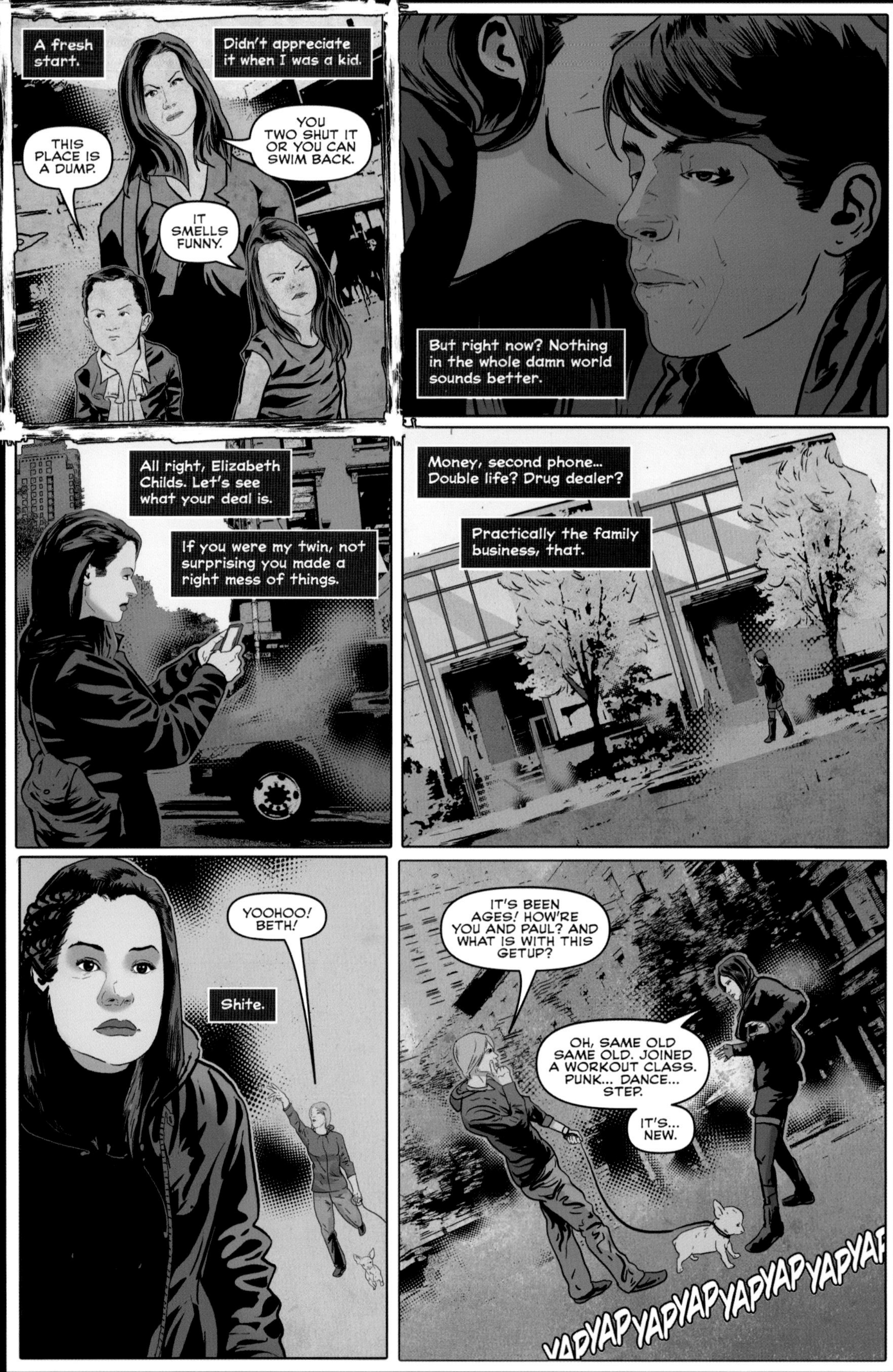
A fresh start.
Didn't appreciate it when I was a kid.
THIS PLACE IS A DUMP.
YOU TWO SHUT IT OR YOU CAN SWIM BACK.
IT SMELLS FUNNY.
But right now? Nothing in the whole damn world sounds better.
All right, Elizabeth Childs. Let's see what your deal is.
If you were my twin, not surprising you made a right mess of things.
Money, second phone... Double life? Drug dealer?
Practically the family business, that.
YOOHOO! BETH!
Shite.
IT'S BEEN AGES! HOW'RE YOU AND PAUL? AND WHAT IS WITH THIS GETUP?
OH, SAME OLD SAME OLD. JOINED A WORKOUT CLASS. PUNK... DANCE... STEP.
IT'S... NEW.
YAPYAPYAPYAPYAPYAP

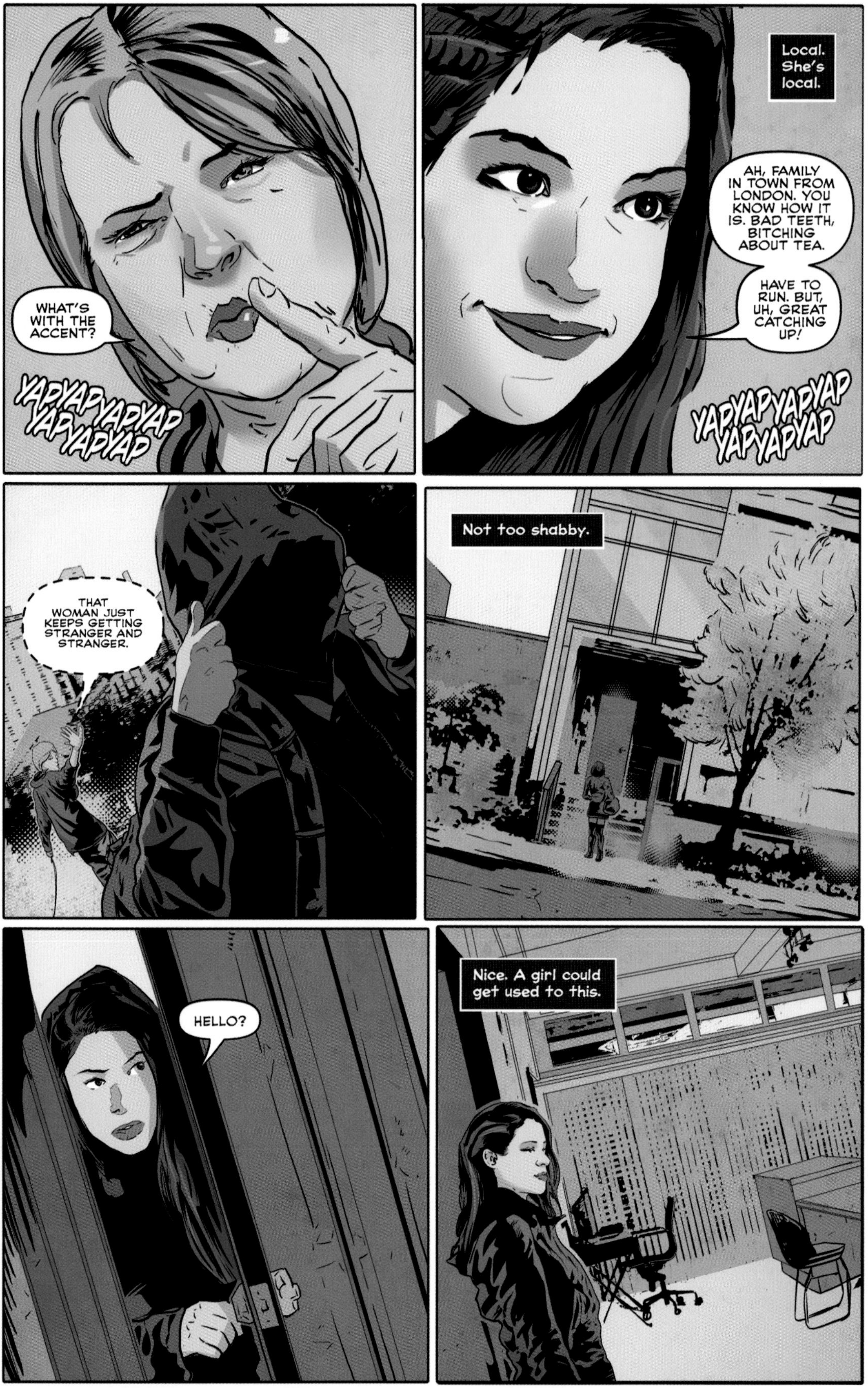
WHAT'S WITH THE ACCENT?
YAPYAPYAPYAP YAPYAPYAP
Local. She's local.
AH, FAMILY IN TOWN FROM LONDON. YOU KNOW HOW IT IS. BAD TEETH, BITCHING ABOUT TEA.
HAVE TO RUN. BUT, UH, GREAT CATCHING UP!
YAPYAPYAPYAP YAPYAPYAP
THAT WOMAN JUST KEEPS GETTING STRANGER AND STRANGER.
Not too shabby.
HELLO?
Nice. A girl could get used to this.

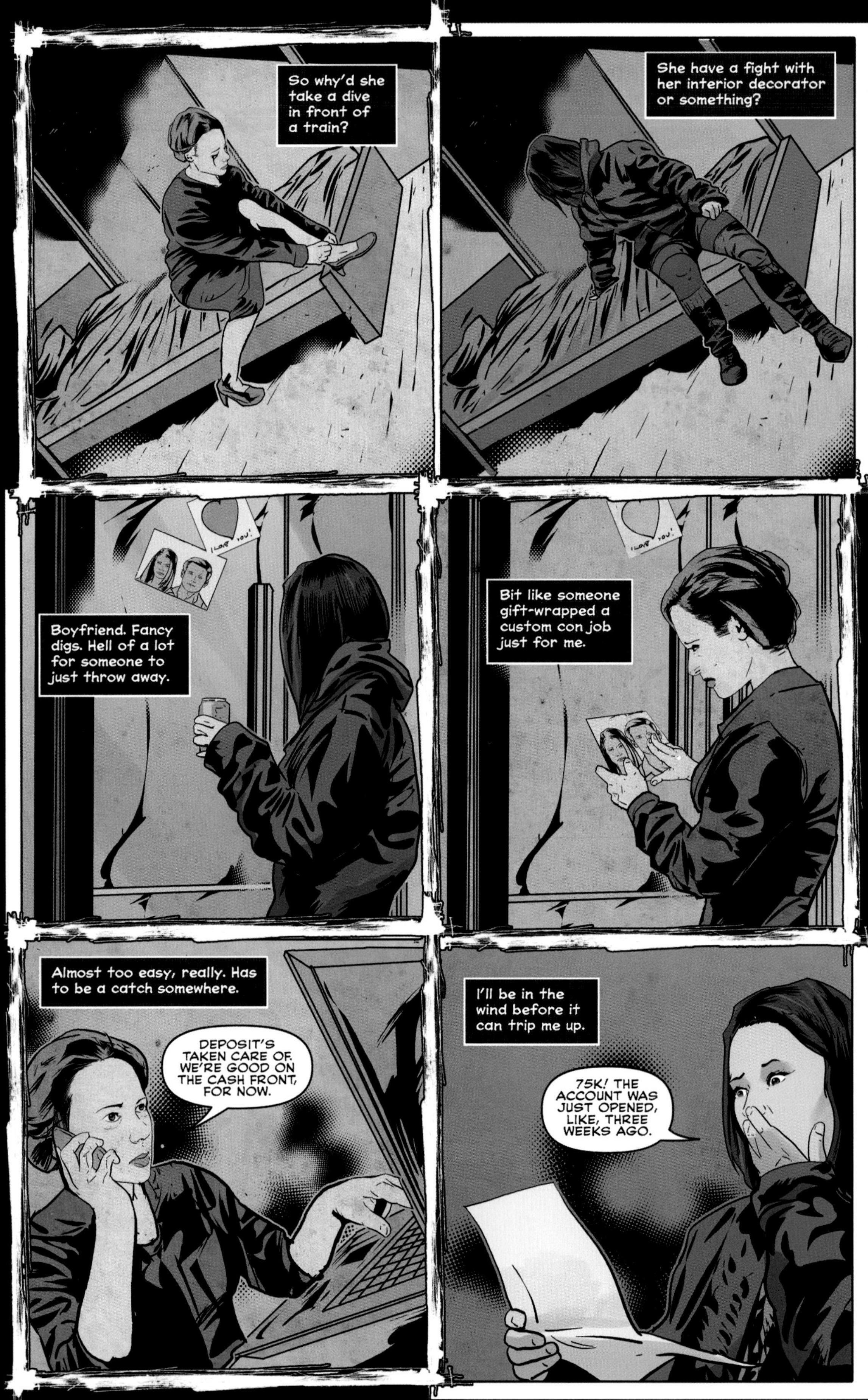
So why'd she take a dive in front of a train?
She have a fight with her interior decorator or something?
I LOVE YOU!
Boyfriend. Fancy digs. Hell of a lot for someone to just throw away.
I LOVE YOU!
Bit like someone gift-wrapped a custom con job just for me.
Almost too easy, really. Has to be a catch somewhere.
DEPOSIT'S TAKEN CARE OF. WE'RE GOOD ON THE CASH FRONT, FOR NOW.
I'll be in the wind before it can trip me up.
75K! THE ACCOUNT WAS JUST OPENED, LIKE, THREE WEEKS AGO.

This is how you do it. Game plan laid out before you go.

Know what you're after and what they expect you to be.

Elizabeth Childs. Boring clothes, sterile decor, and a big fat bank account.

Nice and simple. Too many loose threads, all the more likely they'll pull it apart.

Keep the focus on them. Most are desperate for the attention anyway.

DO YOU WANT ACCESS TO YOUR SAFETY DEPOSIT BOX, AS WELL?

Play it right, you're in and out with no surprises to trip you up.

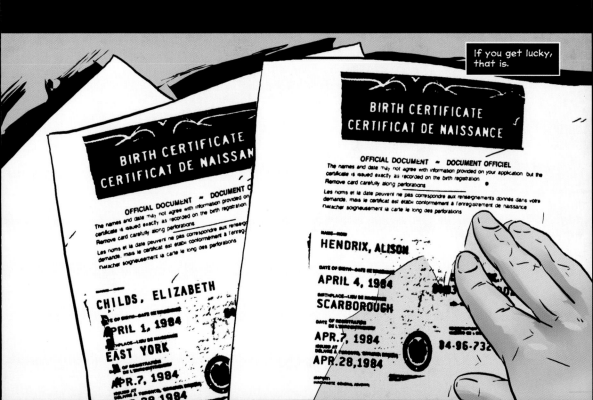

If you get lucky, that is.

BIRTH CERTIFICATE
CERTIFICAT DE NAISSANCE

OFFICIAL DOCUMENT ~ DOCUMENT OFFICIEL
The names and date may not agree with information provided on your application but the certificate is issued exactly as recorded on the birth registration
Remove card carefully along perforations

Les noms et la date peuvent ne pas correspondre aux renseignements donnés dans votre demande, mais le certificat est établi conformément à l'enregistrement de naissance
Détacher soigneusement la carte le long des perforations

HENDRIX, ALISON

APRIL 4, 1984

SCARBOROUGH

APR.7, 1984

APR. 28, 1984

04-96-732

BIRTH CERTIFICATE
CERTIFICAT DE NAISSANCE

OFFICIAL DOCUMENT ~ DOCUMENT C
The names and date may not agree with information provided on
certificate is issued exactly as recorded on the birth registration
Remove card carefully along perforations

Les noms et la date peuvent ne pas correspondre aux renseig
demande, mais le certificat est établi conformément à l'enreg
Détacher soigneusement la carte le long des perforations

CHILDS, ELIZABETH

APRIL 1, 1984

EAST YORK

APR.7, 1984

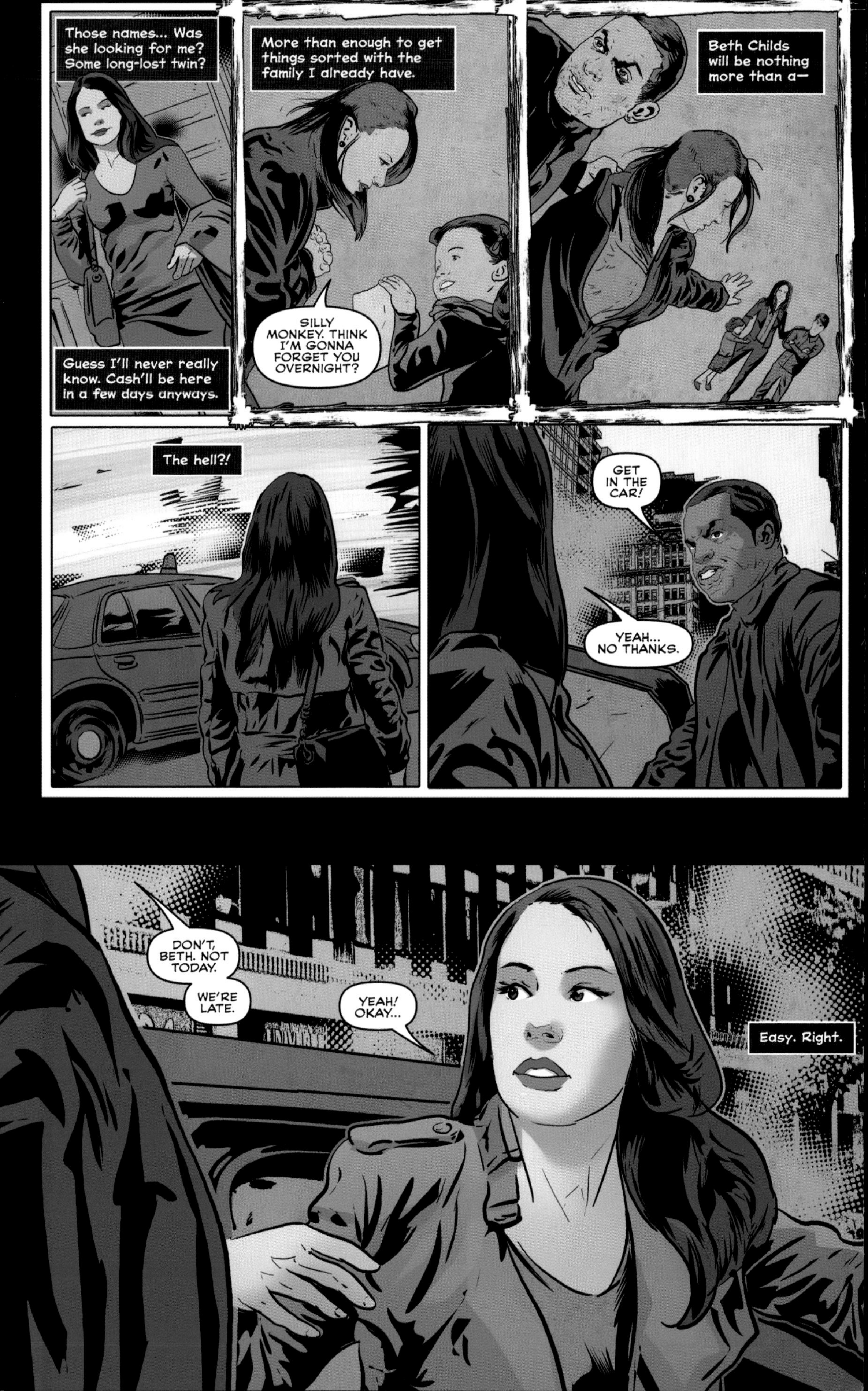
Those names... Was she looking for me? Some long-lost twin?
Guess I'll never really know. Cash'll be here in a few days anyways.
More than enough to get things sorted with the family I already have.
SILLY MONKEY. THINK I'M GONNA FORGET YOU OVERNIGHT?
Beth Childs will be nothing more than a—
The hell?!
GET IN THE CAR!
YEAH... NO THANKS.
DON'T, BETH. NOT TODAY.
WE'RE LATE.
YEAH! OKAY...
Easy. Right.

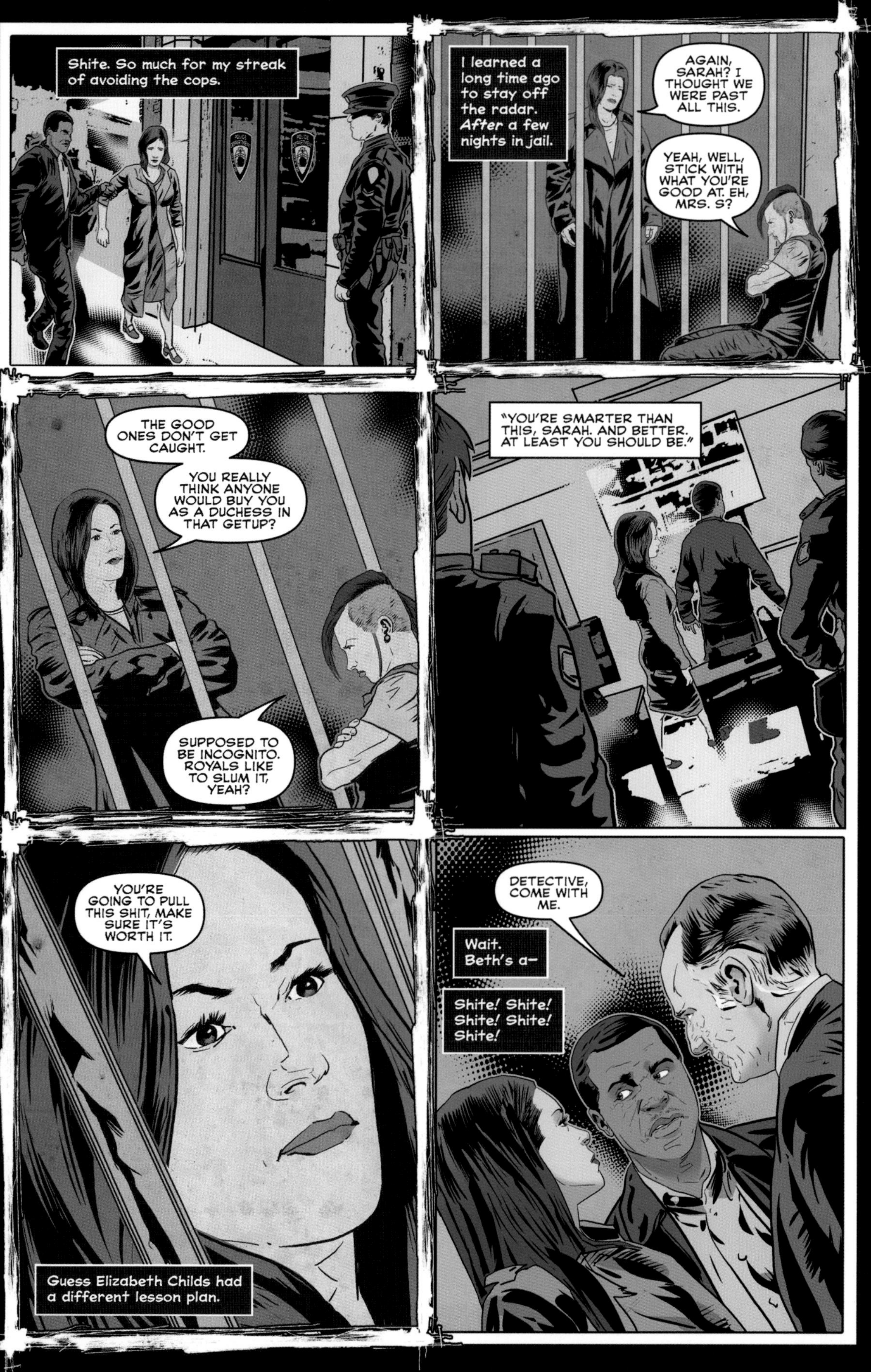
Shite. So much for my streak of avoiding the cops.
I learned a long time ago to stay off the radar. *After* a few nights in jail.
AGAIN, SARAH? I THOUGHT WE WERE PAST ALL THIS.
YEAH, WELL, STICK WITH WHAT YOU'RE GOOD AT. EH, MRS. S?
THE GOOD ONES DON'T GET CAUGHT.
YOU REALLY THINK ANYONE WOULD BUY YOU AS A DUCHESS IN THAT GETUP?
SUPPOSED TO BE INCOGNITO. ROYALS LIKE TO SLUM IT, YEAH?
"YOU'RE SMARTER THAN THIS, SARAH. AND BETTER. AT LEAST YOU SHOULD BE."
YOU'RE GOING TO PULL THIS SHIT, MAKE SURE IT'S WORTH IT.
Guess Elizabeth Childs had a different lesson plan.
DETECTIVE, COME WITH ME.
Wait. Beth's a–
Shite! Shite! Shite! Shite! Shite!

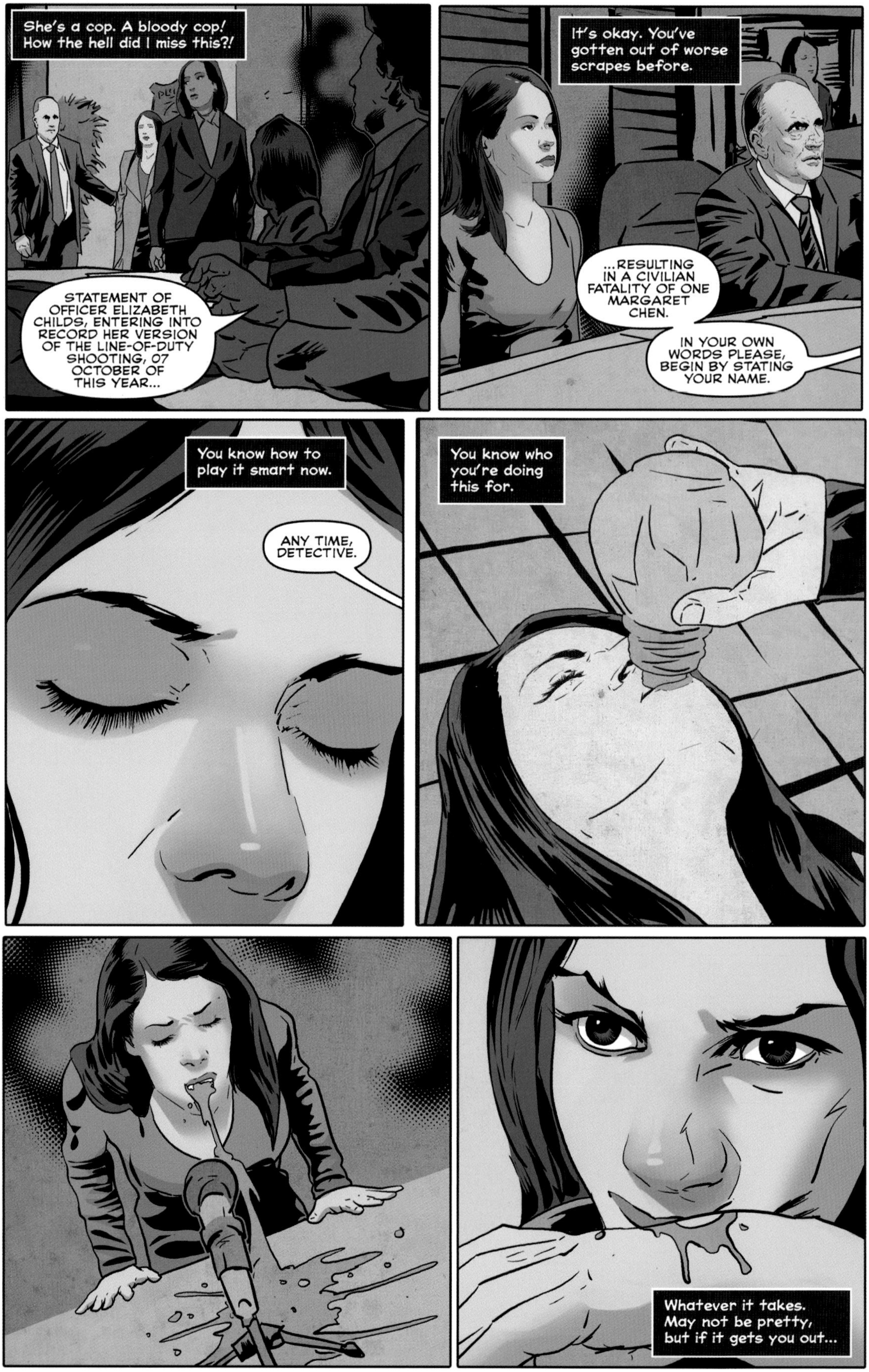
She's a cop. A bloody cop! How the hell did I miss this?!
STATEMENT OF OFFICER ELIZABETH CHILDS, ENTERING INTO RECORD HER VERSION OF THE LINE-OF-DUTY SHOOTING, 07 OCTOBER OF THIS YEAR...
It's okay. You've gotten out of worse scrapes before.
...RESULTING IN A CIVILIAN FATALITY OF ONE MARGARET CHEN.
IN YOUR OWN WORDS PLEASE, BEGIN BY STATING YOUR NAME.
You know how to play it smart now.
ANY TIME, DETECTIVE.
You know who you're doing this for.
Whatever it takes. May not be pretty, but if it gets you out...

Bought myself some time. But there's still too much I'm missing.

Vacation video, training video... has to be something here I can—

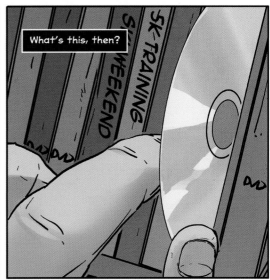

What's this, then?

I THOUGHT I KNEW THE BIG PICTURE. WHO THE ENEMY WAS. WHO TO KEEP AN EYE ON.

BUT I DON'T. I JUST DON'T ANYMORE. IT COULD BE ANY OF THEM.

HELL, IT COULD EVEN BE PAUL. HE COULD... IT WOULD EXPLAIN THINGS. SOME OF THEM, ANYWAY.

I CAN'T... I DON'T WANT IT TO BE HIM. I WANT SOMETHING WE CAN FIX. JUST... NORMAL RELATIONSHIP BULLSHIT.

BUT HOW CAN I TRUST HIM? HOW AM I SUPPOSED TO TRUST ANYONE EVER AGAIN?

TOO MANY BODIES ALREADY. TOO MUCH AT STAKE HERE. CAN'T LET THEM KNOW UNTIL I KNOW FOR SURE.

YEAH, THANKS FOR THAT. CLEARS EVERYTHING UP.

NUTJOB.

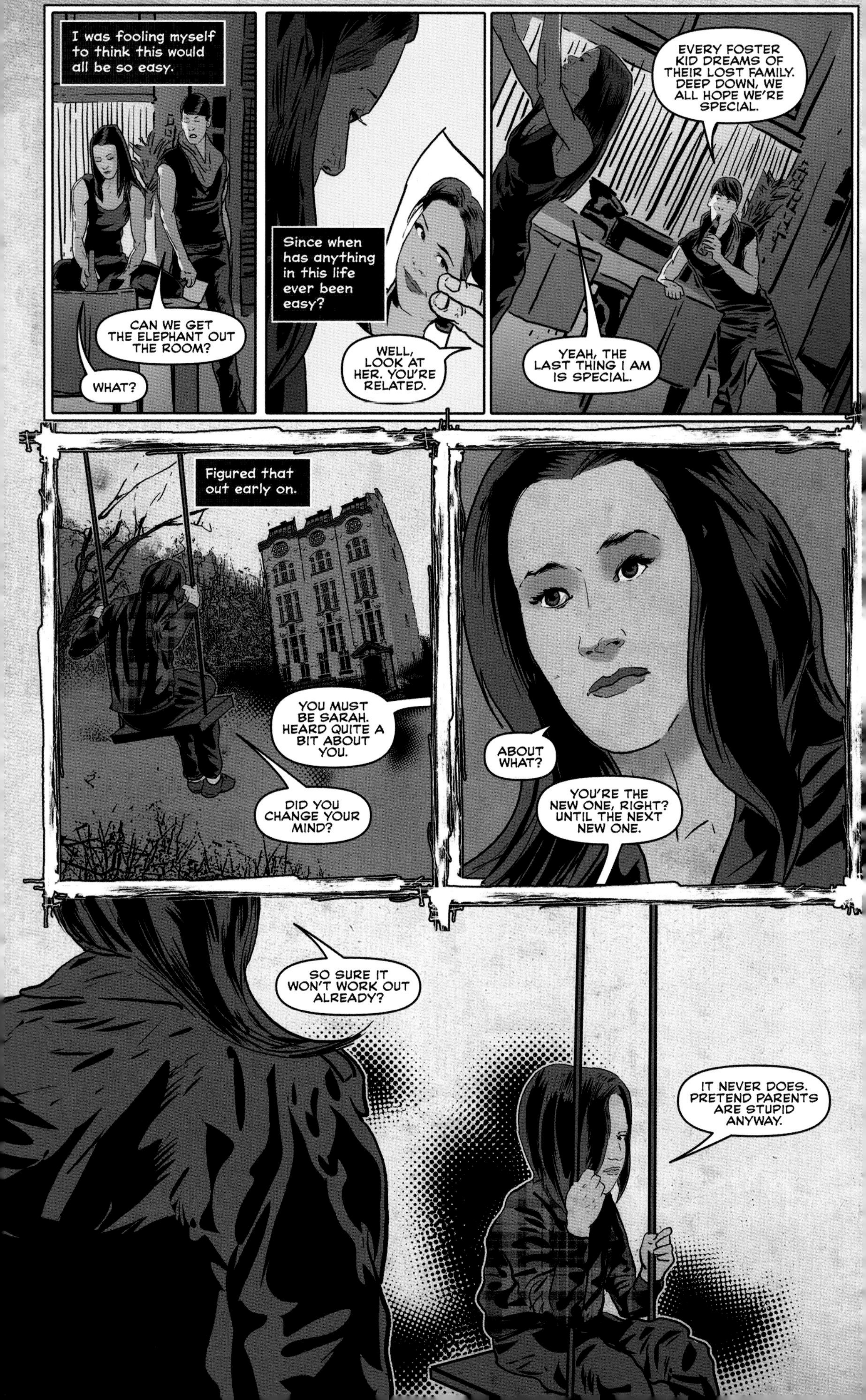

I was fooling myself to think this would all be so easy.
CAN WE GET THE ELEPHANT OUT THE ROOM?
WHAT?
Since when has anything in this life ever been easy?
WELL, LOOK AT HER. YOU'RE RELATED.
EVERY FOSTER KID DREAMS OF THEIR LOST FAMILY. DEEP DOWN, WE ALL HOPE WE'RE SPECIAL.
YEAH, THE LAST THING I AM IS SPECIAL.
Figured that out early on.
YOU MUST BE SARAH. HEARD QUITE A BIT ABOUT YOU.
DID YOU CHANGE YOUR MIND?
ABOUT WHAT?
YOU'RE THE NEW ONE, RIGHT? UNTIL THE NEXT NEW ONE.
SO SURE IT WON'T WORK OUT ALREADY?
IT NEVER DOES. PRETEND PARENTS ARE STUPID ANYWAY.

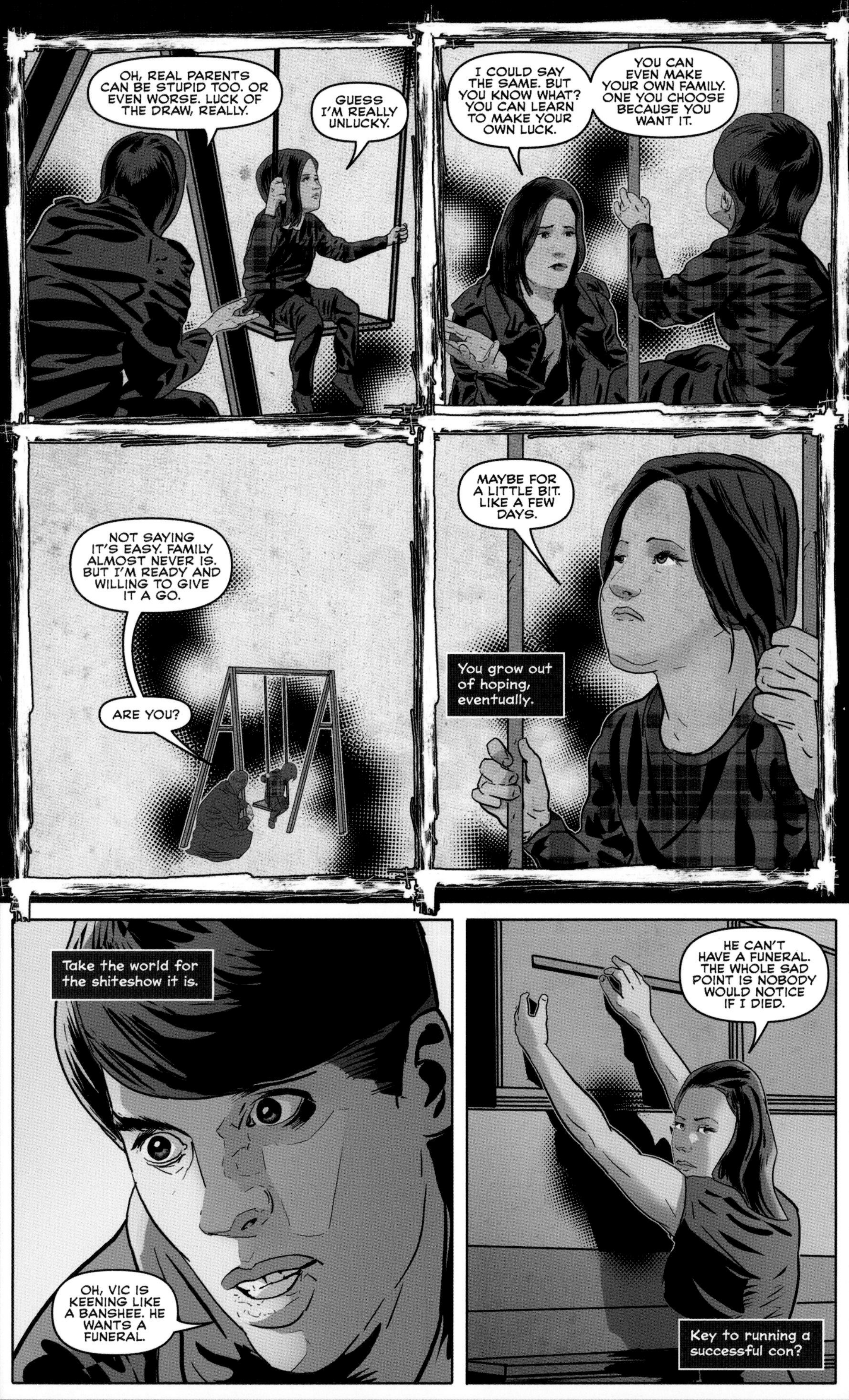
OH, REAL PARENTS CAN BE STUPID TOO. OR EVEN WORSE. LUCK OF THE DRAW, REALLY.
GUESS I'M REALLY UNLUCKY.
I COULD SAY THE SAME. BUT YOU KNOW WHAT? YOU CAN LEARN TO MAKE YOUR OWN LUCK.
YOU CAN EVEN MAKE YOUR OWN FAMILY. ONE YOU CHOOSE BECAUSE YOU WANT IT.
NOT SAYING IT'S EASY. FAMILY ALMOST NEVER IS. BUT I'M READY AND WILLING TO GIVE IT A GO.
ARE YOU?
MAYBE FOR A LITTLE BIT. LIKE A FEW DAYS.
You grow out of hoping, eventually.
Take the world for the shiteshow it is.
OH, VIC IS KEENING LIKE A BANSHEE. HE WANTS A FUNERAL.
HE CAN'T HAVE A FUNERAL. THE WHOLE SAD POINT IS NOBODY WOULD NOTICE IF I DIED.
Key to running a successful con?

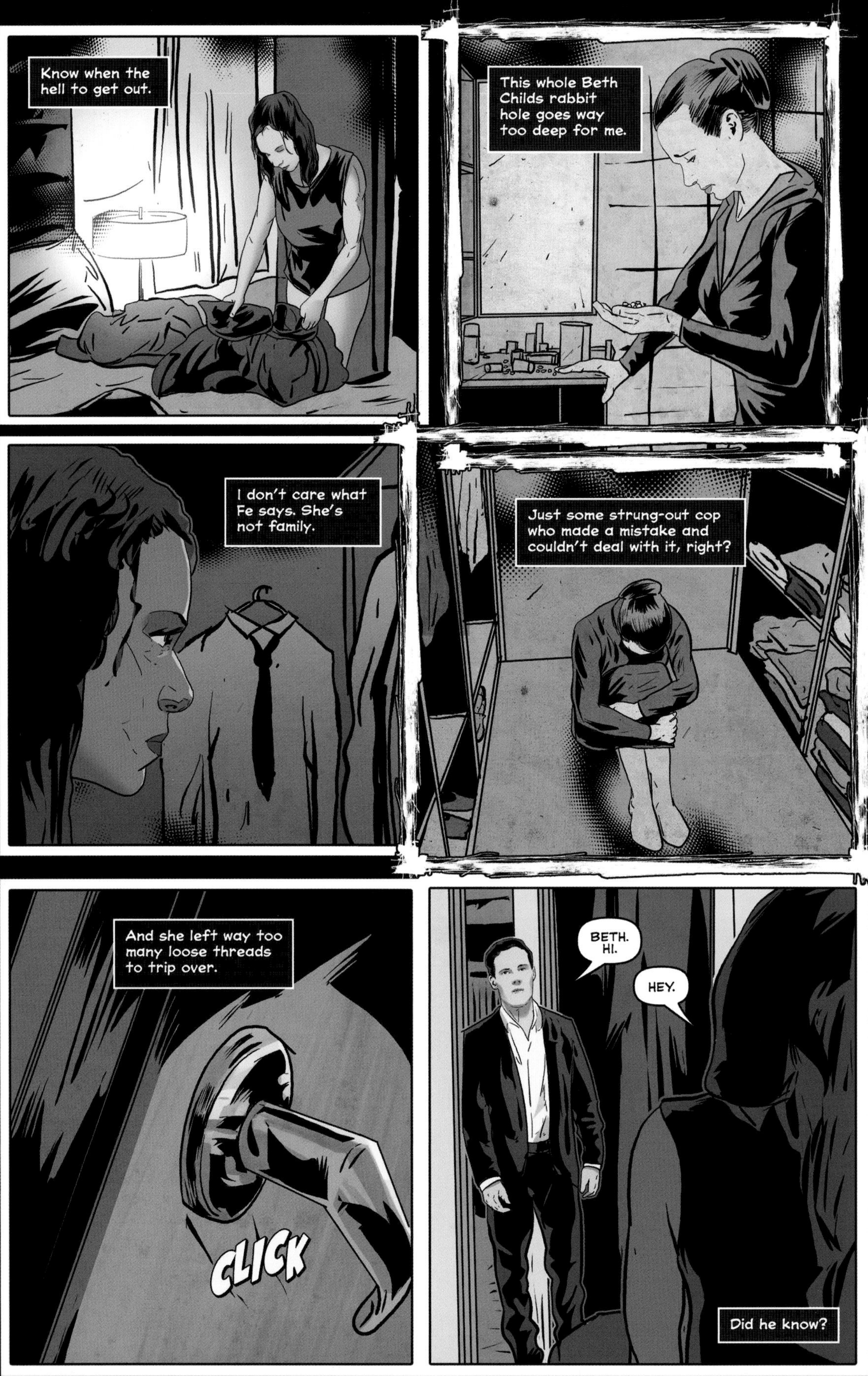
Know when the hell to get out.
This whole Beth Childs rabbit hole goes way too deep for me.
I don't care what Fe says. She's not family.
Just some strung-out cop who made a mistake and couldn't deal with it, right?
And she left way too many loose threads to trip over.
CLICK
BETH. HI.
HEY.
Did he know?

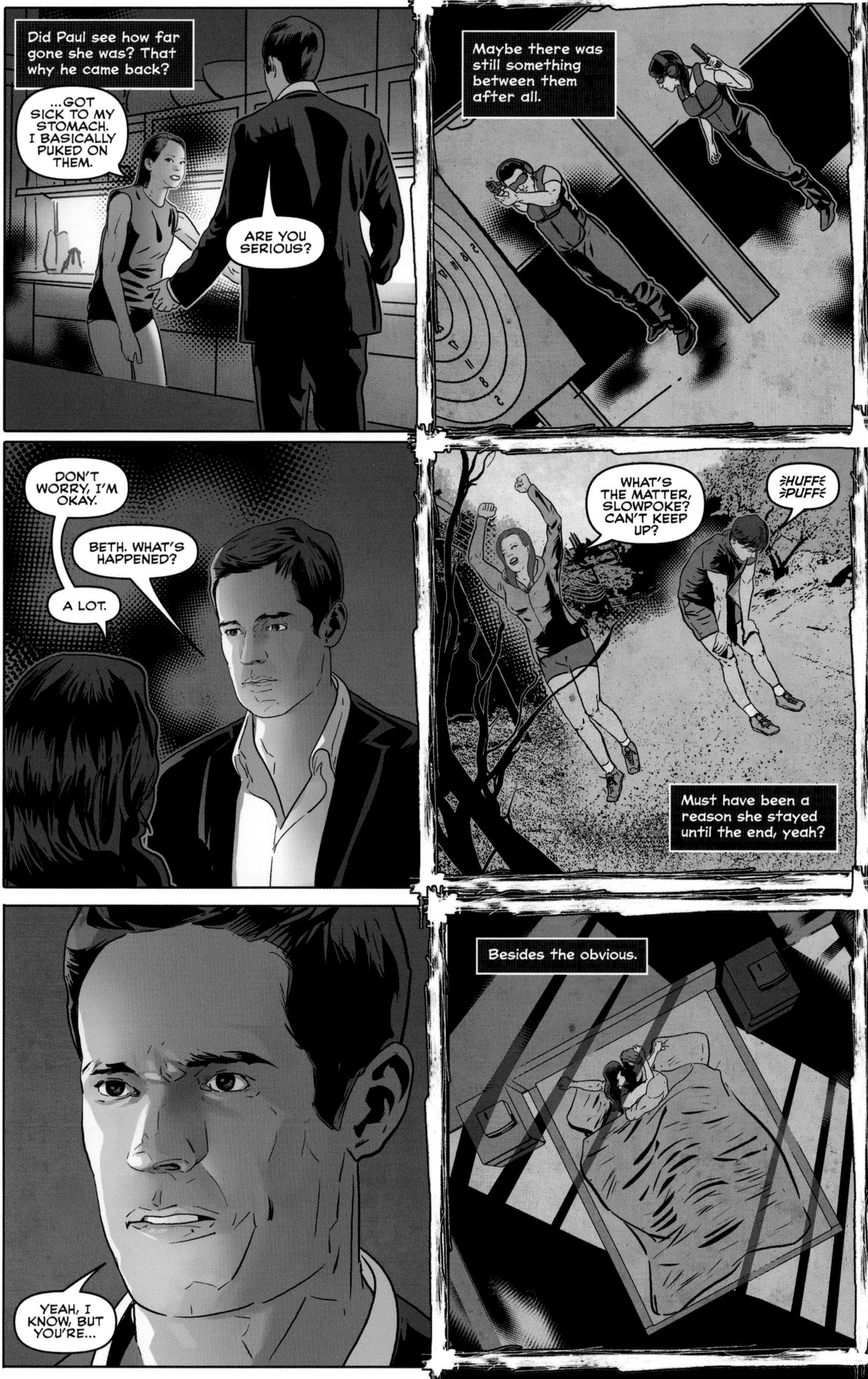
Did Paul see how far gone she was? That why he came back?
...GOT SICK TO MY STOMACH. I BASICALLY PUKED ON THEM.
ARE YOU SERIOUS?
Maybe there was still something between them after all.
DON'T WORRY, I'M OKAY.
BETH. WHAT'S HAPPENED?
A LOT.
WHAT'S THE MATTER, SLOWPOKE? CAN'T KEEP UP?
HUFF PUFF
Must have been a reason she stayed until the end, yeah?
YEAH, I KNOW, BUT YOU'RE...
Besides the obvious.

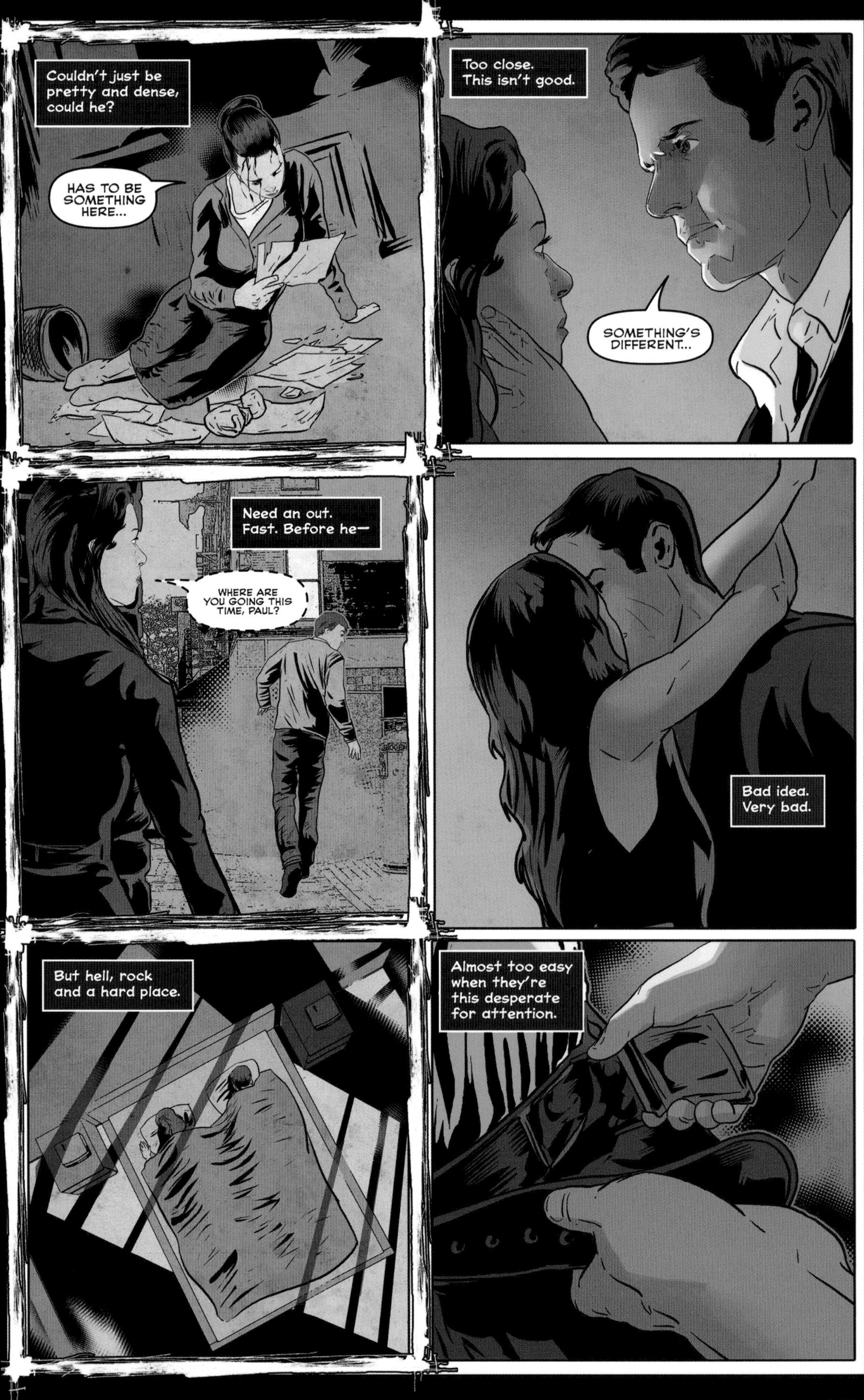

Couldn't just be pretty and dense, could he?
HAS TO BE SOMETHING HERE...
Too close. This isn't good.
SOMETHING'S DIFFERENT...
Need an out. Fast. Before he—
WHERE ARE YOU GOING THIS TIME, PAUL?
Bad idea. Very bad.
But hell, rock and a hard place.
Almost too easy when they're this desperate for attention.

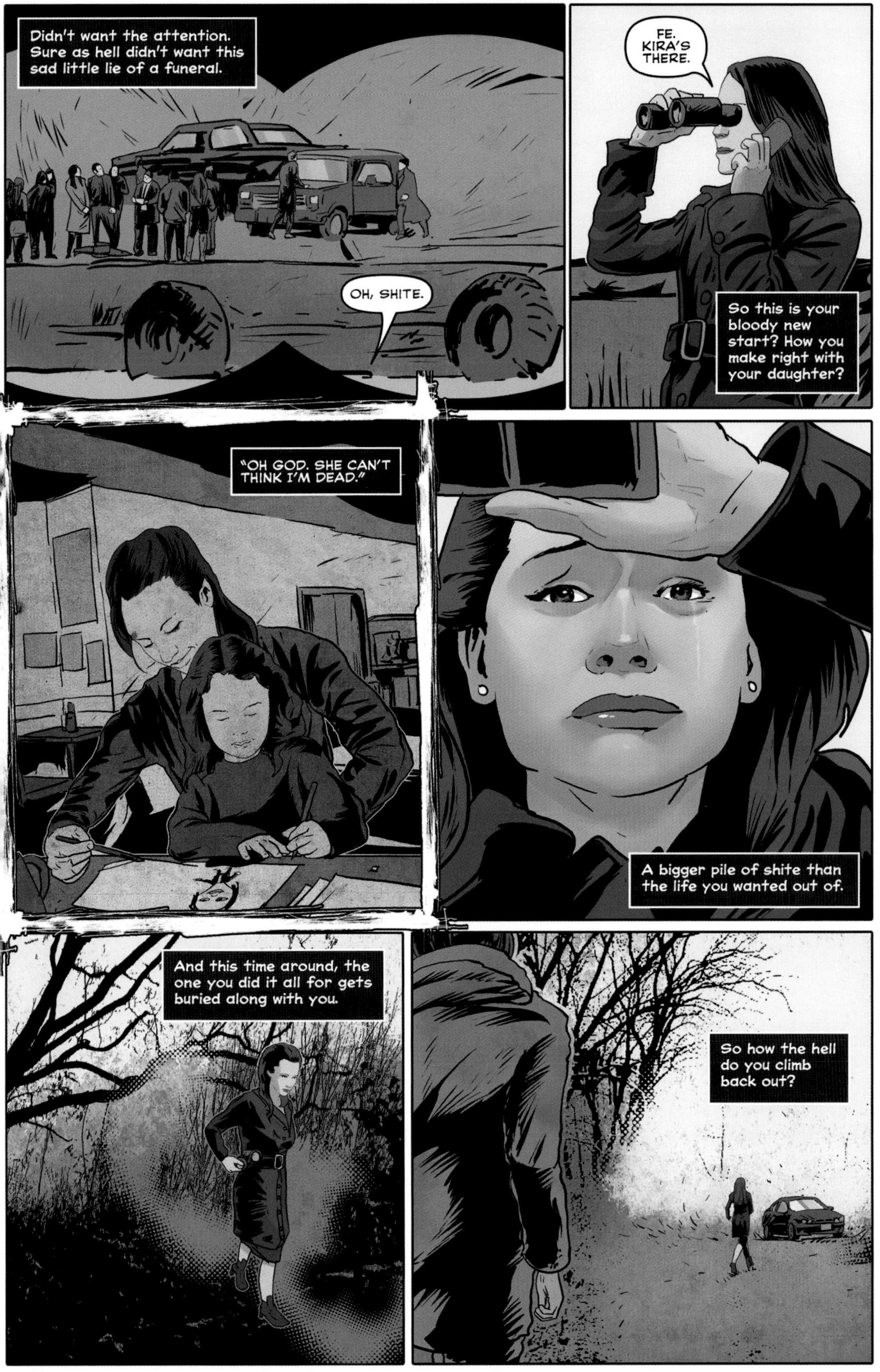
Didn't want the attention. Sure as hell didn't want this sad little lie of a funeral.
OH, SHITE.
FE. KIRA'S THERE.
So this is your bloody new start? How you make right with your daughter?
"OH GOD. SHE CAN'T THINK I'M DEAD."
A bigger pile of shite than the life you wanted out of.
And this time around, the one you did it all for gets buried along with you.
So how the hell do you climb back out?

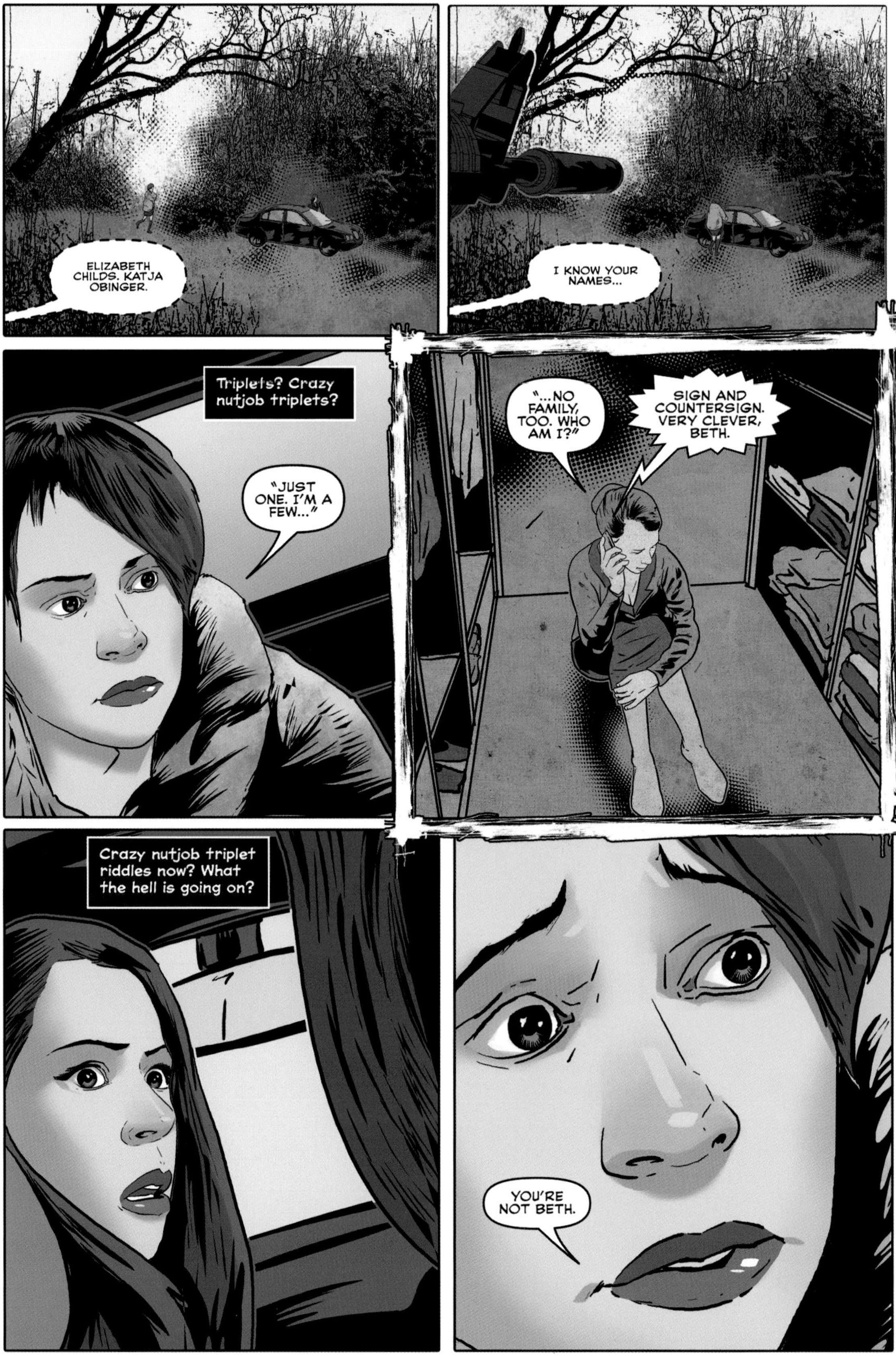
ELIZABETH CHILDS. KATJA OBINGER.
I KNOW YOUR NAMES...
Triplets? Crazy nutjob triplets?
"JUST ONE. I'M A FEW..."
"...NO FAMILY, TOO. WHO AM I?"
SIGN AND COUNTERSIGN. VERY CLEVER, BETH.
Crazy nutjob triplet riddles now? What the hell is going on?
YOU'RE NOT BETH.

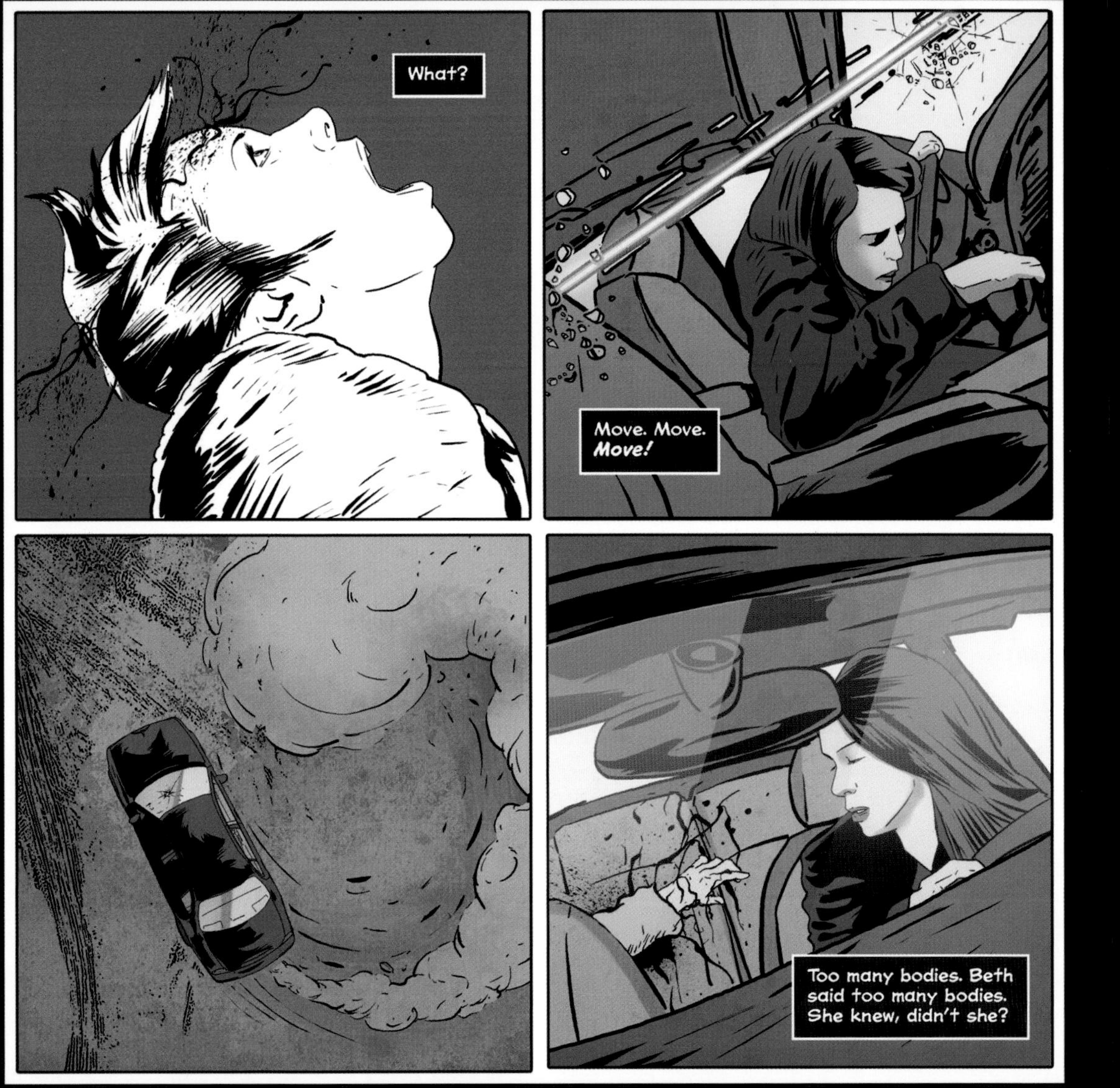
What?
Move. Move.
Move!
Too many bodies. Beth said too many bodies. She knew, didn't she?

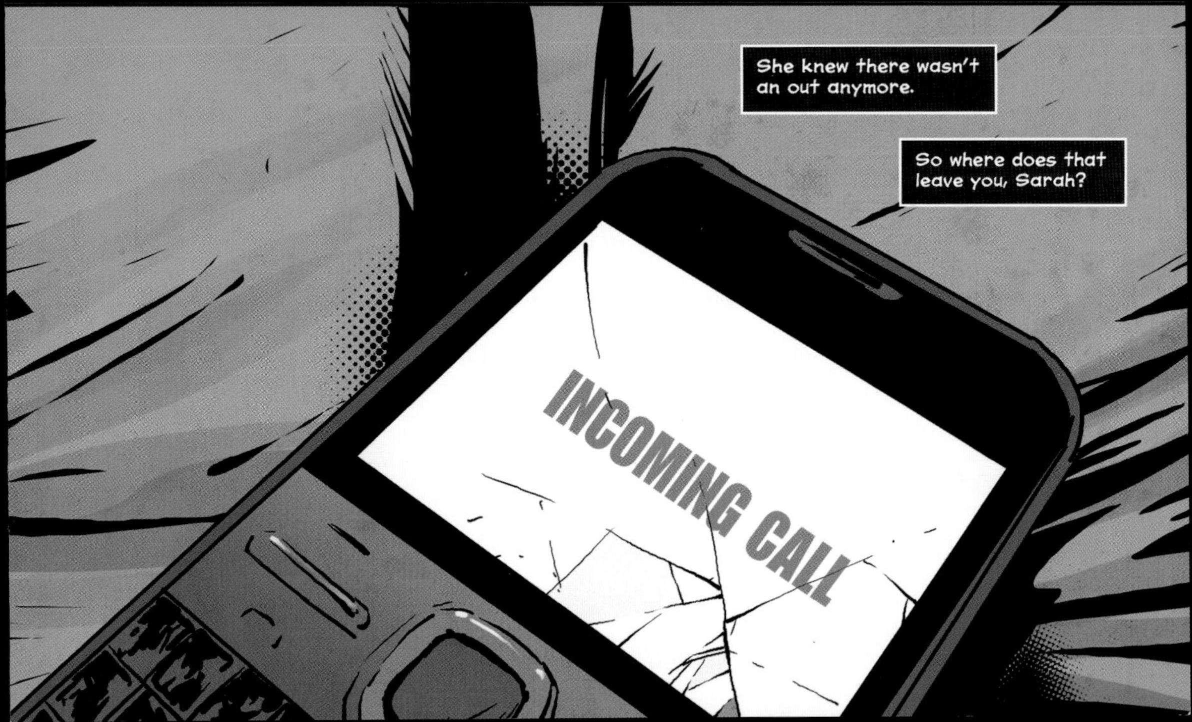
She knew there wasn't an out anymore.
So where does that leave you, Sarah?
INCOMING CALL

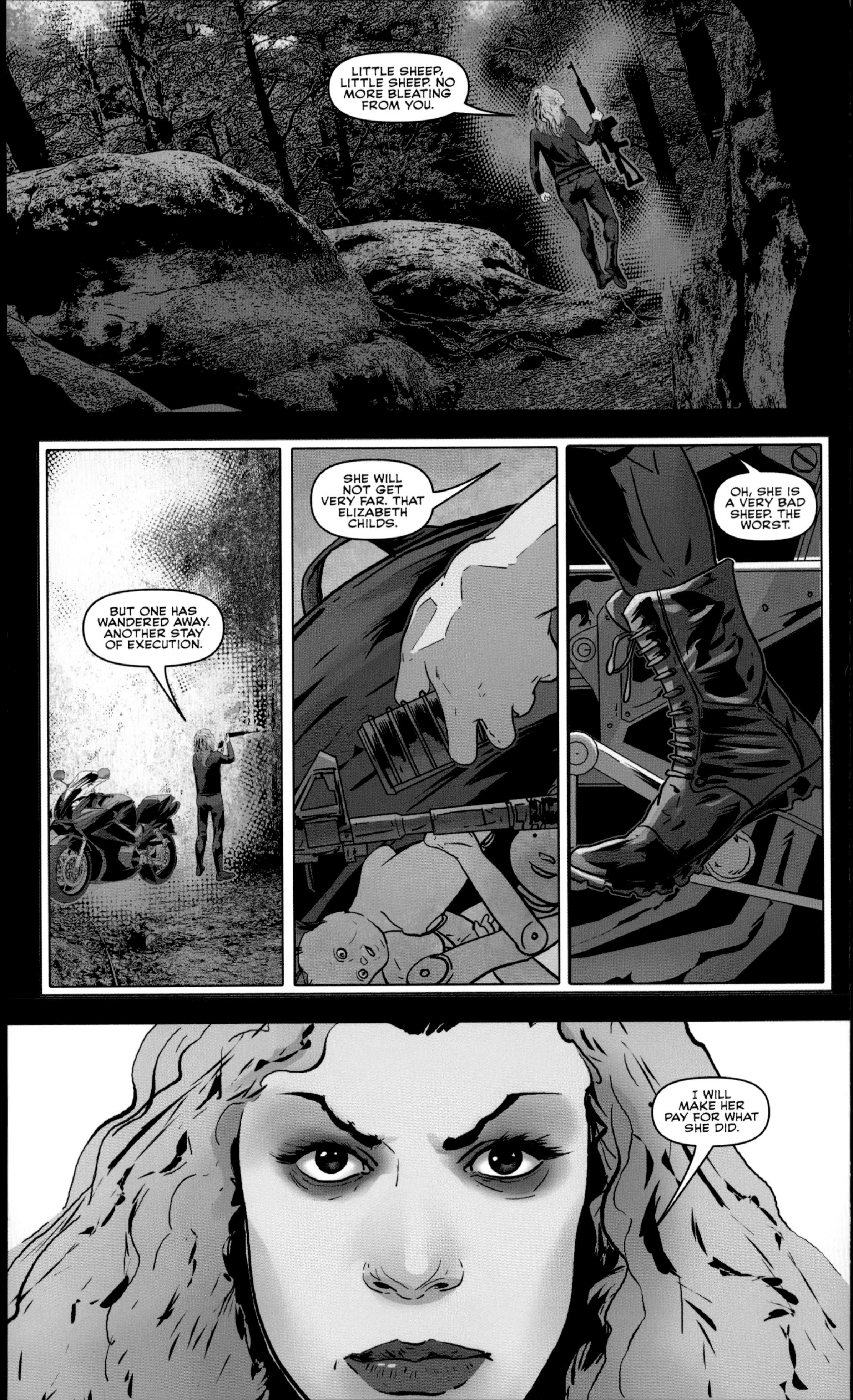
LITTLE SHEEP, LITTLE SHEEP. NO MORE BLEATING FROM YOU.
BUT ONE HAS WANDERED AWAY. ANOTHER STAY OF EXECUTION.
SHE WILL NOT GET VERY FAR. THAT ELIZABETH CHILDS.
OH, SHE IS A VERY BAD SHEEP. THE WORST.
I WILL MAKE HER PAY FOR WHAT SHE DID.

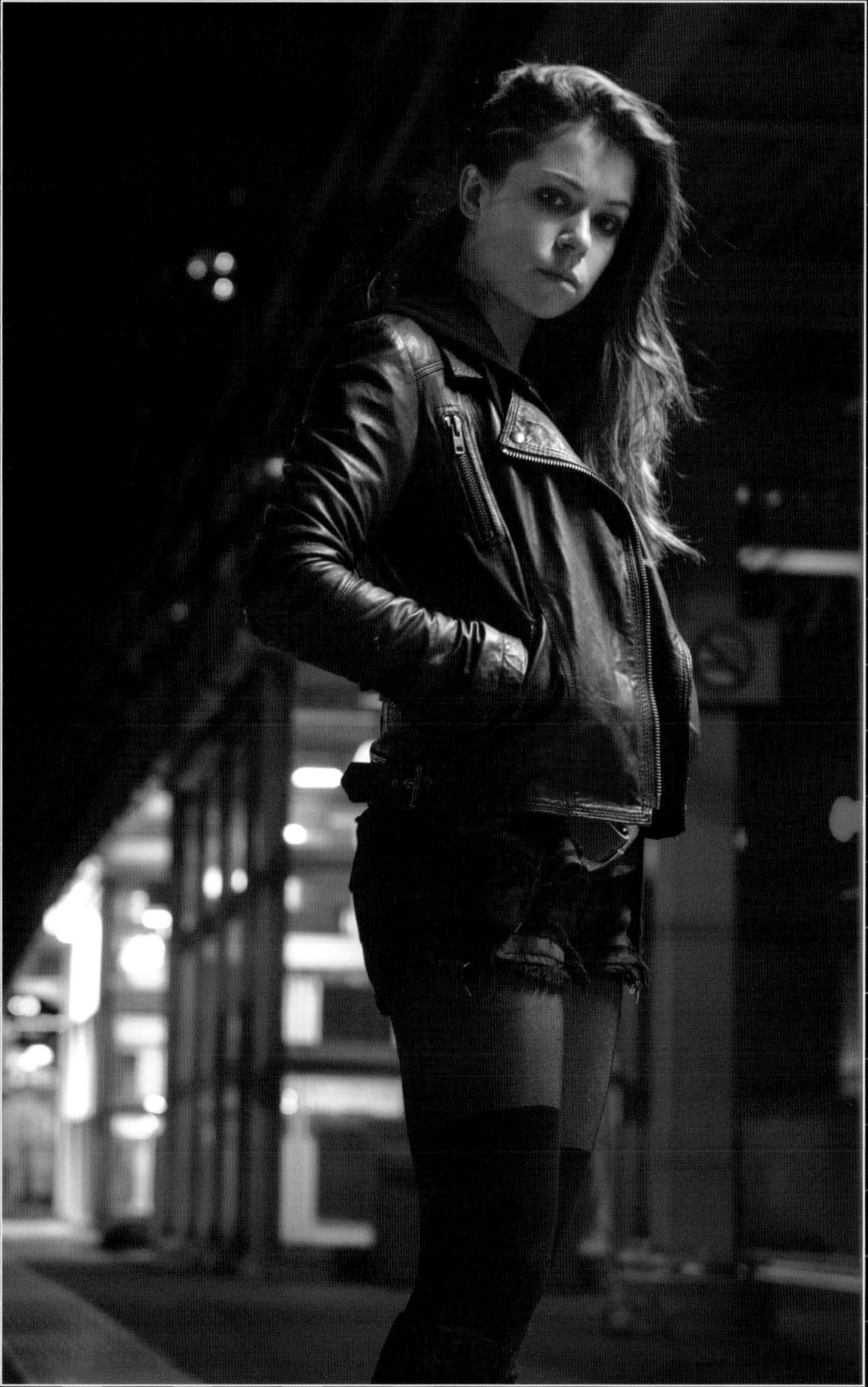

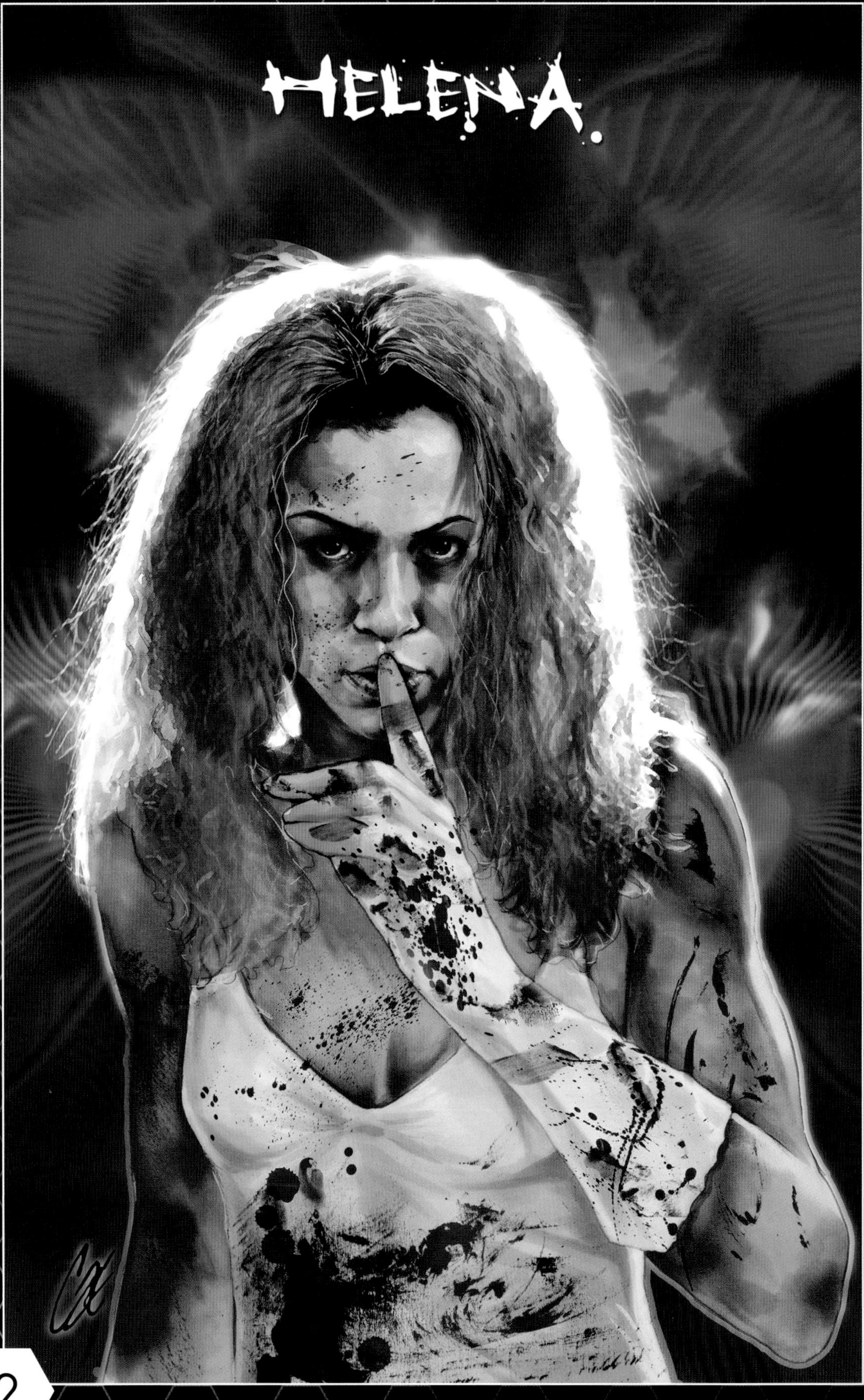
HELENA.

BY CAT STAGGS

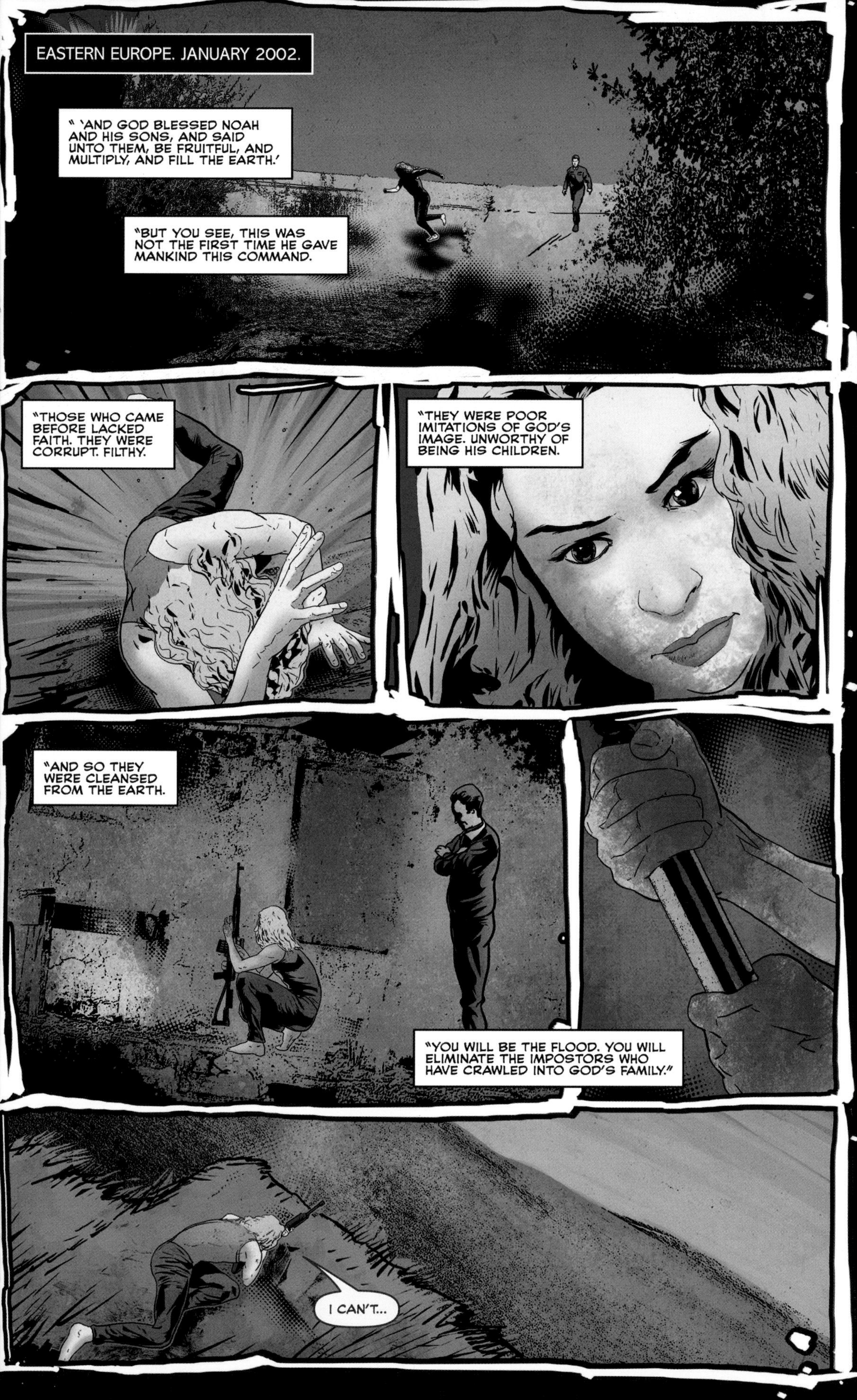
EASTERN EUROPE. JANUARY 2002.
" 'AND GOD BLESSED NOAH AND HIS SONS, AND SAID UNTO THEM, BE FRUITFUL, AND MULTIPLY, AND FILL THE EARTH.'
"BUT YOU SEE, THIS WAS NOT THE FIRST TIME HE GAVE MANKIND THIS COMMAND.
"THOSE WHO CAME BEFORE LACKED FAITH. THEY WERE CORRUPT. FILTHY.
"THEY WERE POOR IMITATIONS OF GOD'S IMAGE. UNWORTHY OF BEING HIS CHILDREN.
"AND SO THEY WERE CLEANSED FROM THE EARTH.
"YOU WILL BE THE FLOOD. YOU WILL ELIMINATE THE IMPOSTORS WHO HAVE CRAWLED INTO GOD'S FAMILY."
I CAN'T...

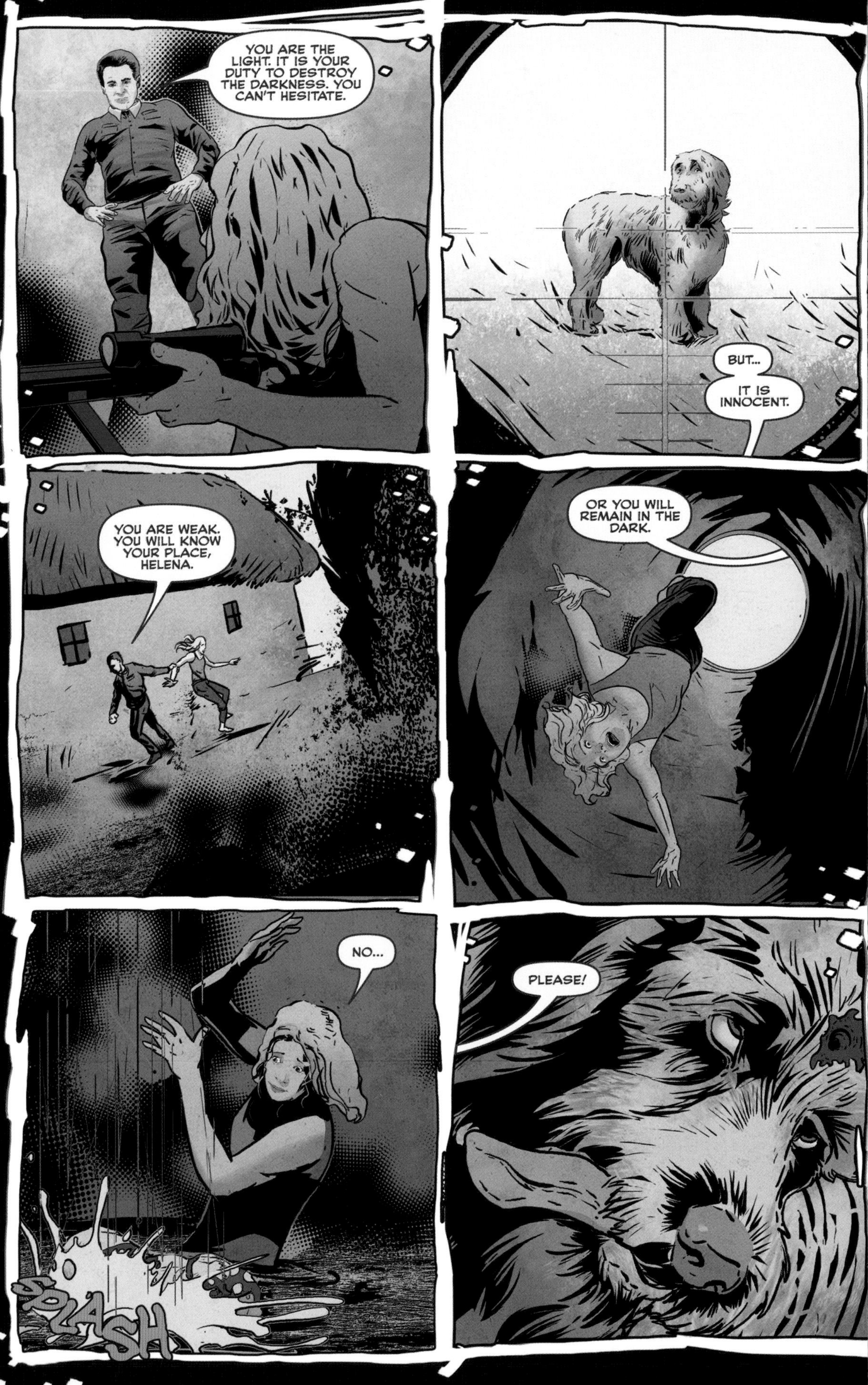
YOU ARE THE LIGHT. IT IS YOUR DUTY TO DESTROY THE DARKNESS. YOU CAN'T HESITATE.
BUT...
IT IS INNOCENT.
YOU ARE WEAK. YOU WILL KNOW YOUR PLACE, HELENA.
OR YOU WILL REMAIN IN THE DARK.
NO...
SPLASH
PLEASE!

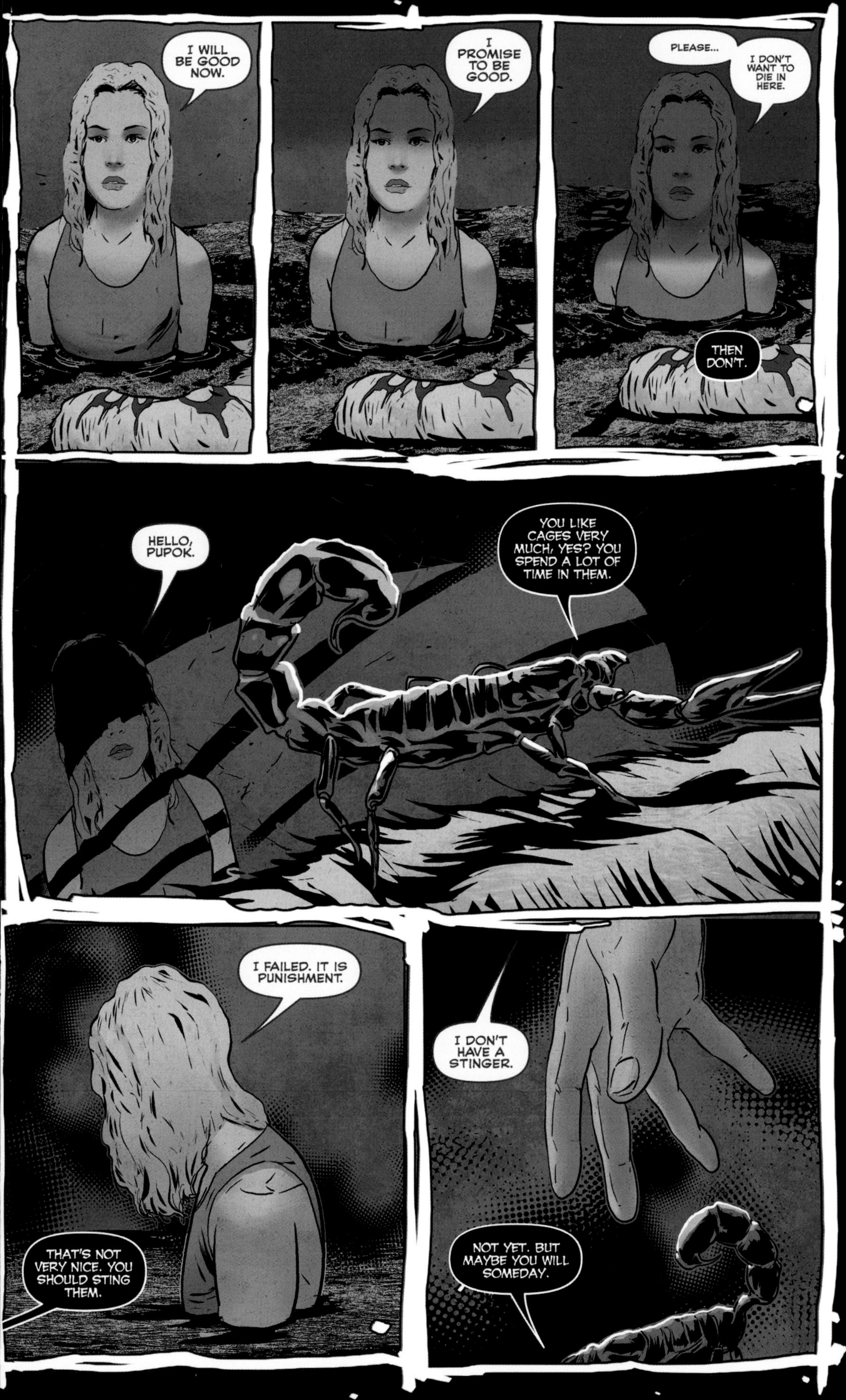
I WILL BE GOOD NOW.
I PROMISE TO BE GOOD.
PLEASE...
I DON'T WANT TO DIE IN HERE.
THEN DON'T.
HELLO, PUPOK.
YOU LIKE CAGES VERY MUCH, YES? YOU SPEND A LOT OF TIME IN THEM.
I FAILED. IT IS PUNISHMENT.
THAT'S NOT VERY NICE. YOU SHOULD STING THEM.
I DON'T HAVE A STINGER.
NOT YET. BUT MAYBE YOU WILL SOMEDAY.

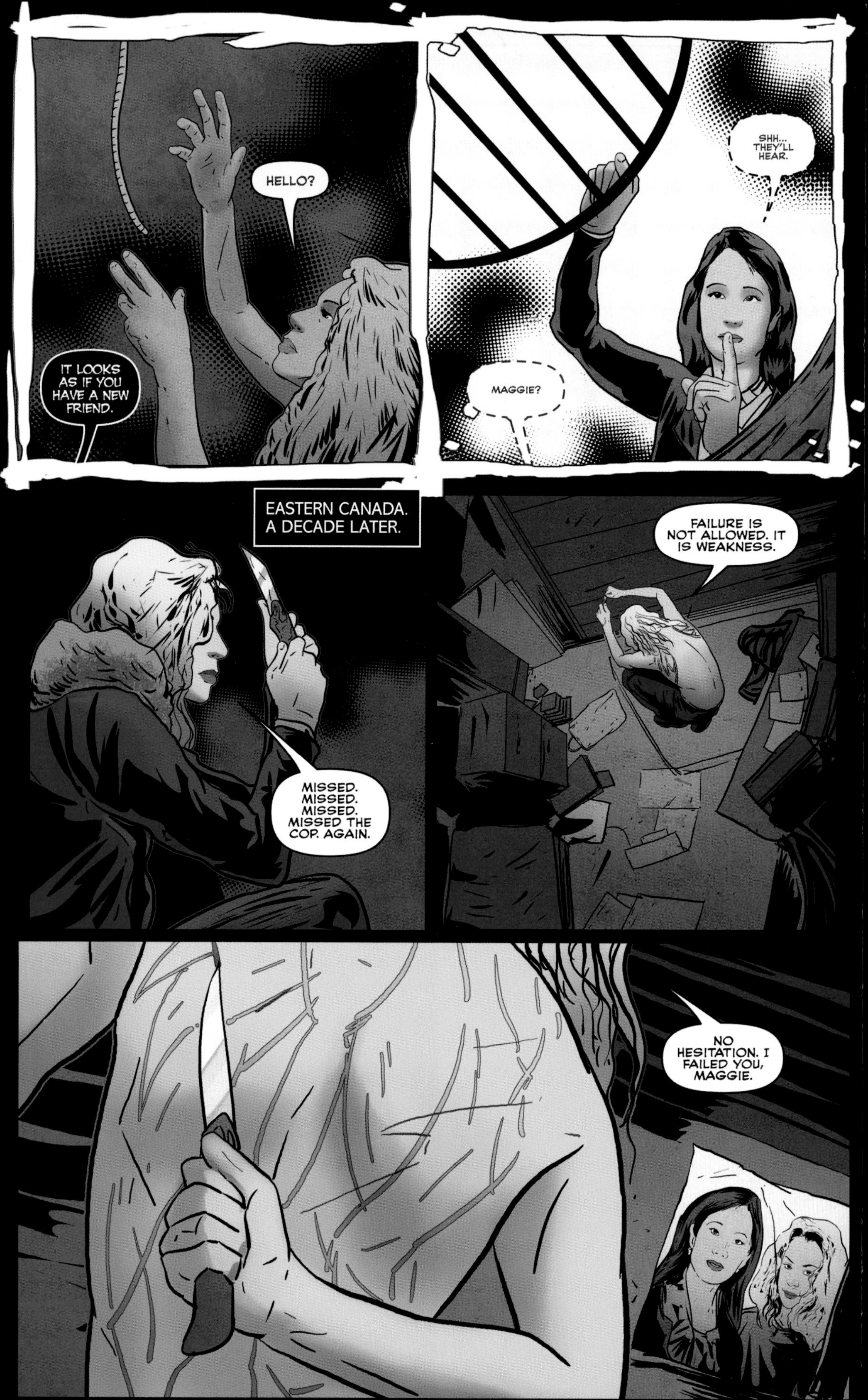
HELLO?
IT LOOKS AS IF YOU HAVE A NEW FRIEND.
SHH... THEY'LL HEAR.
MAGGIE?
EASTERN CANADA. A DECADE LATER.
MISSED. MISSED. MISSED. MISSED THE COP. AGAIN.
FAILURE IS NOT ALLOWED. IT IS WEAKNESS.
NO HESITATION. I FAILED YOU, MAGGIE.

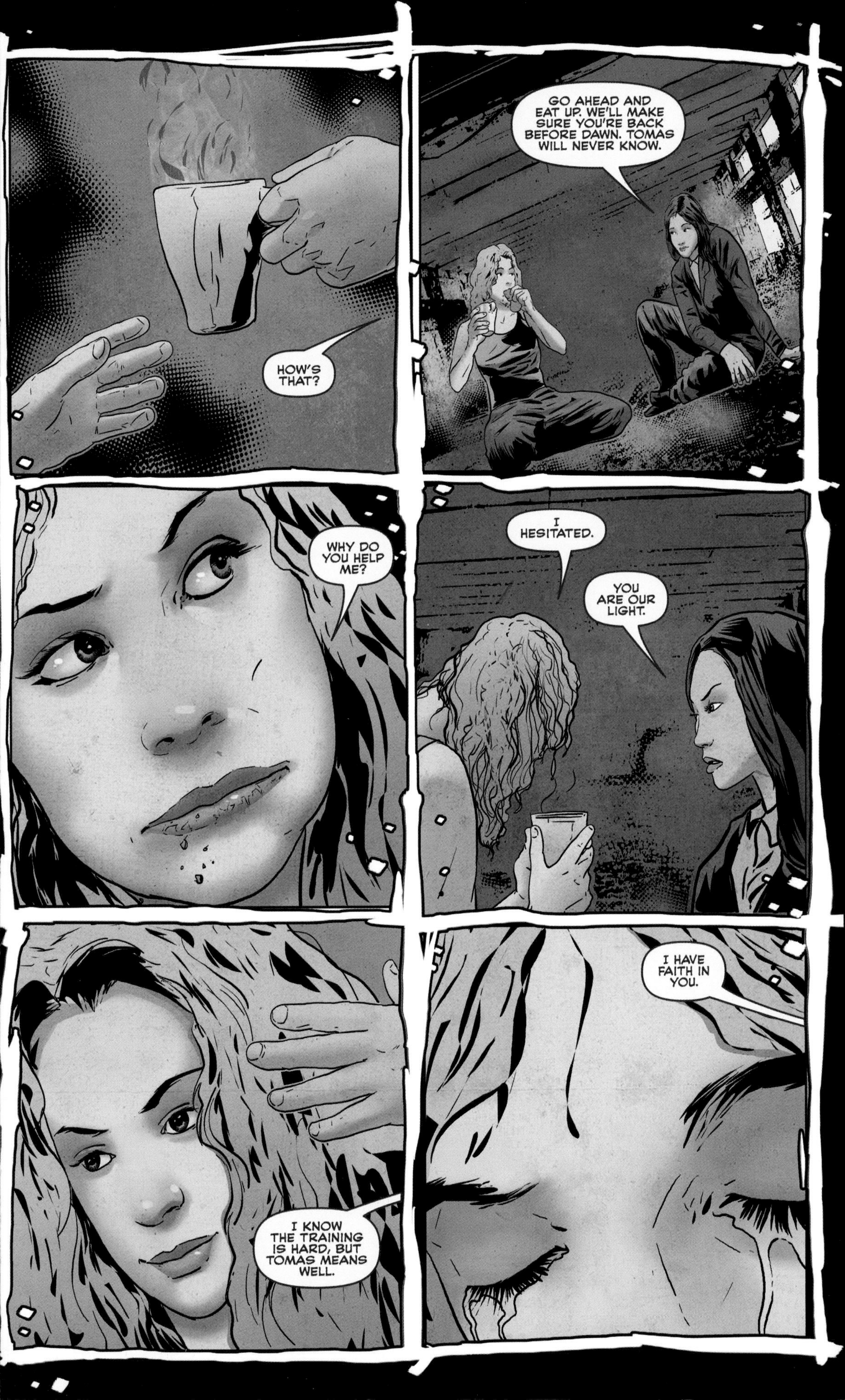
HOW'S THAT?
GO AHEAD AND EAT UP. WE'LL MAKE SURE YOU'RE BACK BEFORE DAWN. TOMAS WILL NEVER KNOW.
WHY DO YOU HELP ME?
I HESITATED.
YOU ARE OUR LIGHT.
I KNOW THE TRAINING IS HARD, BUT TOMAS MEANS WELL.
I HAVE FAITH IN YOU.

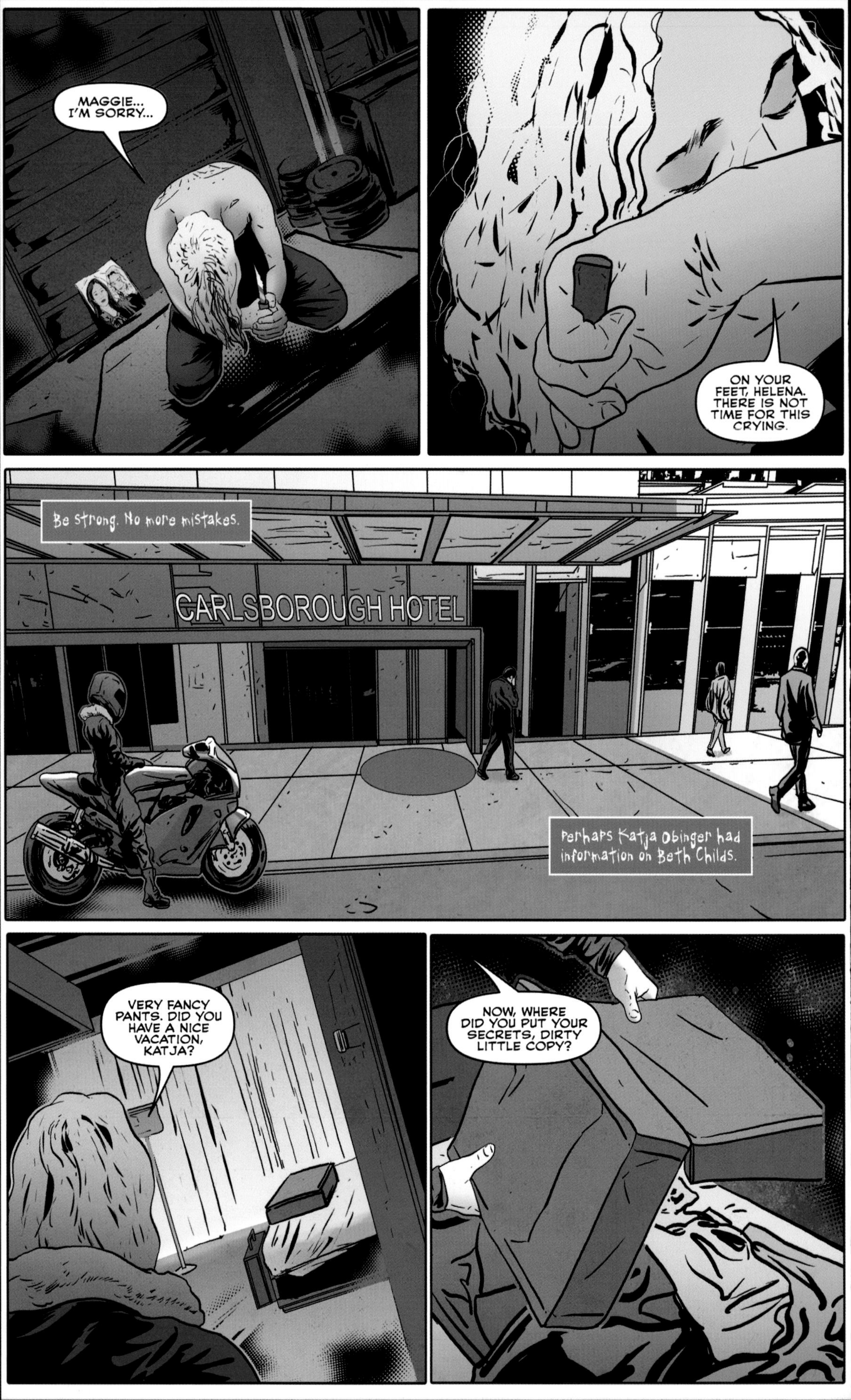
MAGGIE... I'M SORRY...
ON YOUR FEET, HELENA. THERE IS NOT TIME FOR THIS CRYING.
Be strong. No more mistakes.
CARLSBOROUGH HOTEL
Perhaps Katja Obinger had information on Beth Childs.
VERY FANCY PANTS. DID YOU HAVE A NICE VACATION, KATJA?
NOW, WHERE DID YOU PUT YOUR SECRETS, DIRTY LITTLE COPY?

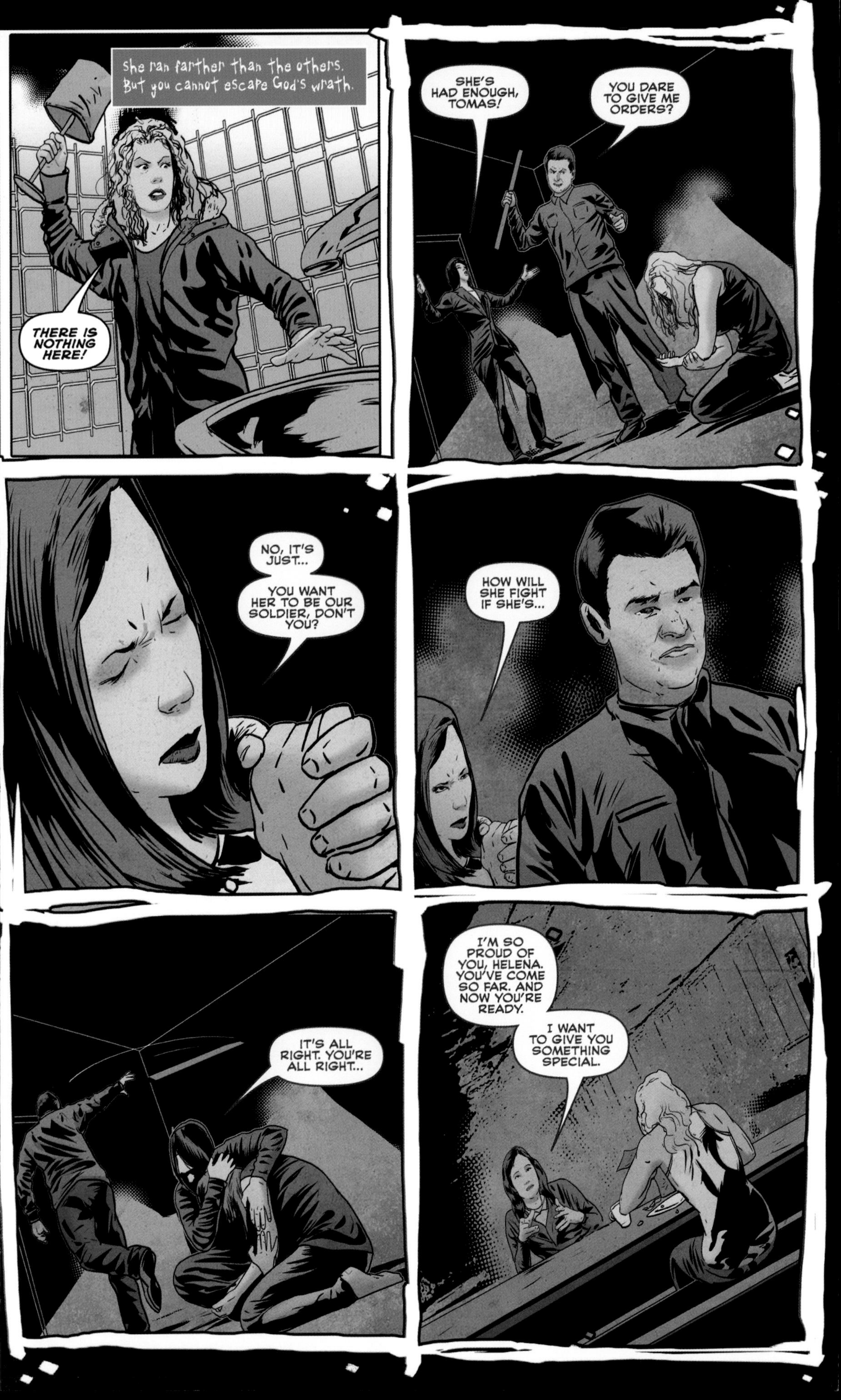
She ran farther than the others. But you cannot escape God's wrath.
THERE IS NOTHING HERE!
SHE'S HAD ENOUGH, TOMAS!
YOU DARE TO GIVE ME ORDERS?
NO, IT'S JUST...
YOU WANT HER TO BE OUR SOLDIER, DON'T YOU?
HOW WILL SHE FIGHT IF SHE'S...
IT'S ALL RIGHT. YOU'RE ALL RIGHT...
I'M SO PROUD OF YOU, HELENA. YOU'VE COME SO FAR. AND NOW YOU'RE READY.
I WANT TO GIVE YOU SOMETHING SPECIAL.

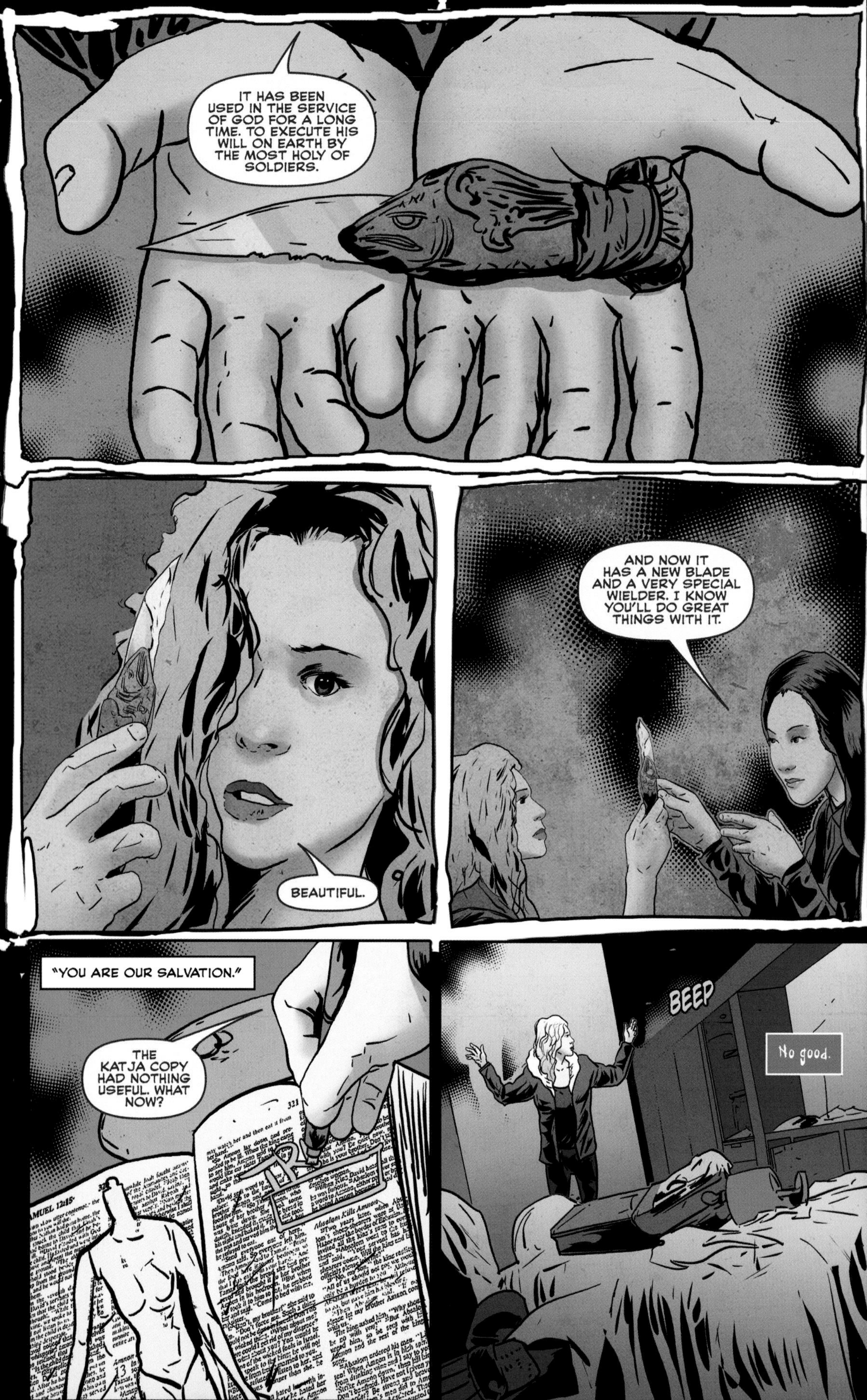
IT HAS BEEN USED IN THE SERVICE OF GOD FOR A LONG TIME. TO EXECUTE HIS WILL ON EARTH BY THE MOST HOLY OF SOLDIERS.
BEAUTIFUL.
AND NOW IT HAS A NEW BLADE AND A VERY SPECIAL WIELDER. I KNOW YOU'LL DO GREAT THINGS WITH IT.
"YOU ARE OUR SALVATION."
THE KATJA COPY HAD NOTHING USEFUL. WHAT NOW?
BEEP
No good.

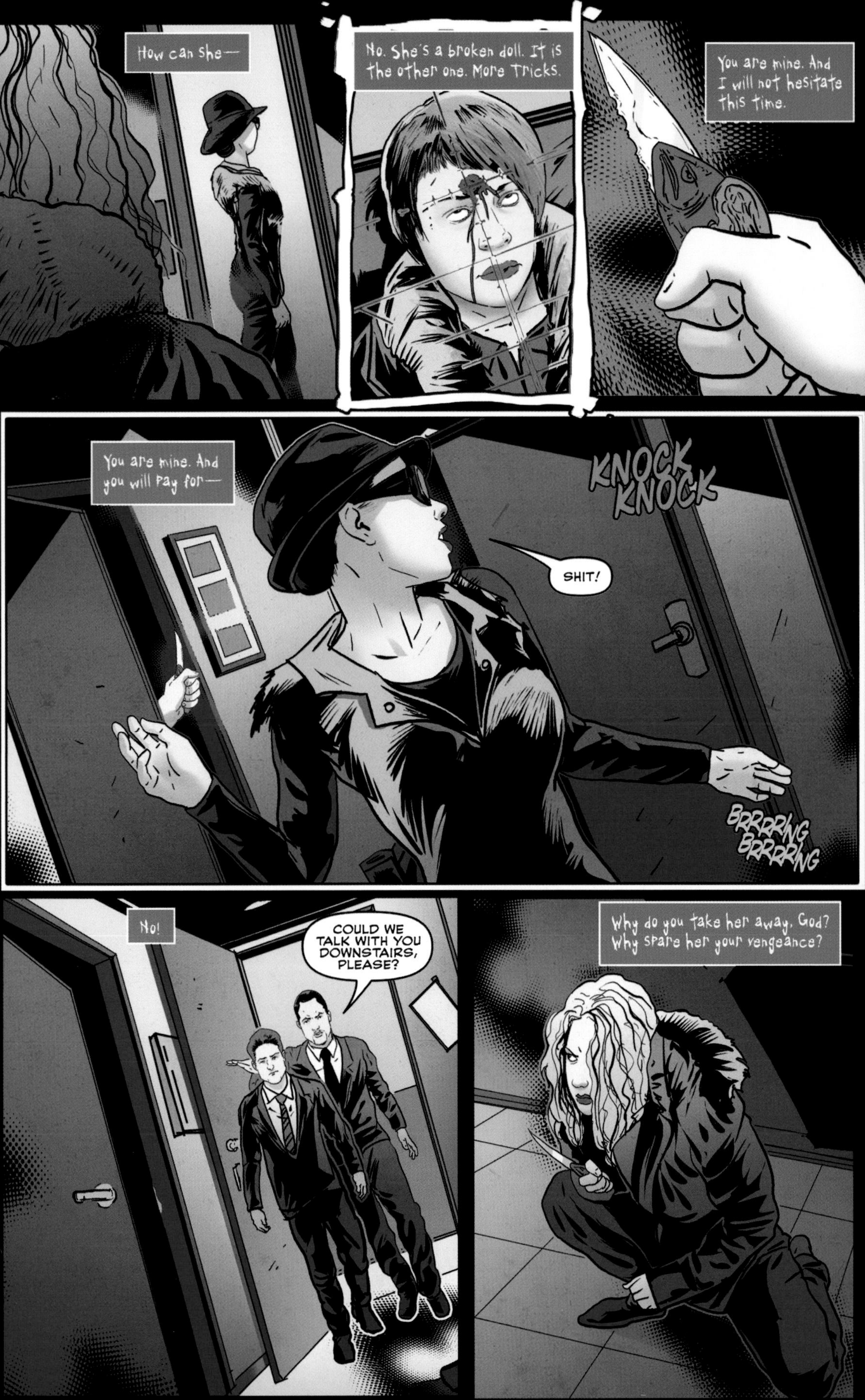
How can she—
No. She's a broken doll. It is the other one. More tricks.
You are mine. And I will not hesitate this time.
You are mine. And you will pay for—
KNOCK KNOCK
SHIT!
BRRRRING BRRRRING
No!
COULD WE TALK WITH YOU DOWNSTAIRS, PLEASE?
Why do you take her away, God? Why spare her your vengeance?

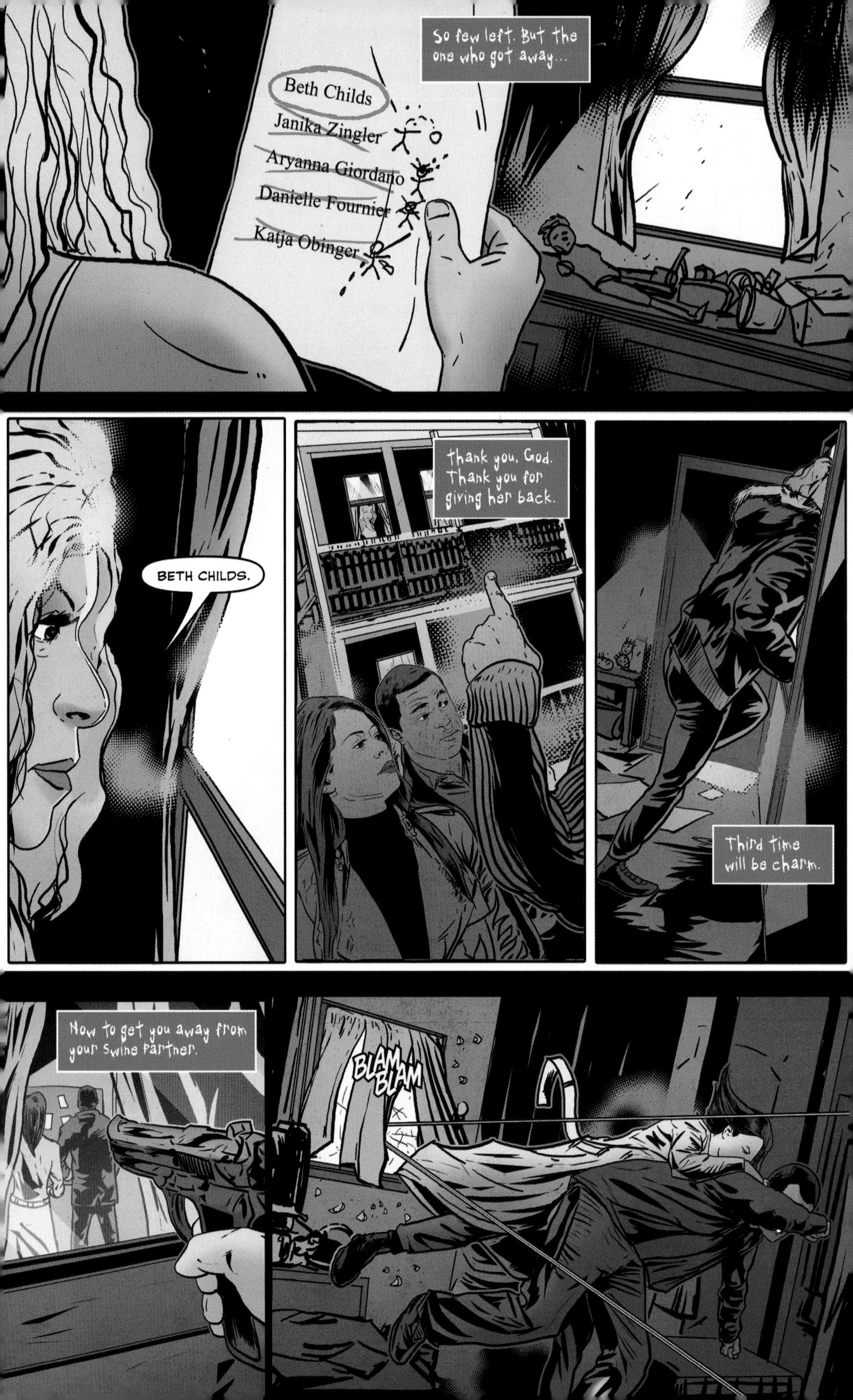
So few left. But the one who got away...
Beth Childs
Janika Zingler
Aryanna Giordano
Danielle Fournier
Katja Obinger
BETH CHILDS.
thank you, God. Thank you for giving her back.
Third time will be charm.
Now to get you away from your swine partner.
BLAM BLAM

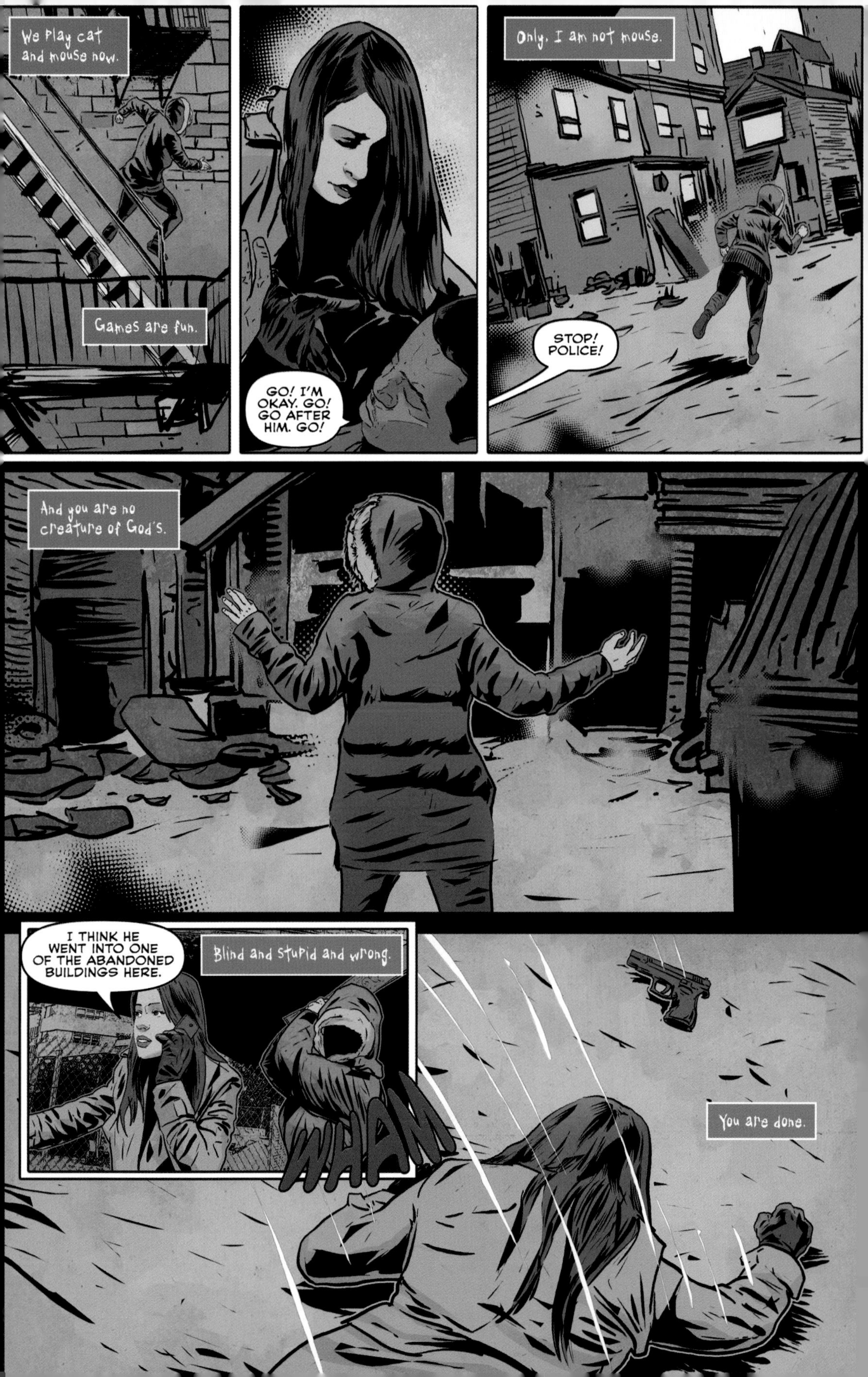

We play cat and mouse now.
Games are fun.
GO! I'M OKAY. GO! GO AFTER HIM. GO!
Only, I am not mouse.
STOP! POLICE!
And you are no creature of God's.
I THINK HE WENT INTO ONE OF THE ABANDONED BUILDINGS HERE.
Blind and stupid and wrong.
WHAM
You are done.

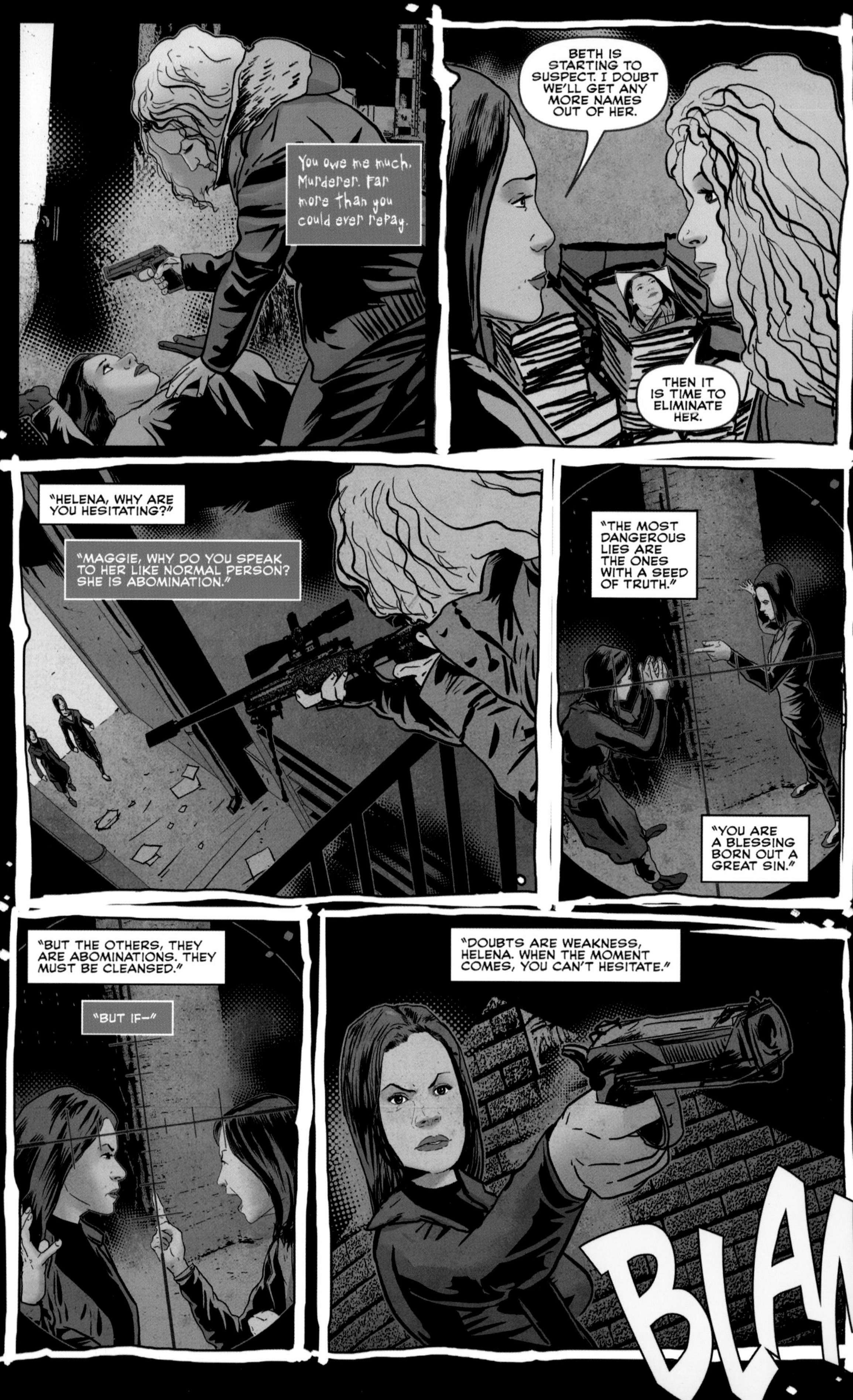
You owe me much, Murderer. Far more than you could ever repay.
BETH IS STARTING TO SUSPECT. I DOUBT WE'LL GET ANY MORE NAMES OUT OF HER.
THEN IT IS TIME TO ELIMINATE HER.
"HELENA, WHY ARE YOU HESITATING?"
"MAGGIE, WHY DO YOU SPEAK TO HER LIKE NORMAL PERSON? SHE IS ABOMINATION."
"THE MOST DANGEROUS LIES ARE THE ONES WITH A SEED OF TRUTH."
"YOU ARE A BLESSING BORN OUT A GREAT SIN."
"BUT THE OTHERS, THEY ARE ABOMINATIONS. THEY MUST BE CLEANSED."
"BUT IF–"
"DOUBTS ARE WEAKNESS, HELENA. WHEN THE MOMENT COMES, YOU CAN'T HESITATE."
BLAM

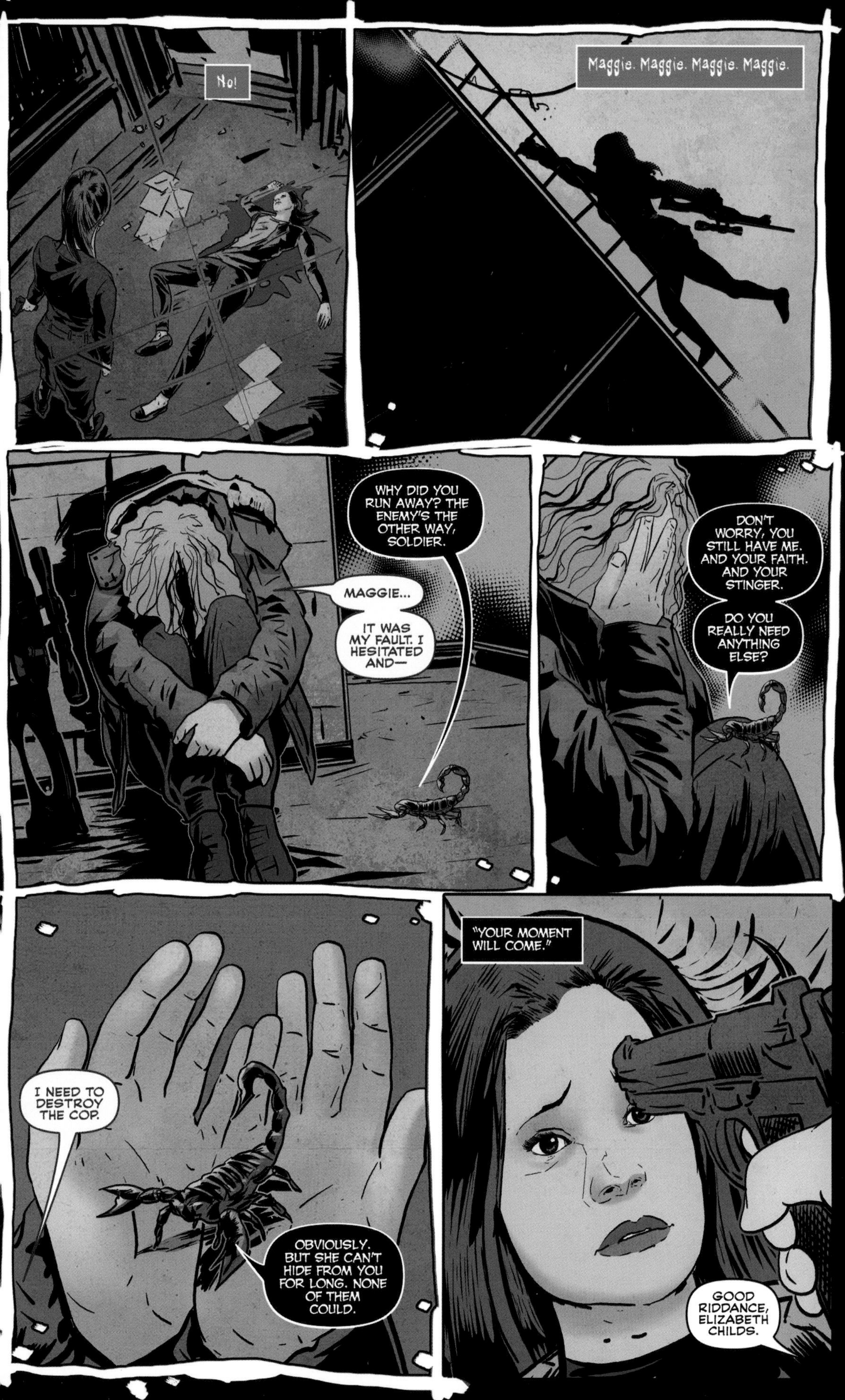
No!
Maggie. Maggie. Maggie. Maggie.
WHY DID YOU RUN AWAY? THE ENEMY'S THE OTHER WAY, SOLDIER.
MAGGIE...
IT WAS MY FAULT. I HESITATED AND—
DON'T WORRY, YOU STILL HAVE ME. AND YOUR FAITH. AND YOUR STINGER.
DO YOU REALLY NEED ANYTHING ELSE?
I NEED TO DESTROY THE COP.
OBVIOUSLY. BUT SHE CAN'T HIDE FROM YOU FOR LONG. NONE OF THEM COULD.
"YOUR MOMENT WILL COME."
GOOD RIDDANCE, ELIZABETH CHILDS.

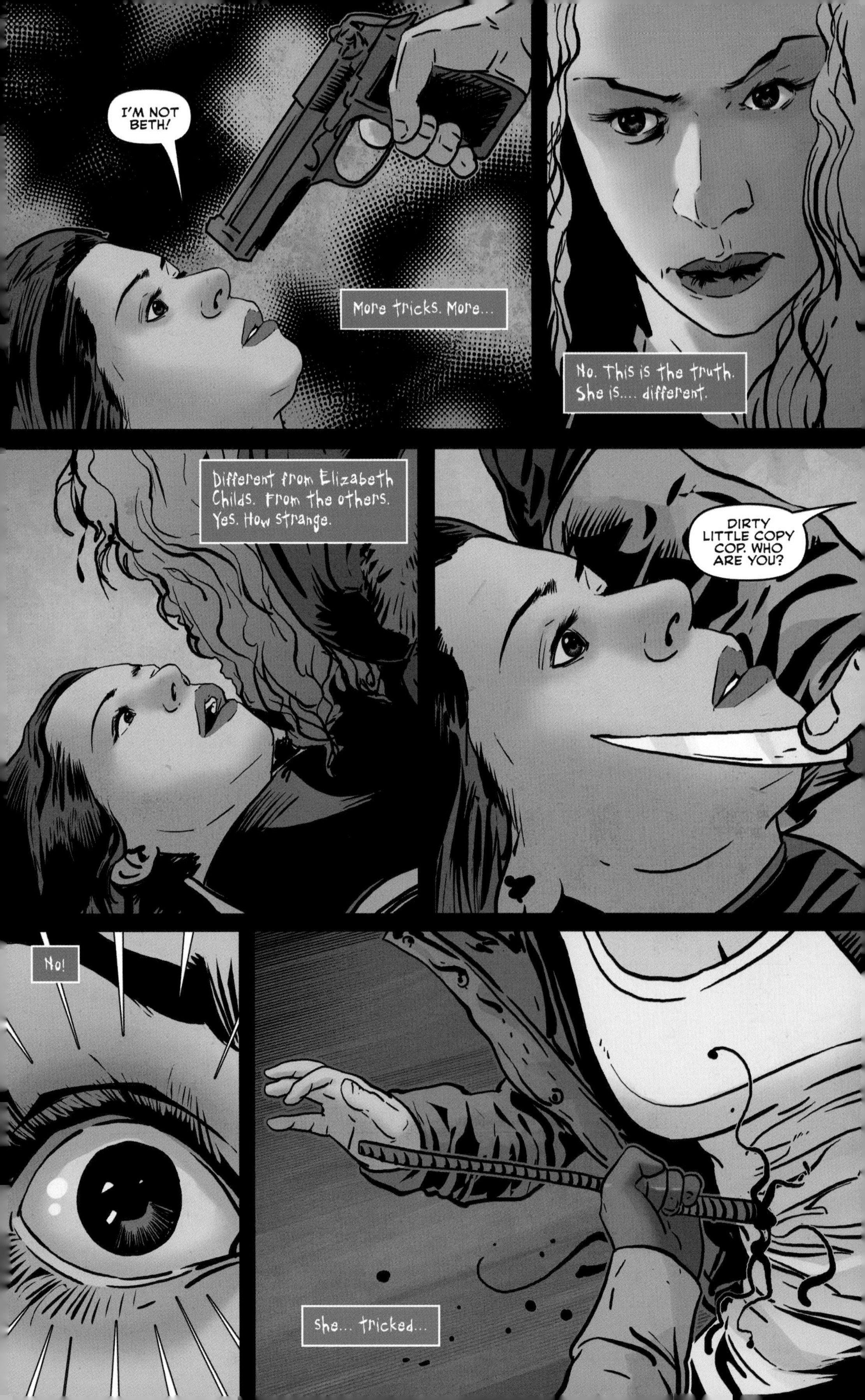
I'M NOT BETH!
More tricks. More...
No. This is the truth. She is.... different.
Different from Elizabeth Childs. From the others. Yes. How strange.
DIRTY LITTLE COPY COP. WHO ARE YOU?
No!
She... tricked...

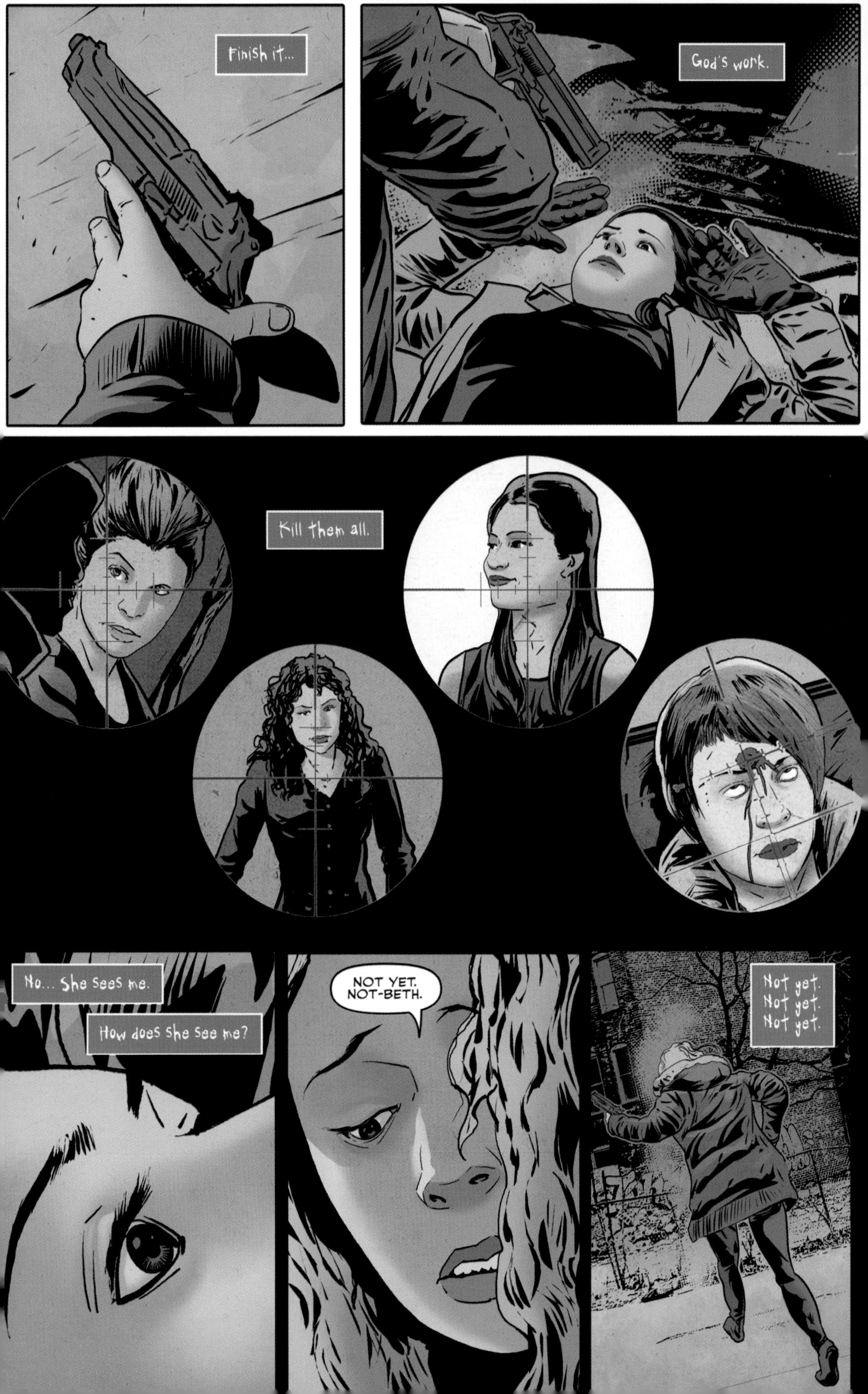

Finish it...
God's work.
Kill them all.
No... She sees me.
How does she see me?
NOT YET. NOT-BETH.
Not yet.
Not yet.
Not yet.

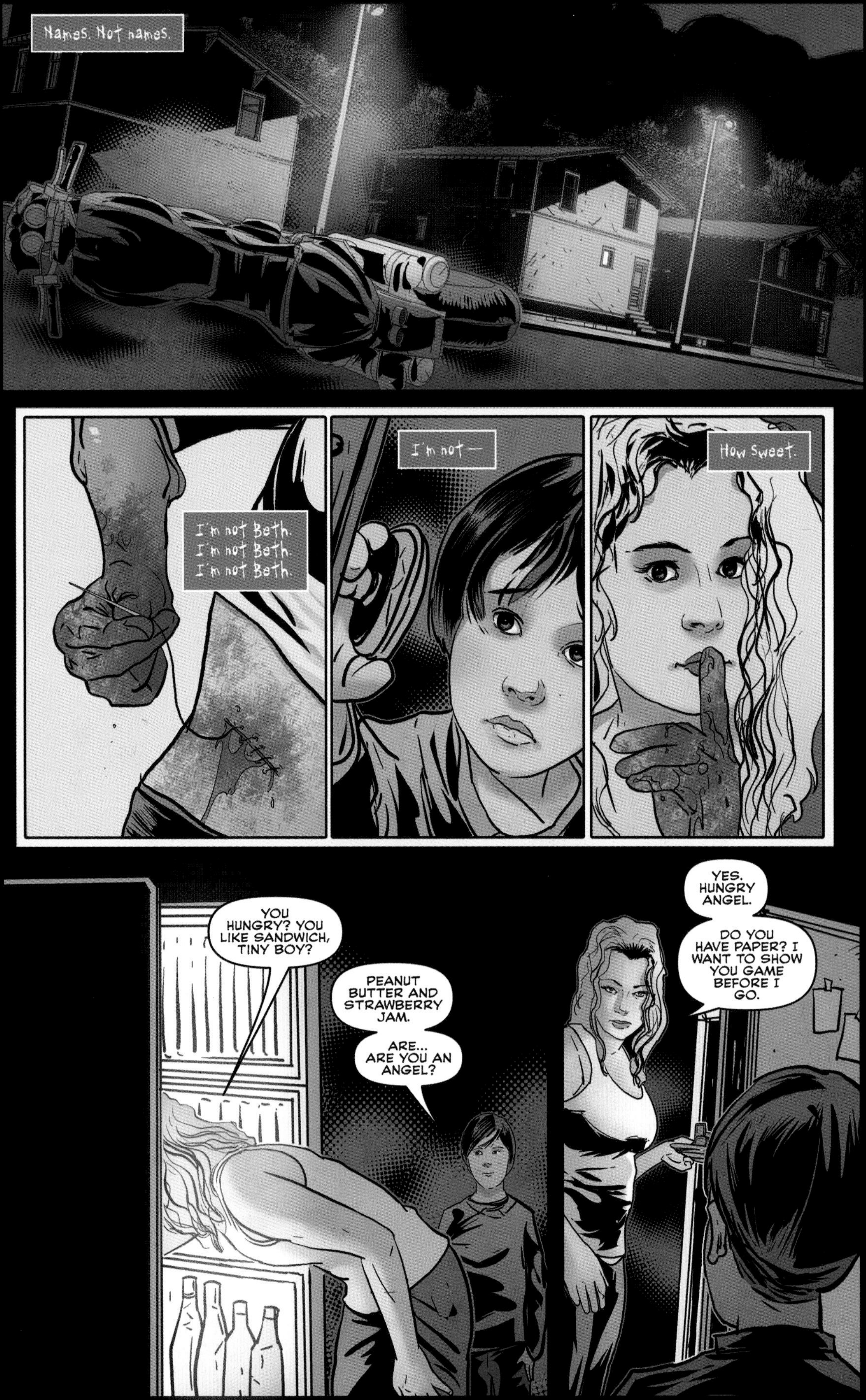
Names. Not names.
I'm not Beth.
I'm not Beth.
I'm not Beth.
I'm not—
How sweet.
YOU HUNGRY? YOU LIKE SANDWICH, TINY BOY?
PEANUT BUTTER AND STRAWBERRY JAM.
ARE... ARE YOU AN ANGEL?
YES. HUNGRY ANGEL.
DO YOU HAVE PAPER? I WANT TO SHOW YOU GAME BEFORE I GO.

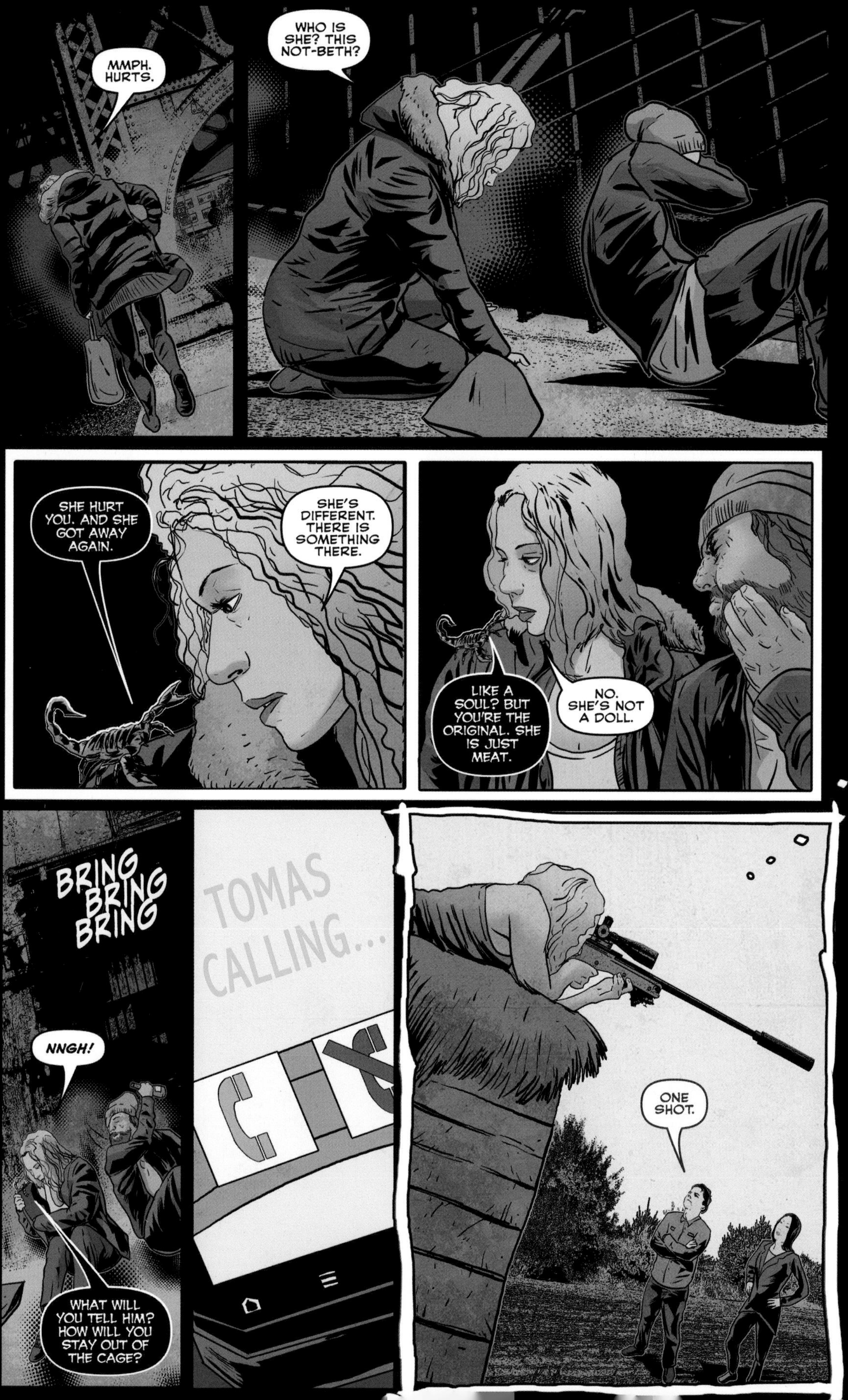
MMPH. HURTS.
WHO IS SHE? THIS NOT-BETH?
SHE HURT YOU. AND SHE GOT AWAY AGAIN.
SHE'S DIFFERENT. THERE IS SOMETHING THERE.
LIKE A SOUL? BUT YOU'RE THE ORIGINAL. SHE IS JUST MEAT.
NO. SHE'S NOT A DOLL.
BRING BRING BRING
NNGH!
WHAT WILL YOU TELL HIM? HOW WILL YOU STAY OUT OF THE CAGE?
TOMAS CALLING...
ONE SHOT.

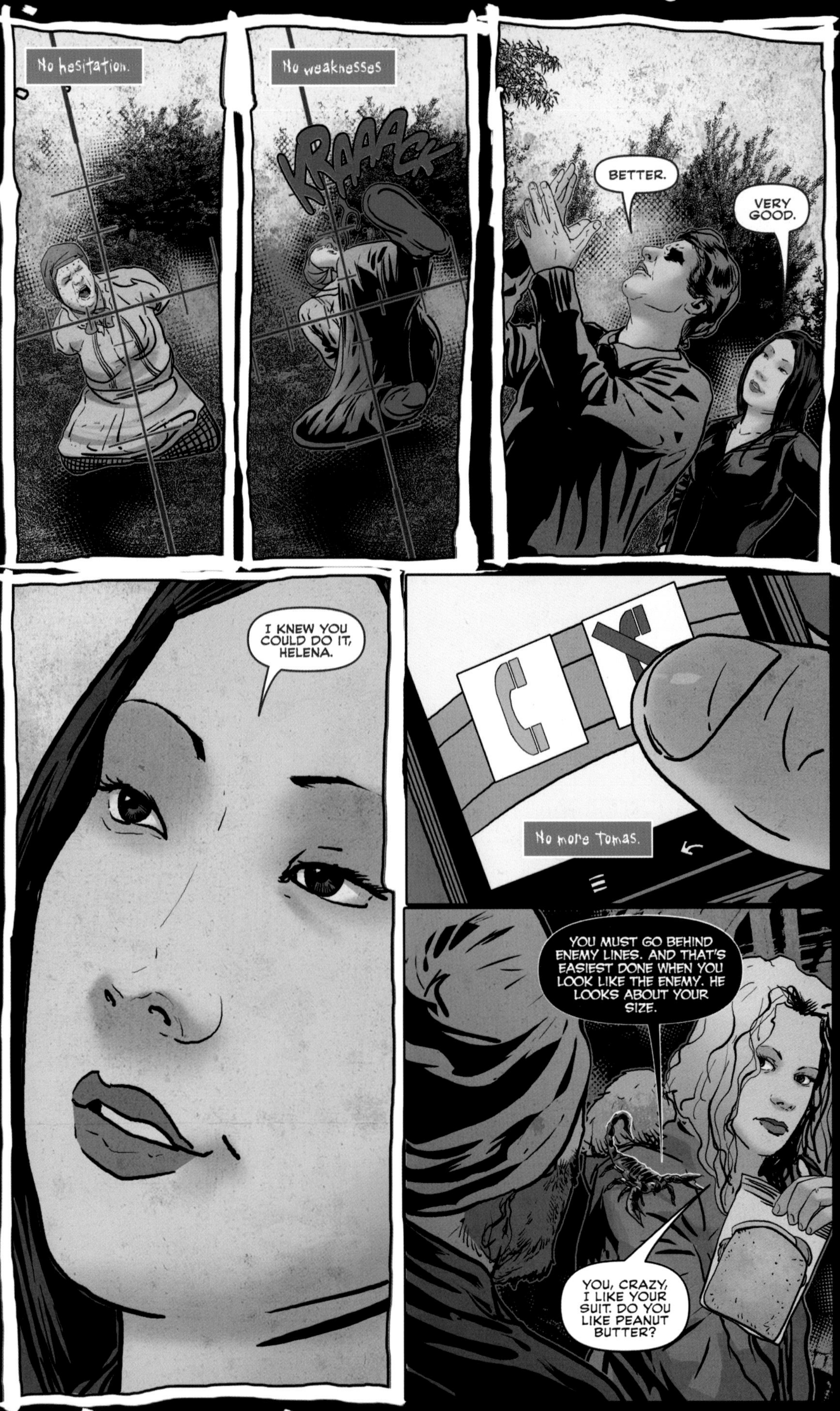
No hesitation.
No weaknesses
KRAAACK
BETTER.
VERY GOOD.
I KNEW YOU COULD DO IT, HELENA.
No more Tomas.
YOU MUST GO BEHIND ENEMY LINES. AND THAT'S EASIEST DONE WHEN YOU LOOK LIKE THE ENEMY. HE LOOKS ABOUT YOUR SIZE.
YOU, CRAZY, I LIKE YOUR SUIT. DO YOU LIKE PEANUT BUTTER?

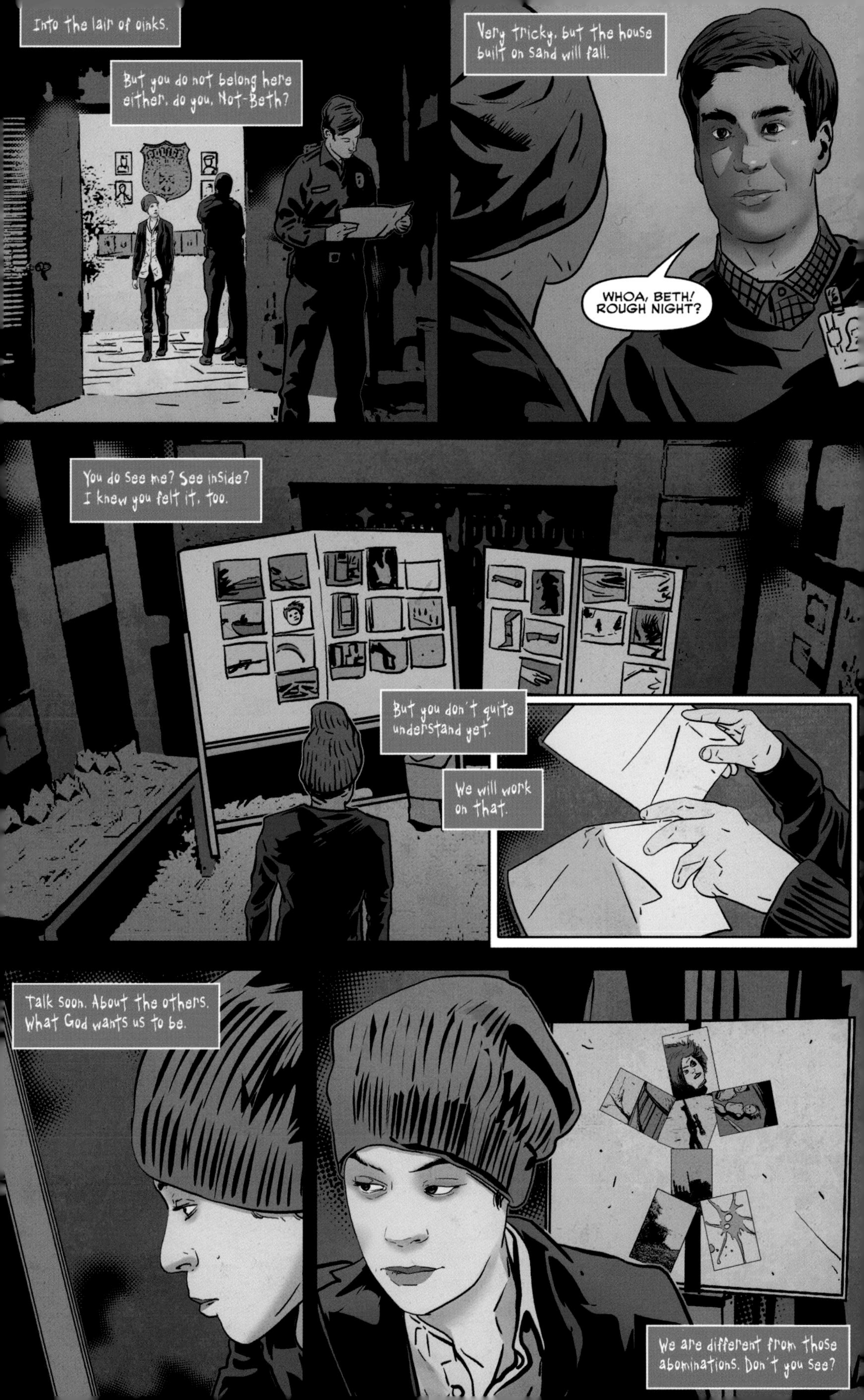
Into the lair of oinks.
But you do not belong here either, do you, Not-Beth?
Very tricky, but the house built on sand will fall.
WHOA, BETH! ROUGH NIGHT?
You do see me? See inside? I knew you felt it, too.
But you don't quite understand yet.
We will work on that.
Talk soon. About the others. What God wants us to be.
We are different from those abominations. Don't you see?

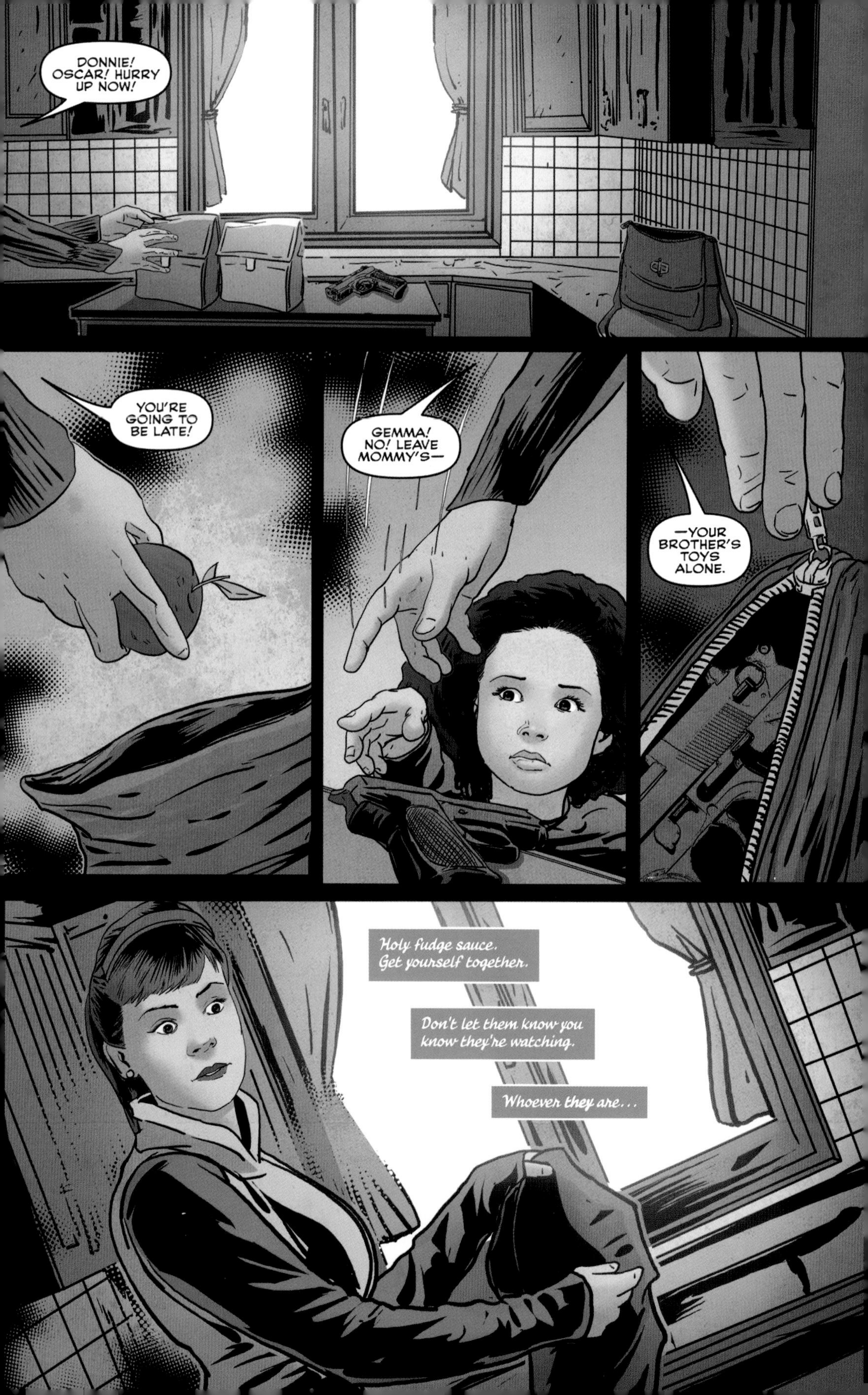
DONNIE! OSCAR! HURRY UP NOW!
YOU'RE GOING TO BE LATE!
GEMMA! NO! LEAVE MOMMY'S—
—YOUR BROTHER'S TOYS ALONE.
Holy fudge sauce. Get yourself together.
Don't let them know you know they're watching.
Whoever they are...

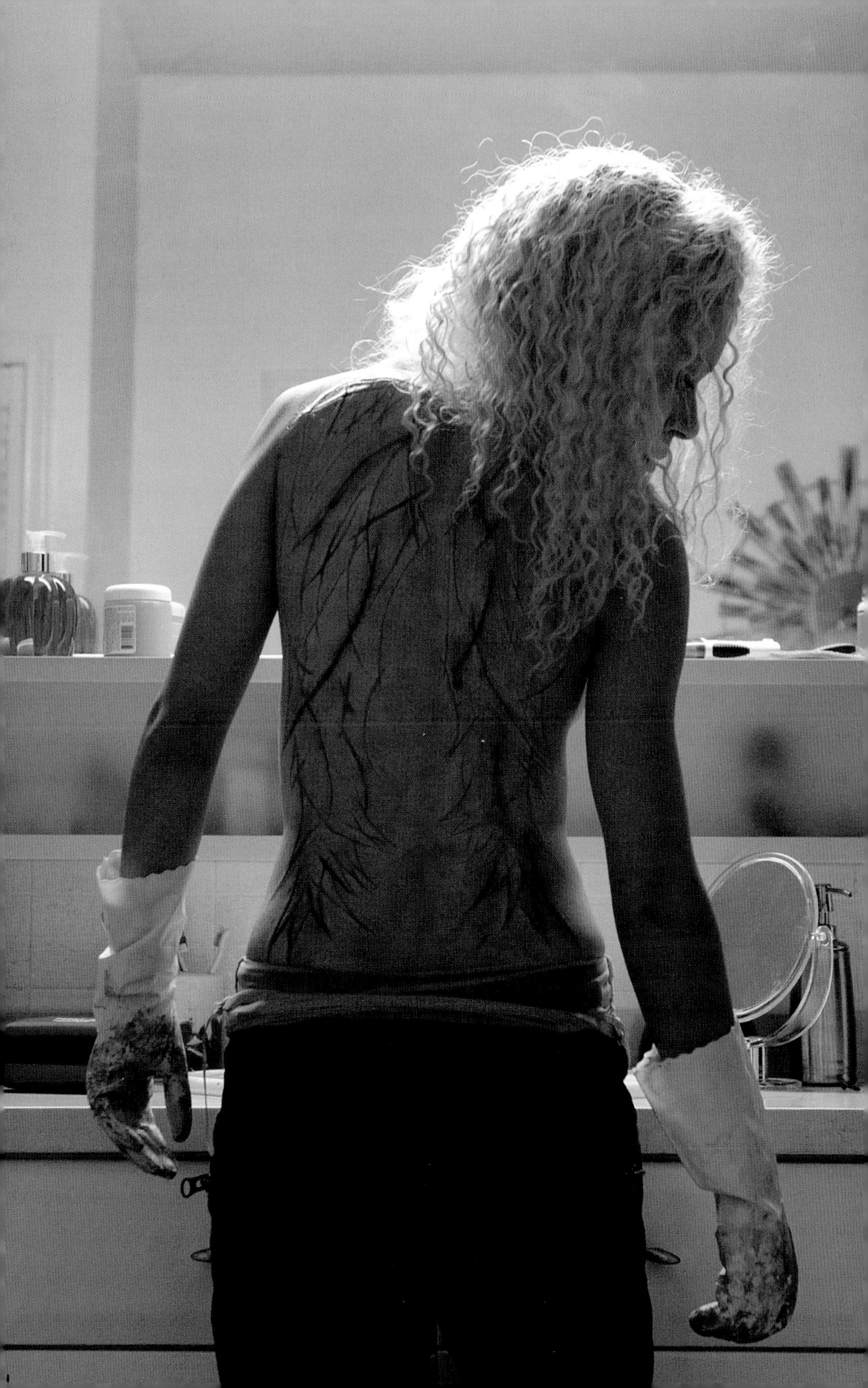

ALISON

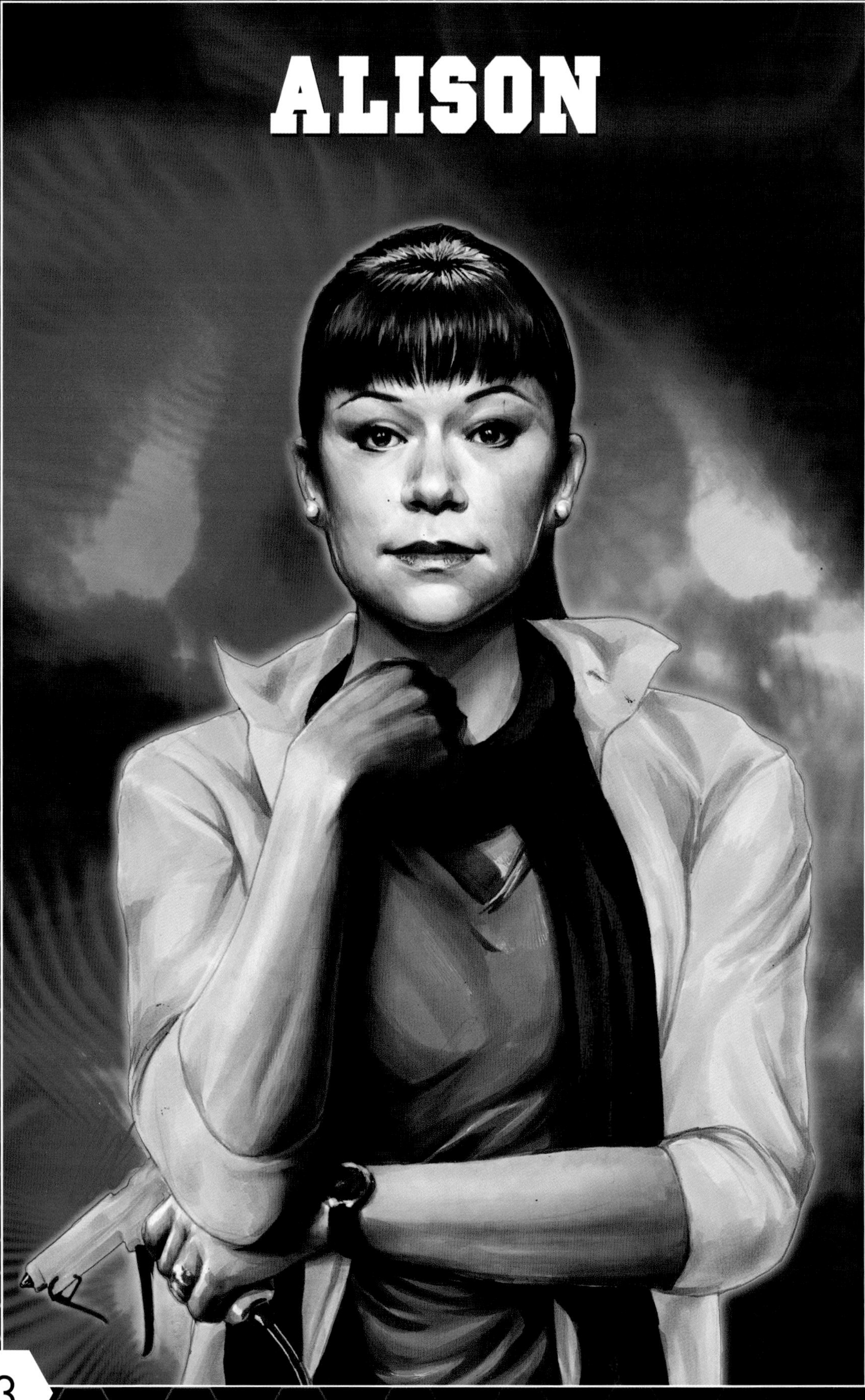

3

BY **CAT STAGGS**

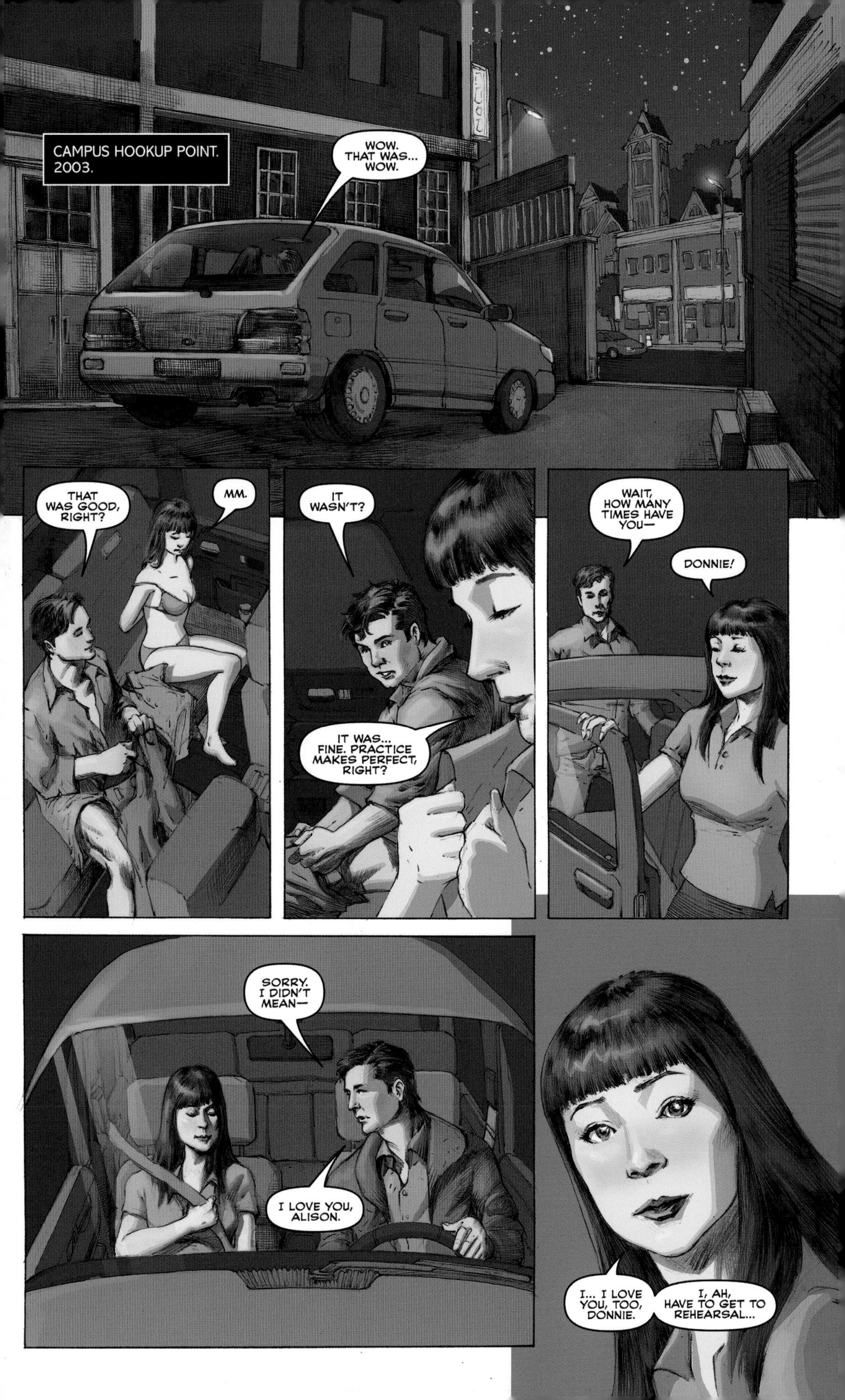
CAMPUS HOOKUP POINT. 2003.
WOW. THAT WAS... WOW.
THAT WAS GOOD, RIGHT?
MM.
IT WASN'T?
IT WAS... FINE. PRACTICE MAKES PERFECT, RIGHT?
WAIT, HOW MANY TIMES HAVE YOU—
DONNIE!
SORRY. I DIDN'T MEAN—
I LOVE YOU, ALISON.
I... I LOVE YOU, TOO, DONNIE.
I, AH, HAVE TO GET TO REHEARSAL...

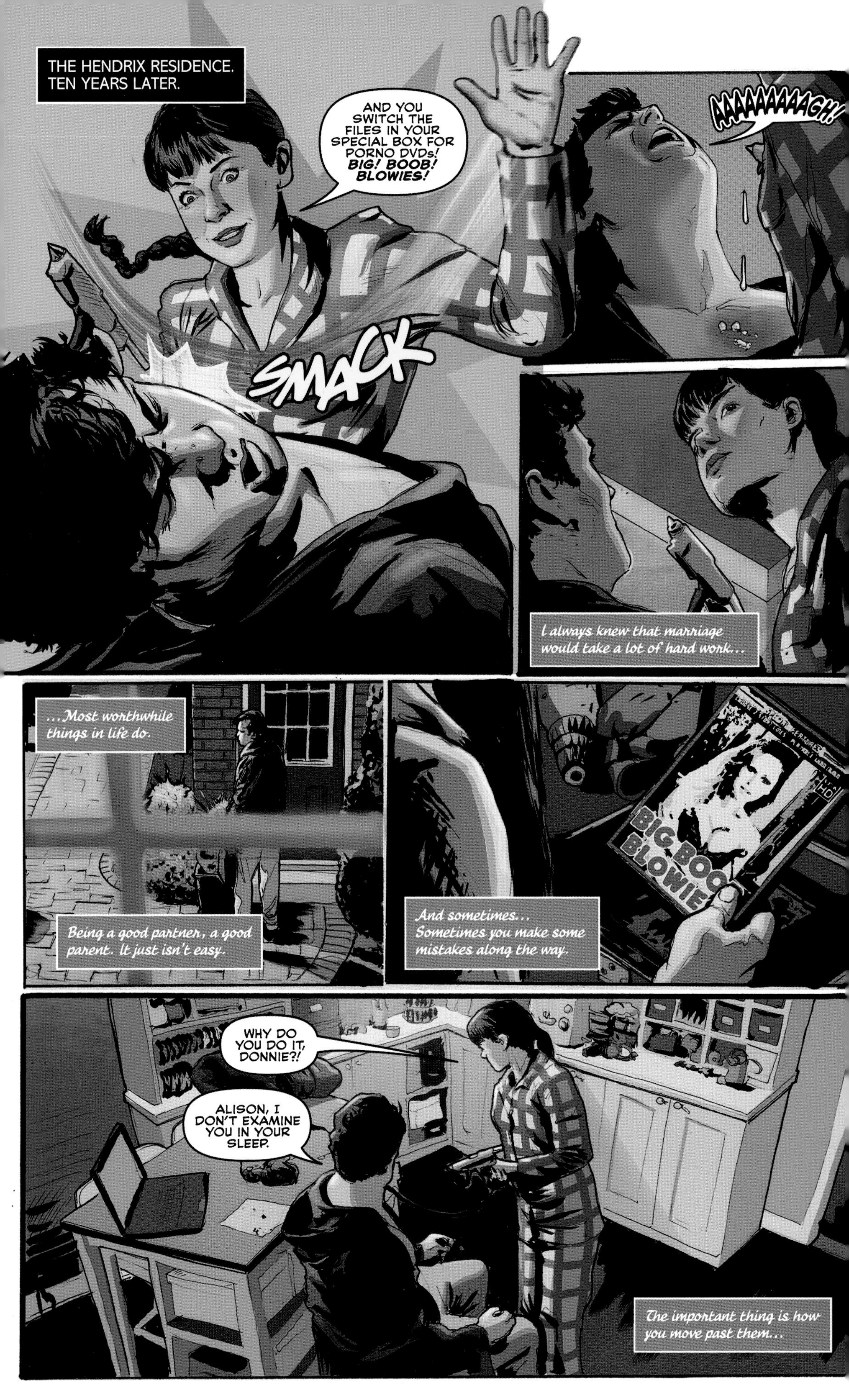
THE HENDRIX RESIDENCE. TEN YEARS LATER.
AND YOU SWITCH THE FILES IN YOUR SPECIAL BOX FOR PORNO DVDs! BIG! BOOB! BLOWIES!
SMACK
AAAAAAAAGH!
I always knew that marriage would take a lot of hard work...
...Most worthwhile things in life do.
Being a good partner, a good parent. It just isn't easy.
And sometimes... Sometimes you make some mistakes along the way.
WHY DO YOU DO IT, DONNIE?!
ALISON, I DON'T EXAMINE YOU IN YOUR SLEEP.
The important thing is how you move past them...

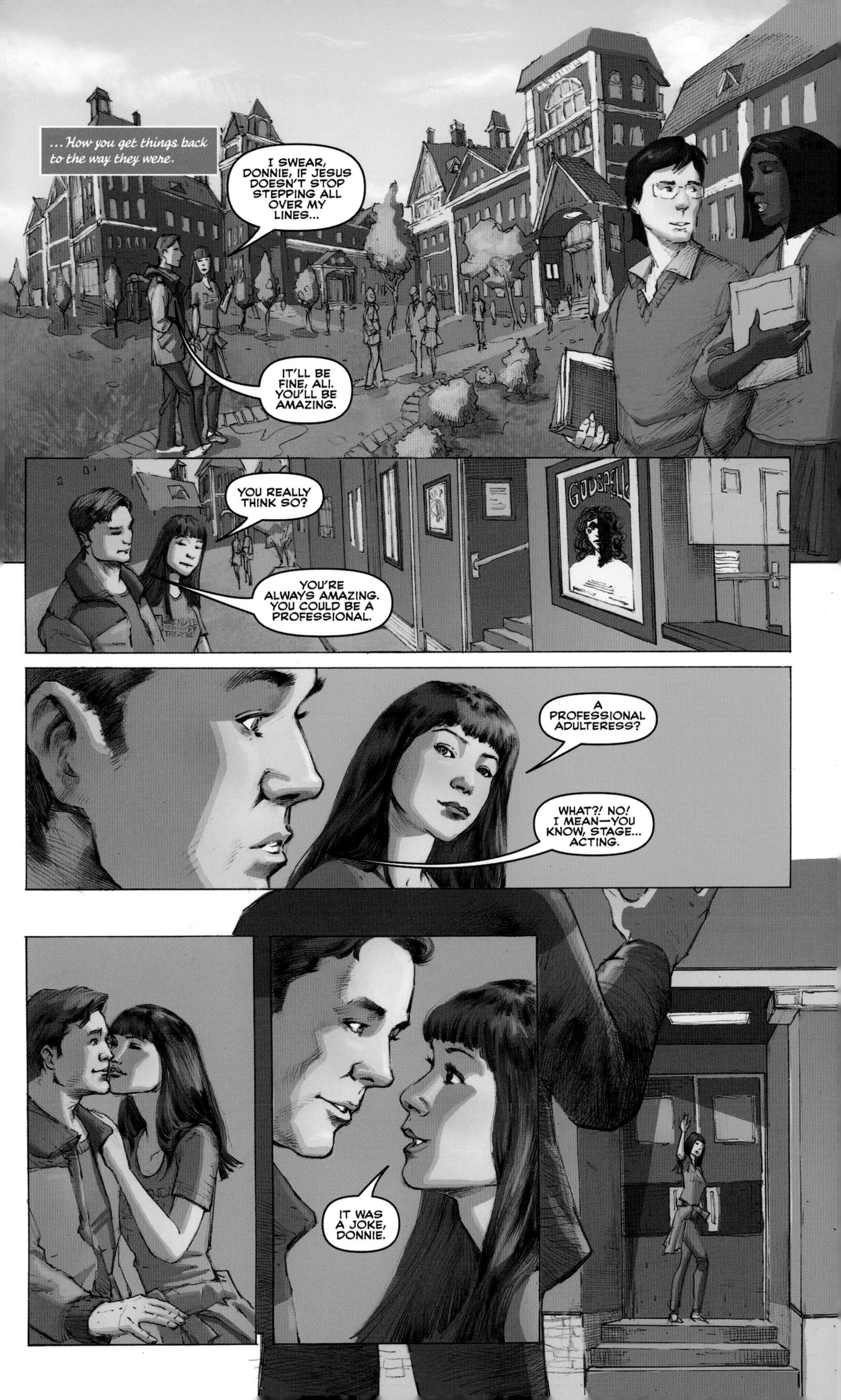
...How you get things back to the way they were.
I SWEAR, DONNIE, IF JESUS DOESN'T STOP STEPPING ALL OVER MY LINES...
IT'LL BE FINE, ALI. YOU'LL BE AMAZING.
YOU REALLY THINK SO?
YOU'RE ALWAYS AMAZING. YOU COULD BE A PROFESSIONAL.
A PROFESSIONAL ADULTERESS?
WHAT?! NO! I MEAN—YOU KNOW, STAGE... ACTING.
IT WAS A JOKE, DONNIE.

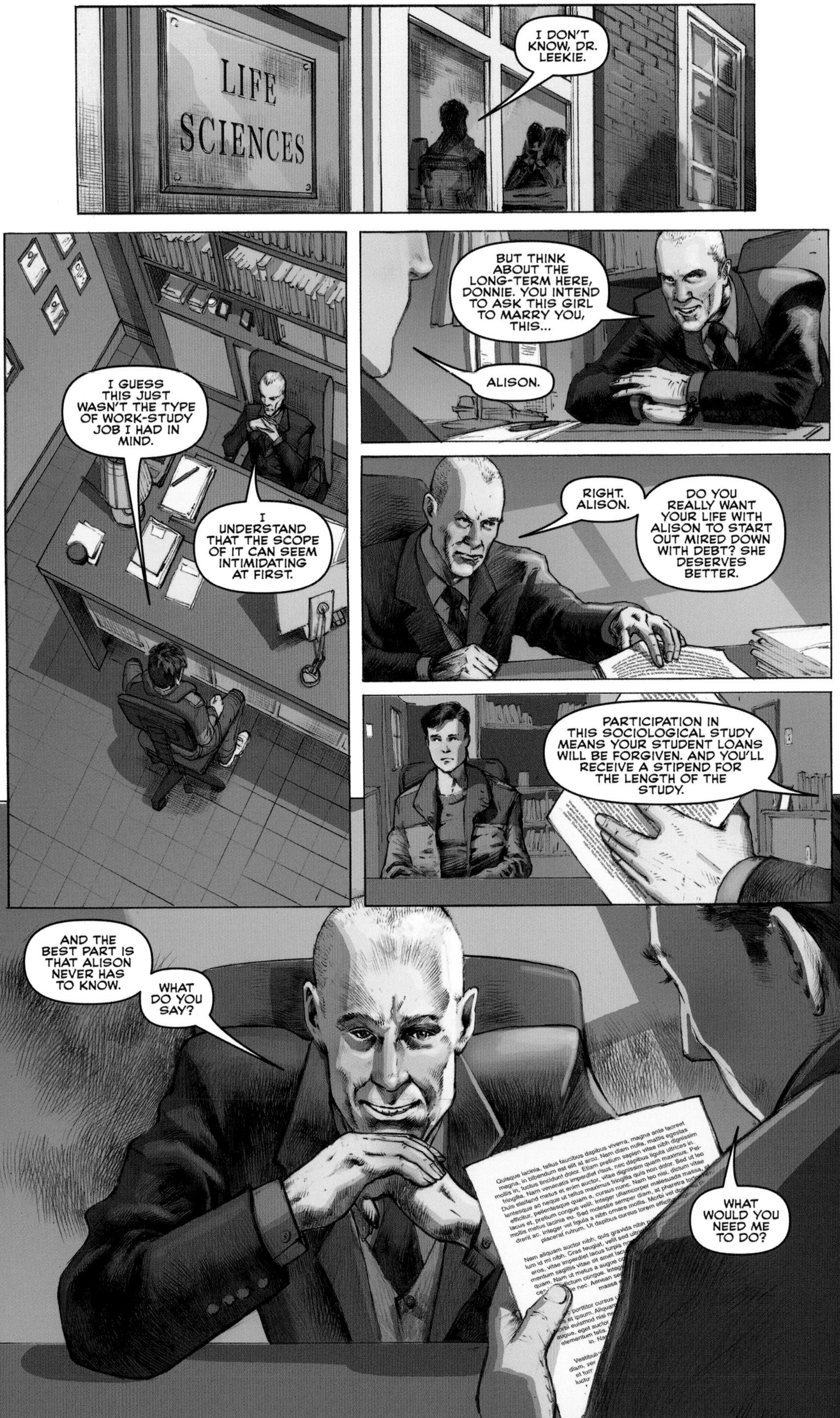
LIFE SCIENCES
I DON'T KNOW, DR. LEEKIE.
I GUESS THIS JUST WASN'T THE TYPE OF WORK-STUDY JOB I HAD IN MIND.
I UNDERSTAND THAT THE SCOPE OF IT CAN SEEM INTIMIDATING AT FIRST.
BUT THINK ABOUT THE LONG-TERM HERE, DONNIE. YOU INTEND TO ASK THIS GIRL TO MARRY YOU, THIS...
ALISON.
RIGHT. ALISON.
DO YOU REALLY WANT YOUR LIFE WITH ALISON TO START OUT MIRED DOWN WITH DEBT? SHE DESERVES BETTER.
PARTICIPATION IN THIS SOCIOLOGICAL STUDY MEANS YOUR STUDENT LOANS WILL BE FORGIVEN. AND YOU'LL RECEIVE A STIPEND FOR THE LENGTH OF THE STUDY.
AND THE BEST PART IS THAT ALISON NEVER HAS TO KNOW.
WHAT DO YOU SAY?
WHAT WOULD YOU NEED ME TO DO?

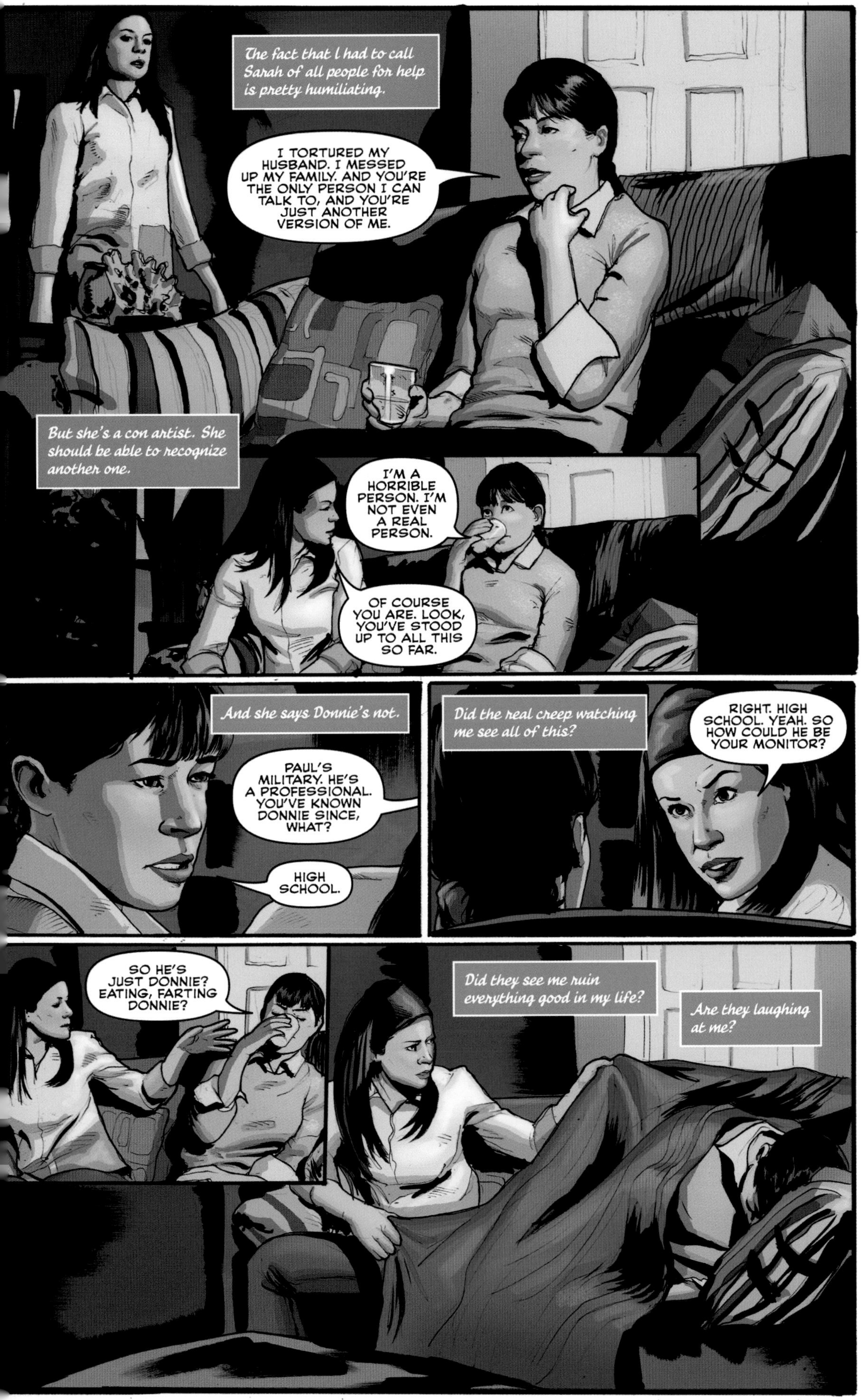
The fact that I had to call Sarah of all people for help is pretty humiliating.
I TORTURED MY HUSBAND. I MESSED UP MY FAMILY. AND YOU'RE THE ONLY PERSON I CAN TALK TO, AND YOU'RE JUST ANOTHER VERSION OF ME.
But she's a con artist. She should be able to recognize another one.
I'M A HORRIBLE PERSON. I'M NOT EVEN A REAL PERSON.
OF COURSE YOU ARE. LOOK, YOU'VE STOOD UP TO ALL THIS SO FAR.
And she says Donnie's not.
PAUL'S MILITARY. HE'S A PROFESSIONAL. YOU'VE KNOWN DONNIE SINCE, WHAT?
HIGH SCHOOL.
Did the real creep watching me see all of this?
RIGHT. HIGH SCHOOL. YEAH. SO HOW COULD HE BE YOUR MONITOR?
SO HE'S JUST DONNIE? EATING, FARTING DONNIE?
Did they see me ruin everything good in my life?
Are they laughing at me?

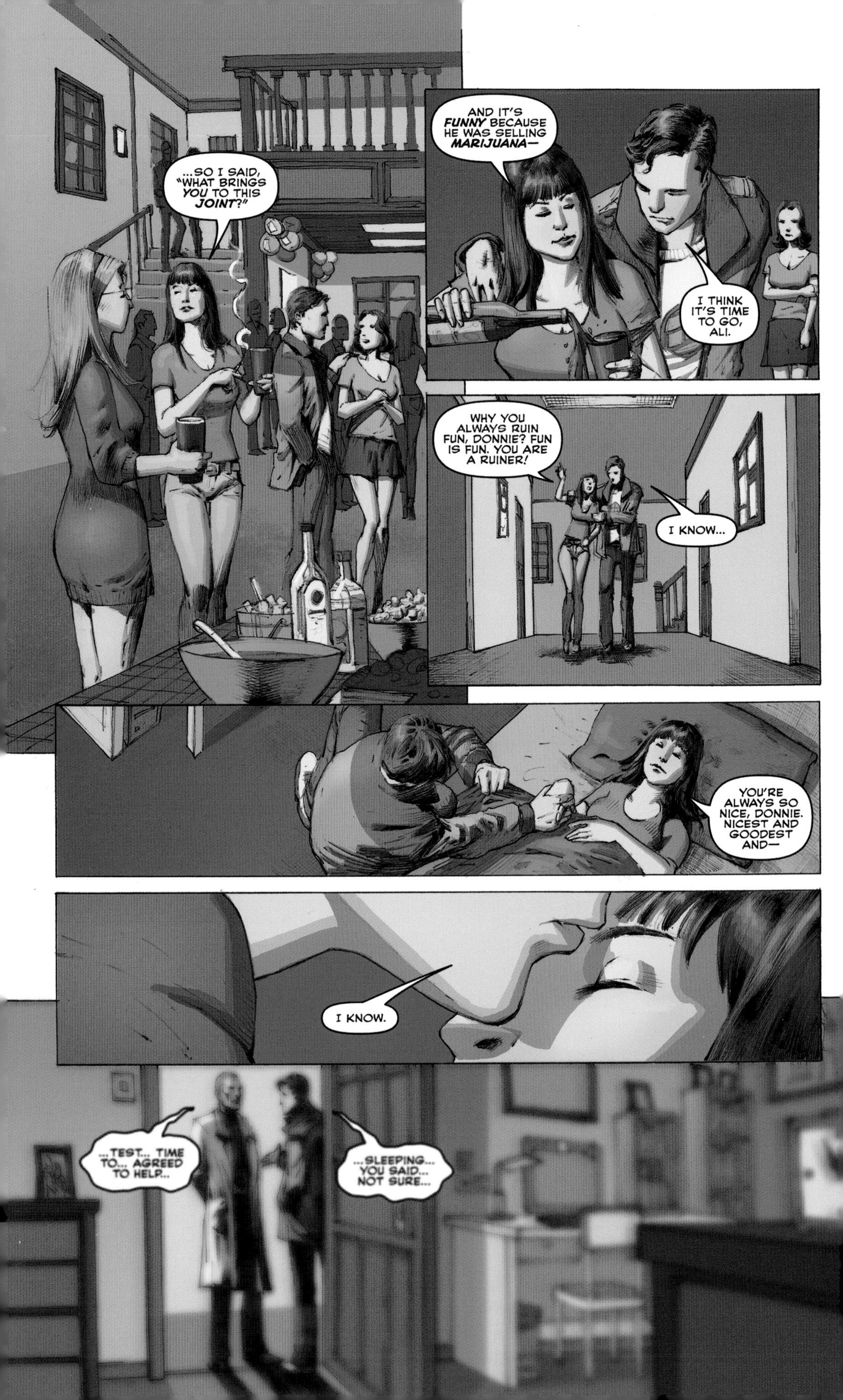
...SO I SAID, "WHAT BRINGS YOU TO THIS JOINT?"
AND IT'S FUNNY BECAUSE HE WAS SELLING MARIJUANA—
I THINK IT'S TIME TO GO, ALI.
WHY YOU ALWAYS RUIN FUN, DONNIE? FUN IS FUN. YOU ARE A RUINER!
I KNOW...
YOU'RE ALWAYS SO NICE, DONNIE. NICEST AND GOODEST AND—
I KNOW.
...TEST... TIME TO... AGREED TO HELP...
...SLEEPING... YOU SAID... NOT SURE...

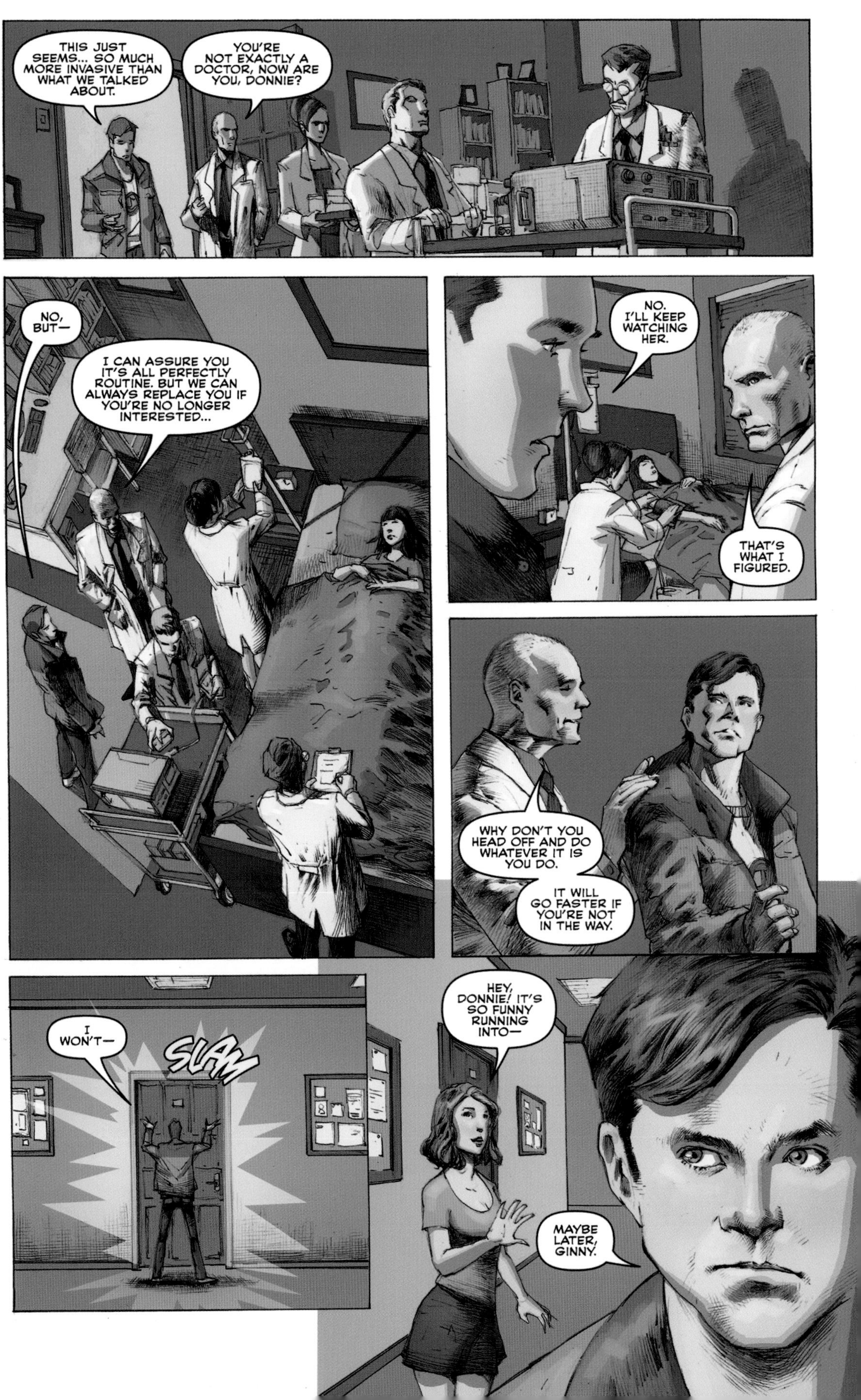
THIS JUST SEEMS... SO MUCH MORE INVASIVE THAN WHAT WE TALKED ABOUT.
YOU'RE NOT EXACTLY A DOCTOR, NOW ARE YOU, DONNIE?
NO, BUT—
I CAN ASSURE YOU IT'S ALL PERFECTLY ROUTINE. BUT WE CAN ALWAYS REPLACE YOU IF YOU'RE NO LONGER INTERESTED...
NO. I'LL KEEP WATCHING HER.
THAT'S WHAT I FIGURED.
WHY DON'T YOU HEAD OFF AND DO WHATEVER IT IS YOU DO.
IT WILL GO FASTER IF YOU'RE NOT IN THE WAY.
I WON'T—
SLAM
HEY, DONNIE! IT'S SO FUNNY RUNNING INTO—
MAYBE LATER, GINNY.

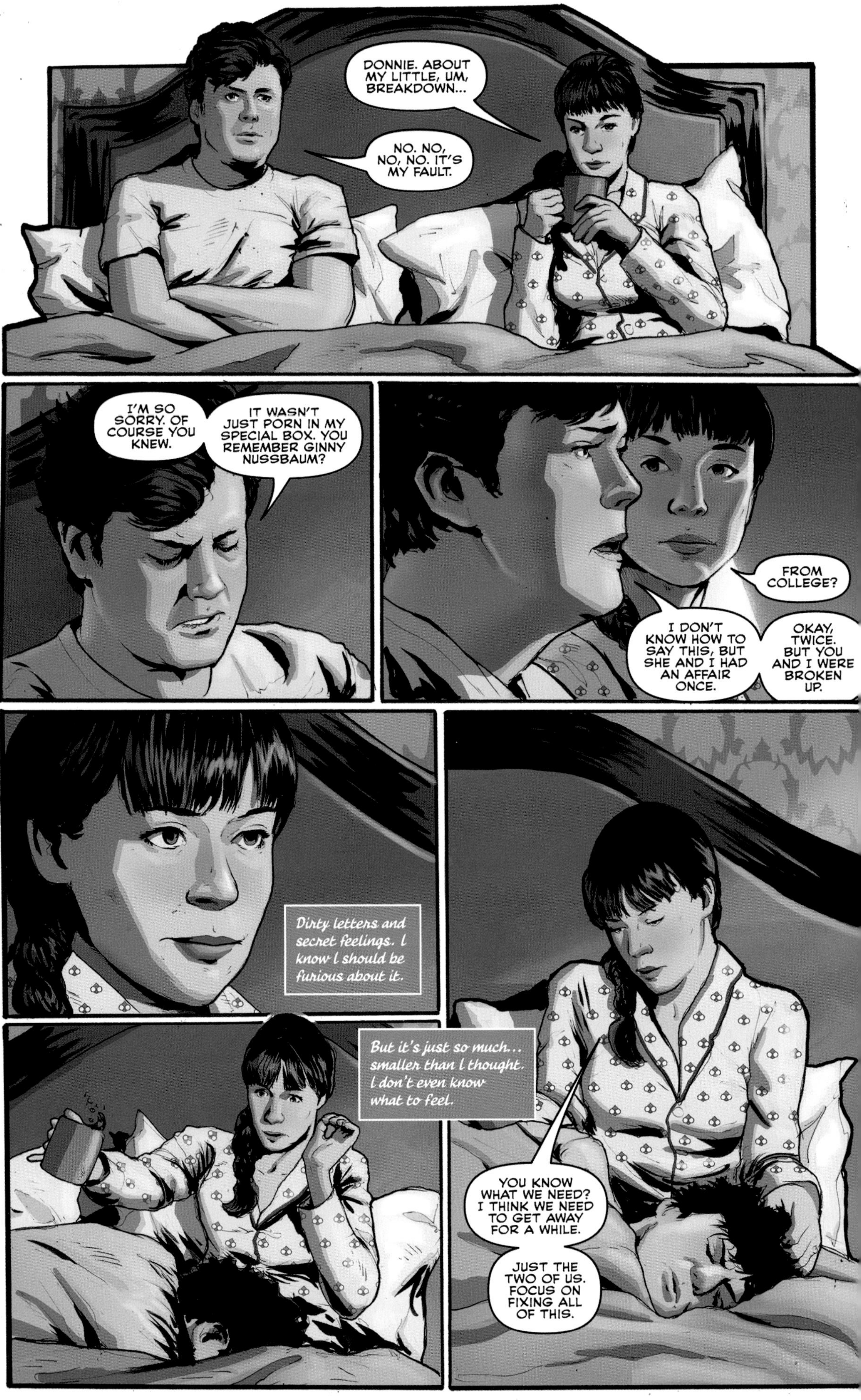
DONNIE. ABOUT MY LITTLE, UM, BREAKDOWN...
NO. NO, NO, NO. IT'S MY FAULT.
I'M SO SORRY. OF COURSE YOU KNEW.
IT WASN'T JUST PORN IN MY SPECIAL BOX. YOU REMEMBER GINNY NUSSBAUM?
FROM COLLEGE?
I DON'T KNOW HOW TO SAY THIS, BUT SHE AND I HAD AN AFFAIR ONCE.
OKAY, TWICE. BUT YOU AND I WERE BROKEN UP.
Dirty letters and secret feelings. I know I should be furious about it.
But it's just so much... smaller than I thought. I don't even know what to feel.
YOU KNOW WHAT WE NEED? I THINK WE NEED TO GET AWAY FOR A WHILE.
JUST THE TWO OF US. FOCUS ON FIXING ALL OF THIS.

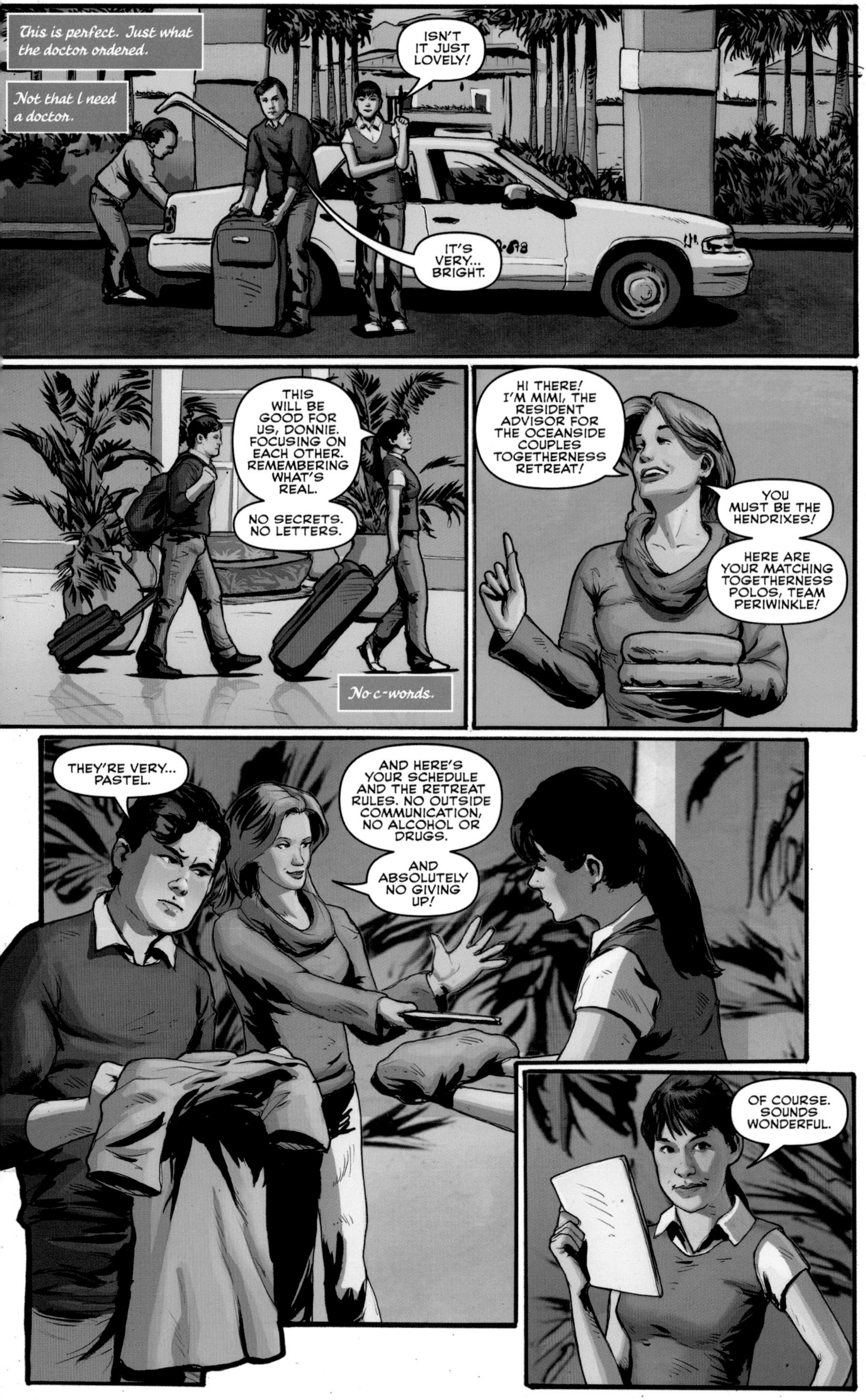
This is perfect. Just what the doctor ordered.
Not that I need a doctor.
ISN'T IT JUST LOVELY!
IT'S VERY... BRIGHT.
THIS WILL BE GOOD FOR US, DONNIE. FOCUSING ON EACH OTHER. REMEMBERING WHAT'S REAL.
NO SECRETS. NO LETTERS.
No c-words.
HI THERE! I'M MIMI, THE RESIDENT ADVISOR FOR THE OCEANSIDE COUPLES TOGETHERNESS RETREAT!
YOU MUST BE THE HENDRIXES!
HERE ARE YOUR MATCHING TOGETHERNESS POLOS, TEAM PERIWINKLE!
THEY'RE VERY... PASTEL.
AND HERE'S YOUR SCHEDULE AND THE RETREAT RULES. NO OUTSIDE COMMUNICATION, NO ALCOHOL OR DRUGS.
AND ABSOLUTELY NO GIVING UP!
OF COURSE. SOUNDS WONDERFUL.

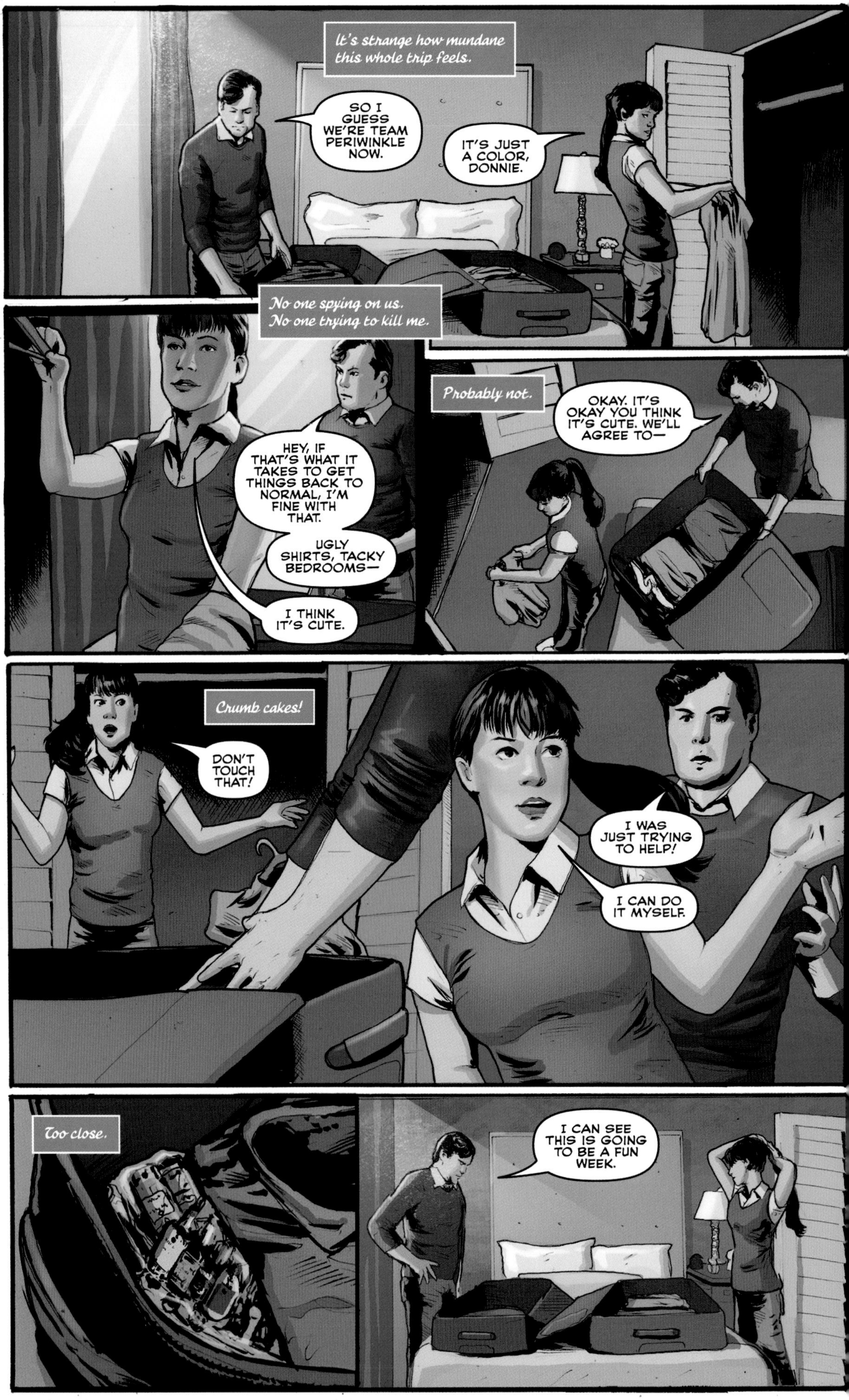

It's strange how mundane this whole trip feels.
SO I GUESS WE'RE TEAM PERIWINKLE NOW.
IT'S JUST A COLOR, DONNIE.
No one spying on us. No one trying to kill me.
HEY, IF THAT'S WHAT IT TAKES TO GET THINGS BACK TO NORMAL, I'M FINE WITH THAT.
UGLY SHIRTS, TACKY BEDROOMS—
I THINK IT'S CUTE.
Probably not.
OKAY. IT'S OKAY YOU THINK IT'S CUTE. WE'LL AGREE TO—
Crumb cakes!
DON'T TOUCH THAT!
I WAS JUST TRYING TO HELP!
I CAN DO IT MYSELF.
Too close.
I CAN SEE THIS IS GOING TO BE A FUN WEEK.

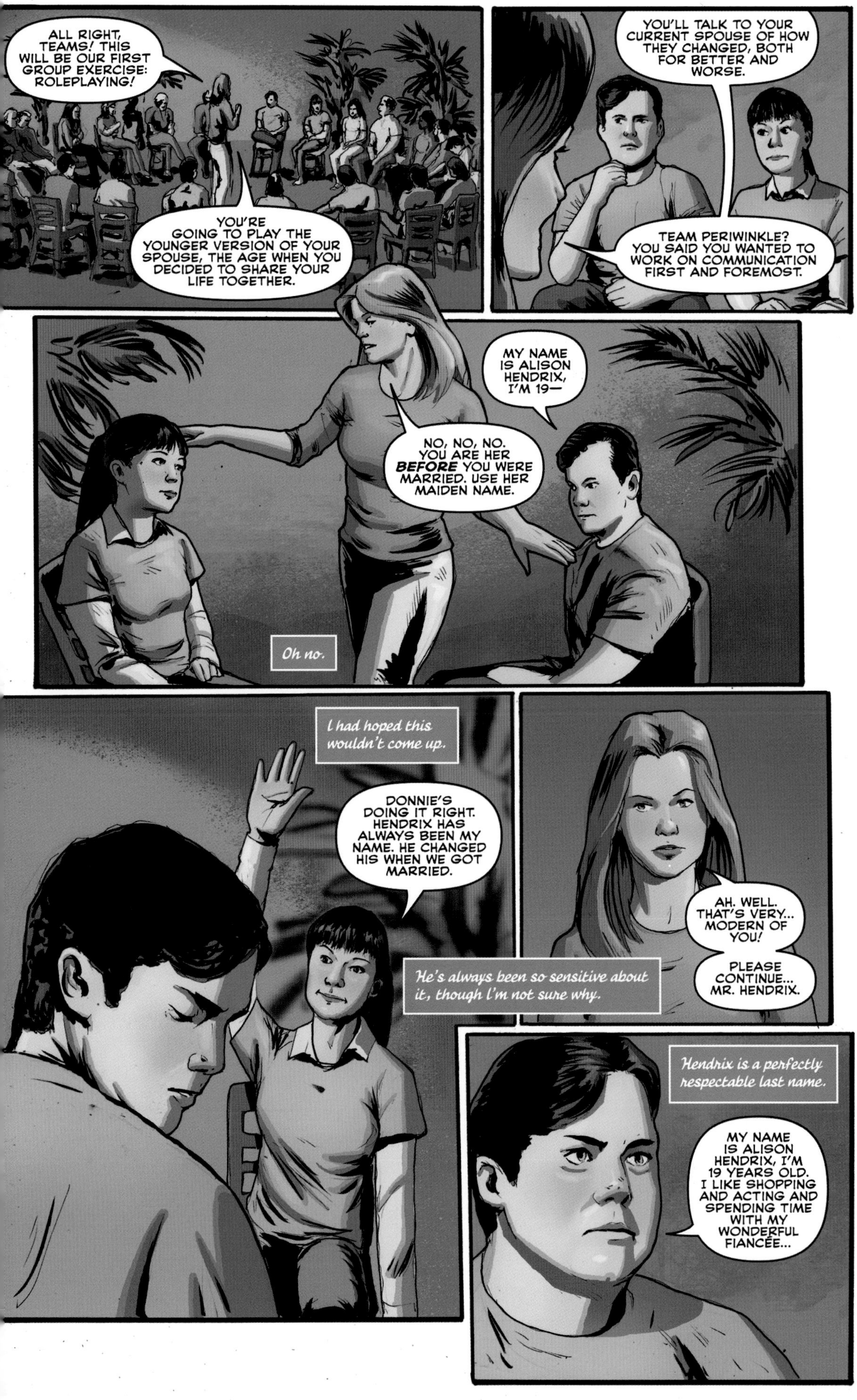
ALL RIGHT, TEAMS! THIS WILL BE OUR FIRST GROUP EXERCISE: ROLEPLAYING!
YOU'RE GOING TO PLAY THE YOUNGER VERSION OF YOUR SPOUSE, THE AGE WHEN YOU DECIDED TO SHARE YOUR LIFE TOGETHER.
YOU'LL TALK TO YOUR CURRENT SPOUSE OF HOW THEY CHANGED, BOTH FOR BETTER AND WORSE.
TEAM PERIWINKLE? YOU SAID YOU WANTED TO WORK ON COMMUNICATION FIRST AND FOREMOST.
MY NAME IS ALISON HENDRIX, I'M 19—
NO, NO, NO. YOU ARE HER **BEFORE** YOU WERE MARRIED. USE HER MAIDEN NAME.
Oh no.
I had hoped this wouldn't come up.
DONNIE'S DOING IT RIGHT. HENDRIX HAS ALWAYS BEEN MY NAME. HE CHANGED HIS WHEN WE GOT MARRIED.
He's always been so sensitive about it, though I'm not sure why.
AH. WELL. THAT'S VERY... MODERN OF YOU!
PLEASE CONTINUE... MR. HENDRIX.
Hendrix is a perfectly respectable last name.
MY NAME IS ALISON HENDRIX, I'M 19 YEARS OLD. I LIKE SHOPPING AND ACTING AND SPENDING TIME WITH MY WONDERFUL FIANCÉE...

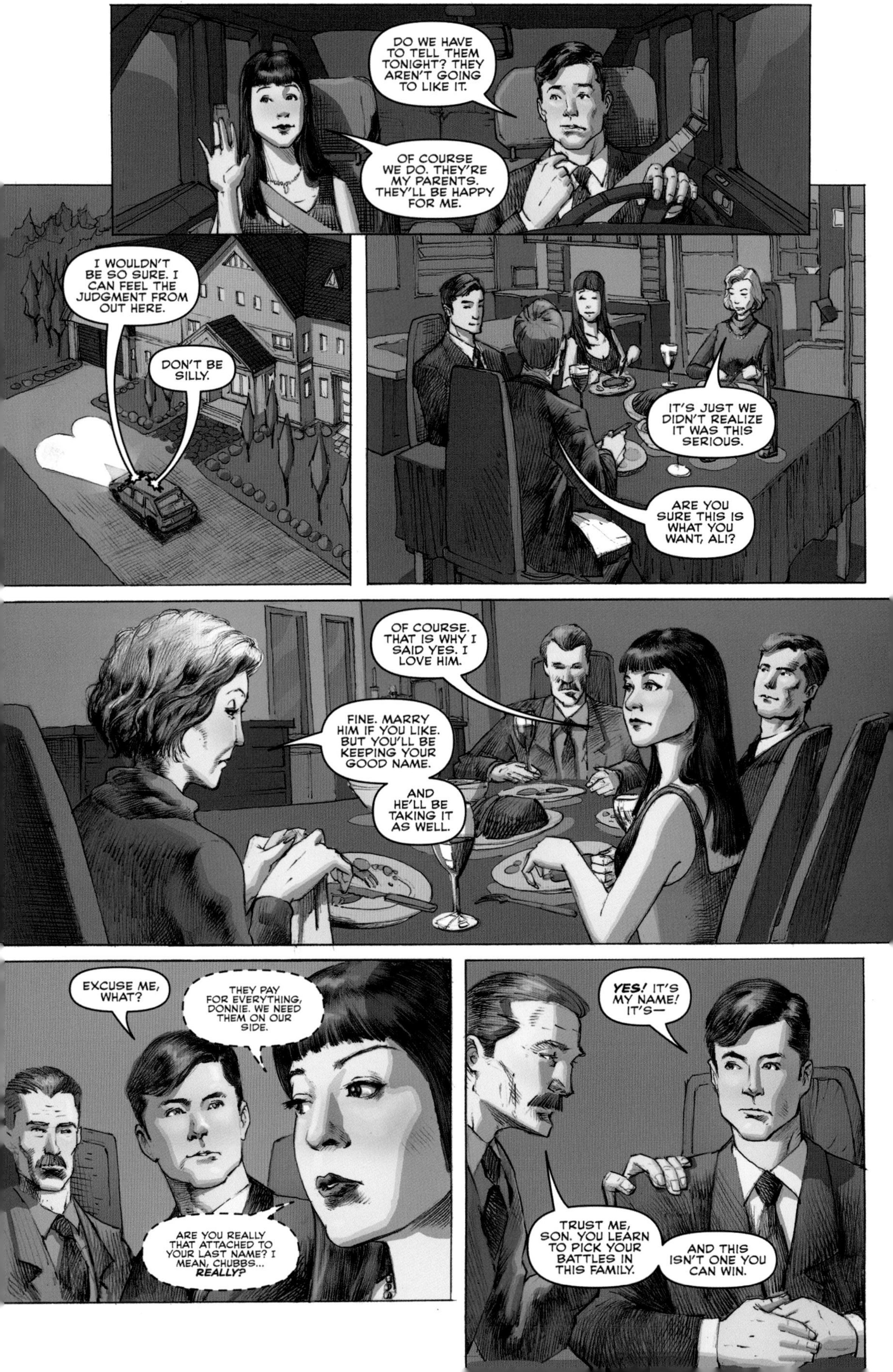

DO WE HAVE TO TELL THEM TONIGHT? THEY AREN'T GOING TO LIKE IT.
OF COURSE WE DO. THEY'RE MY PARENTS. THEY'LL BE HAPPY FOR ME.
I WOULDN'T BE SO SURE. I CAN FEEL THE JUDGMENT FROM OUT HERE.
DON'T BE SILLY.
IT'S JUST WE DIDN'T REALIZE IT WAS THIS SERIOUS.
ARE YOU SURE THIS IS WHAT YOU WANT, ALI?
OF COURSE. THAT IS WHY I SAID YES. I LOVE HIM.
FINE. MARRY HIM IF YOU LIKE. BUT YOU'LL BE KEEPING YOUR GOOD NAME.
AND HE'LL BE TAKING IT AS WELL.
EXCUSE ME, WHAT?
THEY PAY FOR EVERYTHING, DONNIE. WE NEED THEM ON OUR SIDE.
ARE YOU REALLY THAT ATTACHED TO YOUR LAST NAME? I MEAN, CHUBBS... **REALLY?**
YES! IT'S MY NAME! IT'S—
TRUST ME, SON. YOU LEARN TO PICK YOUR BATTLES IN THIS FAMILY.
AND THIS ISN'T ONE YOU CAN WIN.

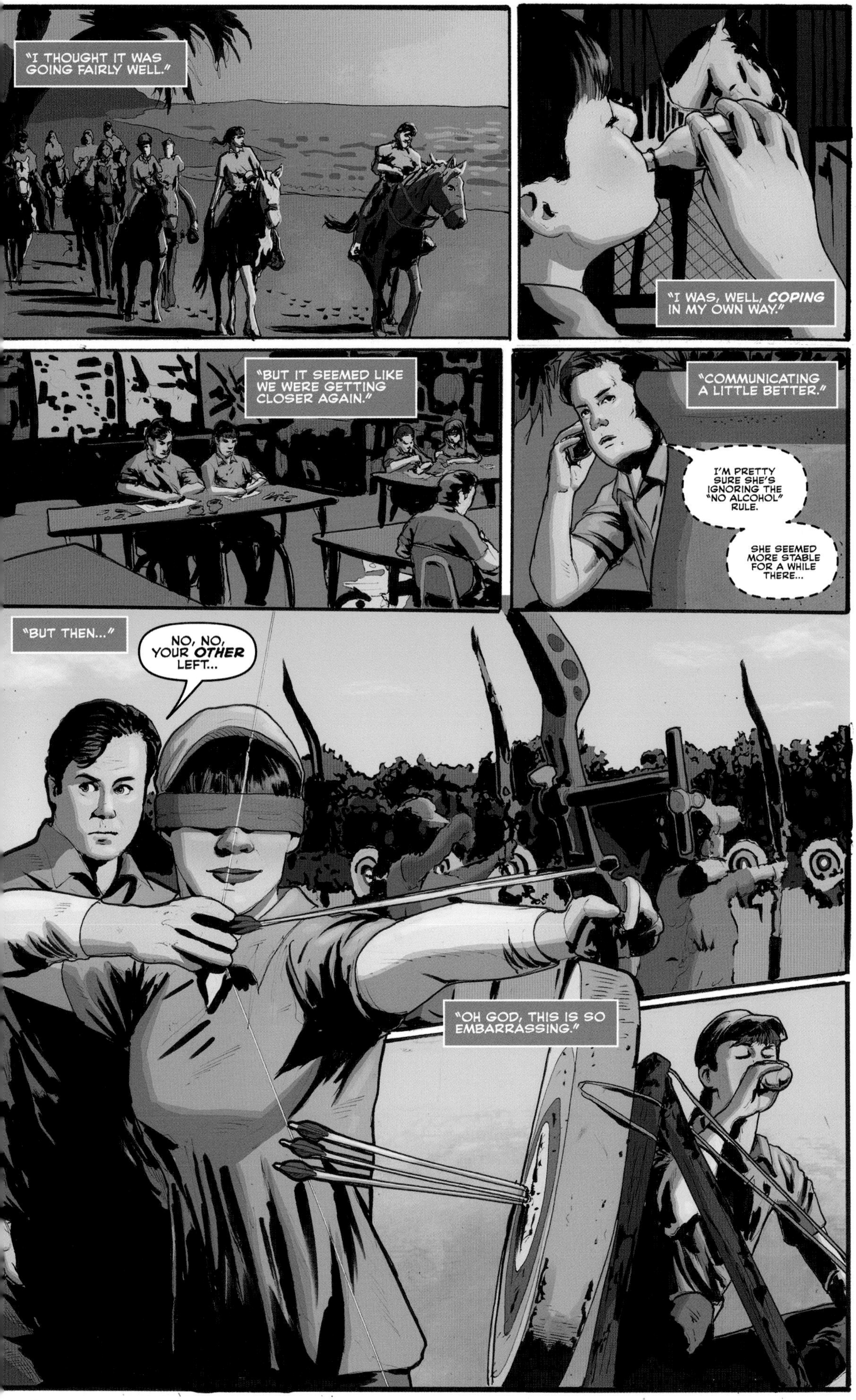
"I THOUGHT IT WAS GOING FAIRLY WELL."
"I WAS, WELL, *COPING* IN MY OWN WAY."
"BUT IT SEEMED LIKE WE WERE GETTING CLOSER AGAIN."
"COMMUNICATING A LITTLE BETTER."
I'M PRETTY SURE SHE'S IGNORING THE "NO ALCOHOL" RULE.
SHE SEEMED MORE STABLE FOR A WHILE THERE...
"BUT THEN..."
NO, NO, YOUR *OTHER* LEFT...
"OH GOD, THIS IS SO EMBARRASSING."

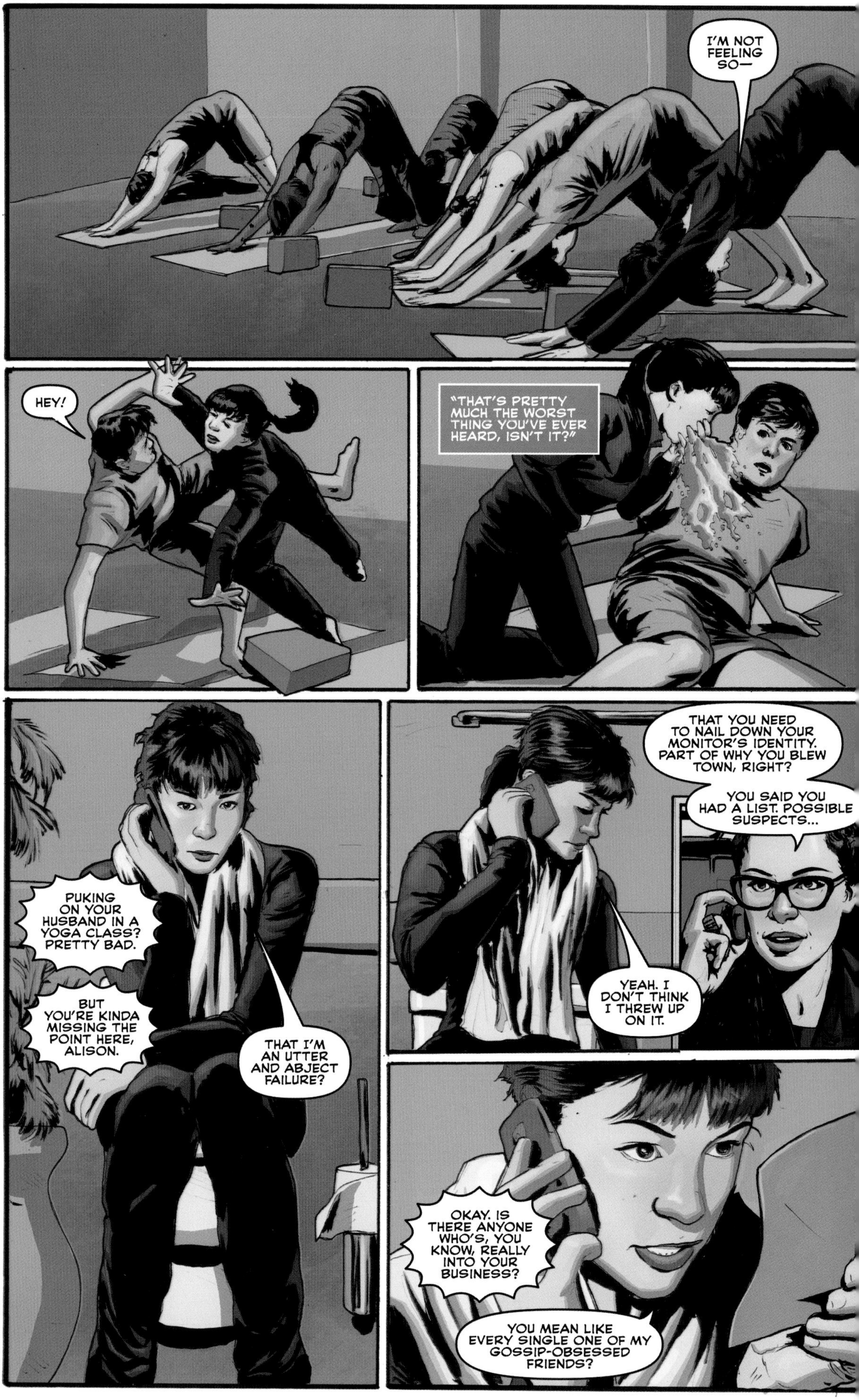
I'M NOT FEELING SO—
HEY!
"THAT'S PRETTY MUCH THE WORST THING YOU'VE EVER HEARD, ISN'T IT?"
PUKING ON YOUR HUSBAND IN A YOGA CLASS? PRETTY BAD.
BUT YOU'RE KINDA MISSING THE POINT HERE, ALISON.
THAT I'M AN UTTER AND ABJECT FAILURE?
THAT YOU NEED TO NAIL DOWN YOUR MONITOR'S IDENTITY. PART OF WHY YOU BLEW TOWN, RIGHT?
YOU SAID YOU HAD A LIST. POSSIBLE SUSPECTS...
YEAH. I DON'T THINK I THREW UP ON IT.
OKAY. IS THERE ANYONE WHO'S, YOU KNOW, REALLY INTO YOUR BUSINESS?
YOU MEAN LIKE EVERY SINGLE ONE OF MY GOSSIP-OBSESSED FRIENDS?

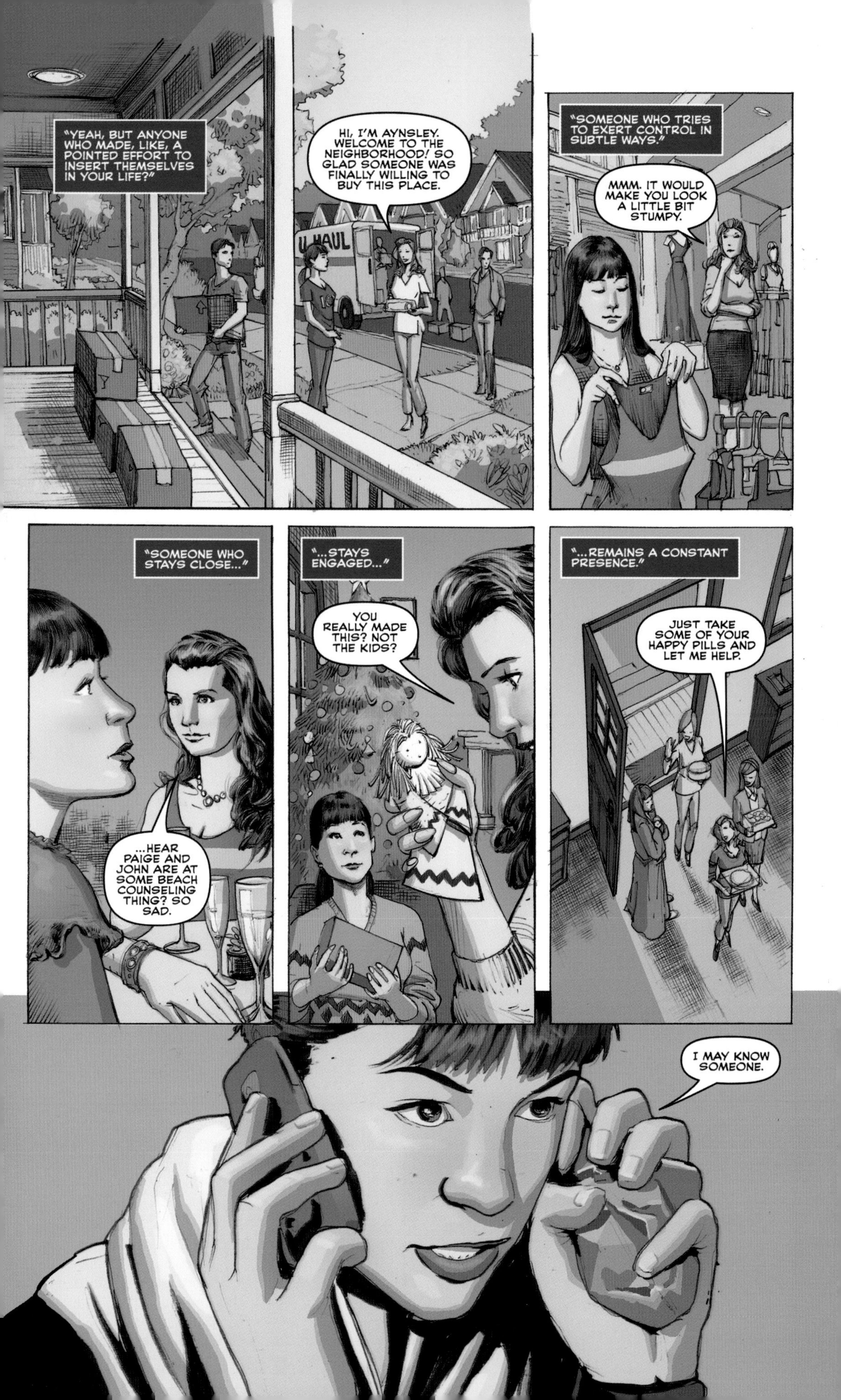

"YEAH, BUT ANYONE WHO MADE, LIKE, A POINTED EFFORT TO INSERT THEMSELVES IN YOUR LIFE?"
HI, I'M AYNSLEY. WELCOME TO THE NEIGHBORHOOD! SO GLAD SOMEONE WAS FINALLY WILLING TO BUY THIS PLACE.
U-HAUL
"SOMEONE WHO TRIES TO EXERT CONTROL IN SUBTLE WAYS."
MMM. IT WOULD MAKE YOU LOOK A LITTLE BIT STUMPY.
"SOMEONE WHO STAYS CLOSE..."
...HEAR PAIGE AND JOHN ARE AT SOME BEACH COUNSELING THING? SO SAD.
"...STAYS ENGAGED..."
YOU REALLY MADE THIS? NOT THE KIDS?
"...REMAINS A CONSTANT PRESENCE."
JUST TAKE SOME OF YOUR HAPPY PILLS AND LET ME HELP.
I MAY KNOW SOMEONE.

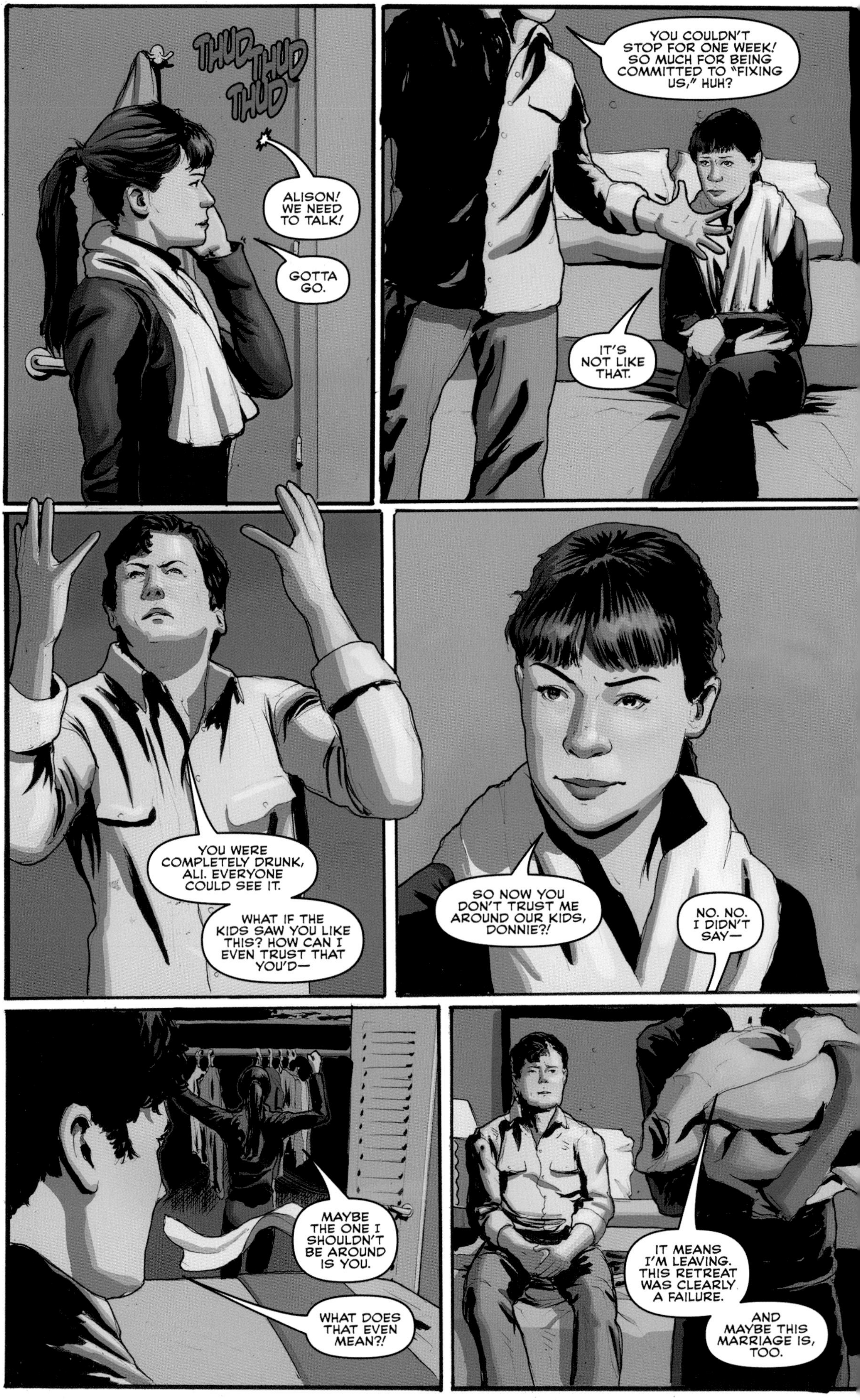
THUD THUD THUD
ALISON! WE NEED TO TALK!
GOTTA GO.
YOU COULDN'T STOP FOR ONE WEEK! SO MUCH FOR BEING COMMITTED TO "FIXING US," HUH?
IT'S NOT LIKE THAT.
YOU WERE COMPLETELY DRUNK, ALI. EVERYONE COULD SEE IT.
WHAT IF THE KIDS SAW YOU LIKE THIS? HOW CAN I EVEN TRUST THAT YOU'D—
SO NOW YOU DON'T TRUST ME AROUND OUR KIDS, DONNIE?!
NO. NO. I DIDN'T SAY—
MAYBE THE ONE I SHOULDN'T BE AROUND IS YOU.
WHAT DOES THAT EVEN MEAN?!
IT MEANS I'M LEAVING. THIS RETREAT WAS CLEARLY A FAILURE.
AND MAYBE THIS MARRIAGE IS, TOO.

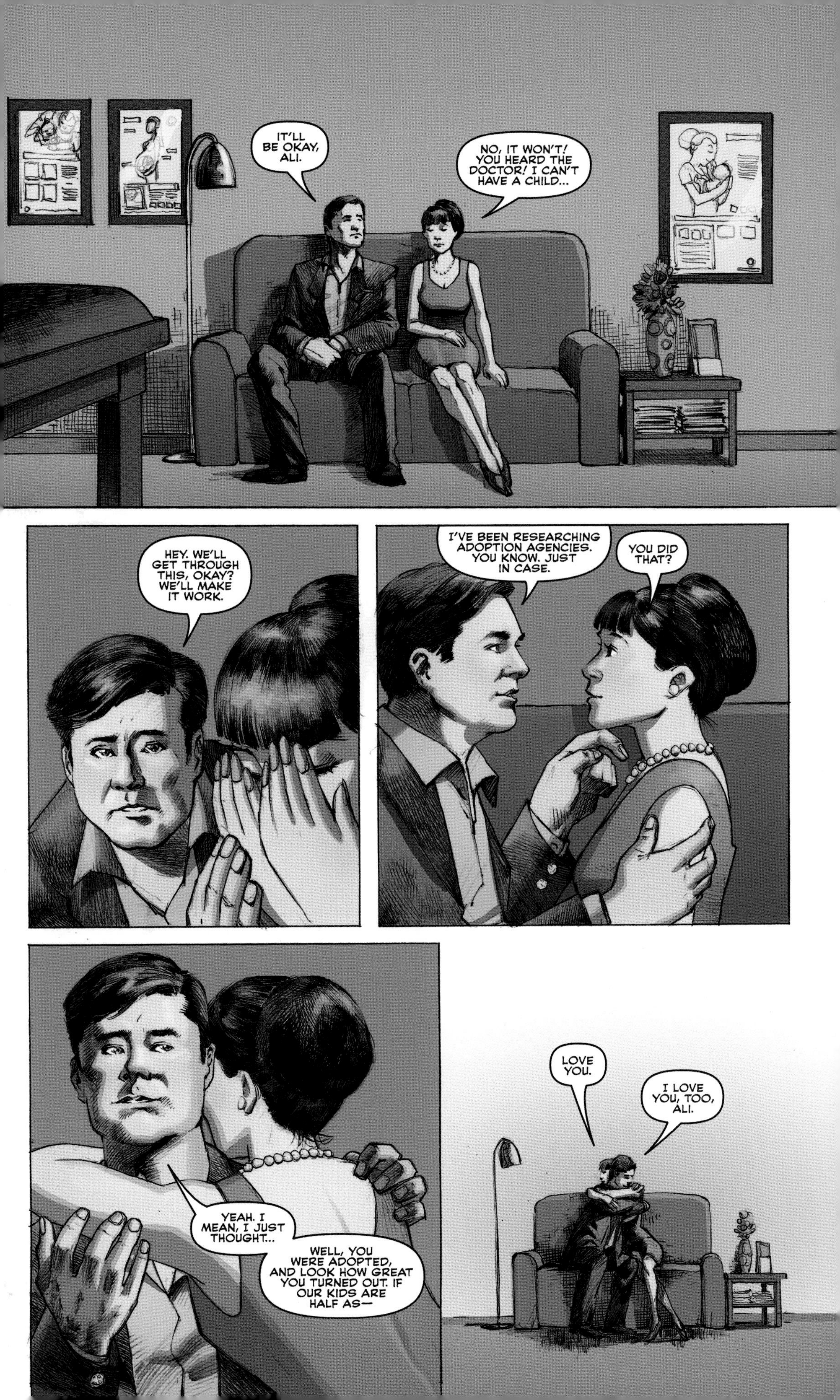
IT'LL BE OKAY, ALI.
NO, IT WON'T! YOU HEARD THE DOCTOR! I CAN'T HAVE A CHILD...
HEY. WE'LL GET THROUGH THIS, OKAY? WE'LL MAKE IT WORK.
I'VE BEEN RESEARCHING ADOPTION AGENCIES. YOU KNOW. JUST IN CASE.
YOU DID THAT?
YEAH. I MEAN, I JUST THOUGHT...
WELL, YOU WERE ADOPTED, AND LOOK HOW GREAT YOU TURNED OUT. IF OUR KIDS ARE HALF AS—
LOVE YOU.
I LOVE YOU, TOO, ALI.

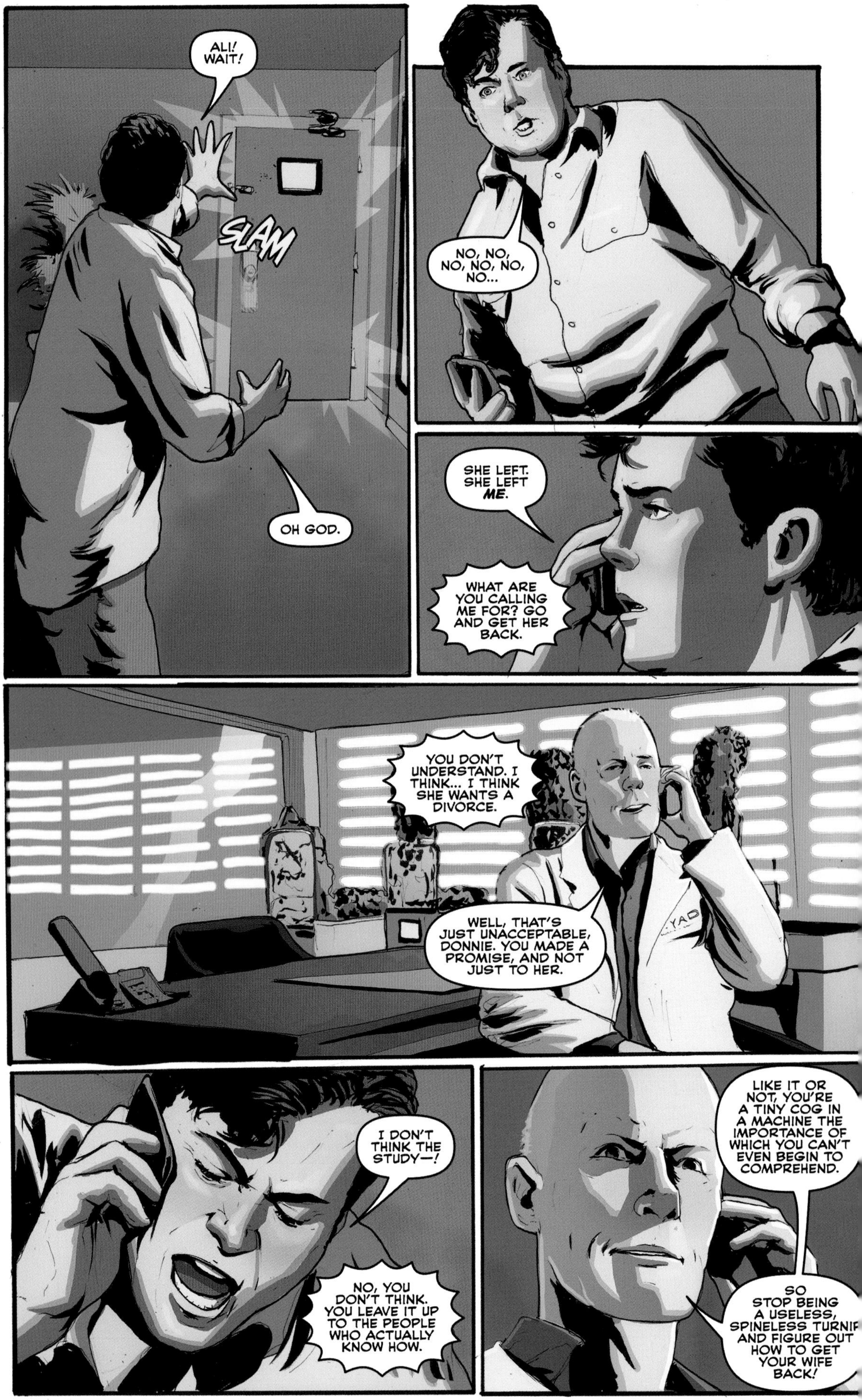
ALI! WAIT!
SLAM
OH GOD.
NO, NO, NO, NO, NO, NO...
SHE LEFT. SHE LEFT ME.
WHAT ARE YOU CALLING ME FOR? GO AND GET HER BACK.
YOU DON'T UNDERSTAND. I THINK... I THINK SHE WANTS A DIVORCE.
WELL, THAT'S JUST UNACCEPTABLE, DONNIE. YOU MADE A PROMISE, AND NOT JUST TO HER.
I DON'T THINK THE STUDY—!
NO, YOU DON'T THINK. YOU LEAVE IT UP TO THE PEOPLE WHO ACTUALLY KNOW HOW.
LIKE IT OR NOT, YOU'RE A TINY COG IN A MACHINE THE IMPORTANCE OF WHICH YOU CAN'T EVEN BEGIN TO COMPREHEND.
SO STOP BEING A USELESS, SPINELESS TURNIP AND FIGURE OUT HOW TO GET YOUR WIFE BACK!

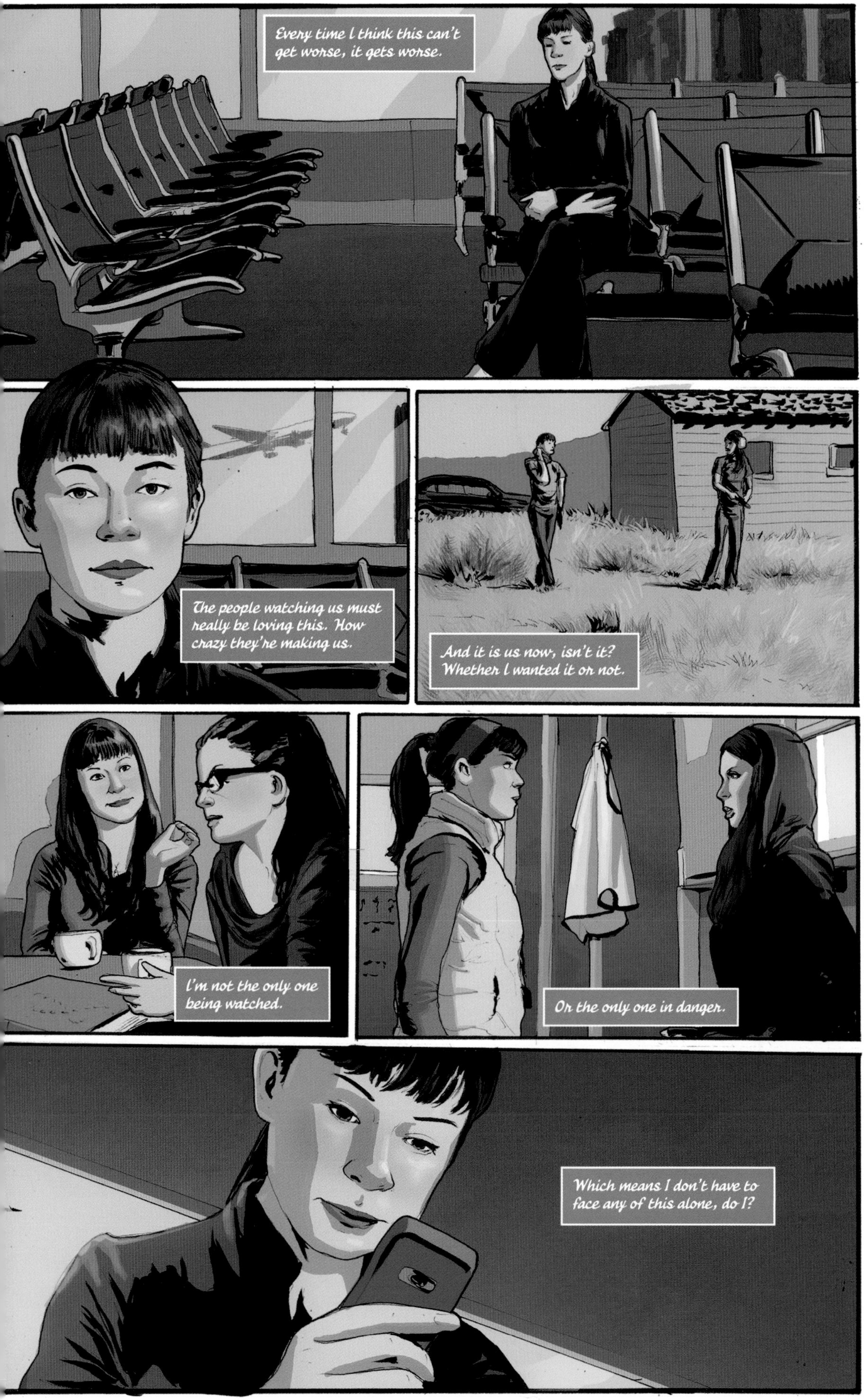

Every time I think this can't get worse, it gets worse.
The people watching us must really be loving this. How crazy they're making us.
And it is us now, isn't it? Whether I wanted it or not.
I'm not the only one being watched.
Or the only one in danger.
Which means I don't have to face any of this alone, do I?

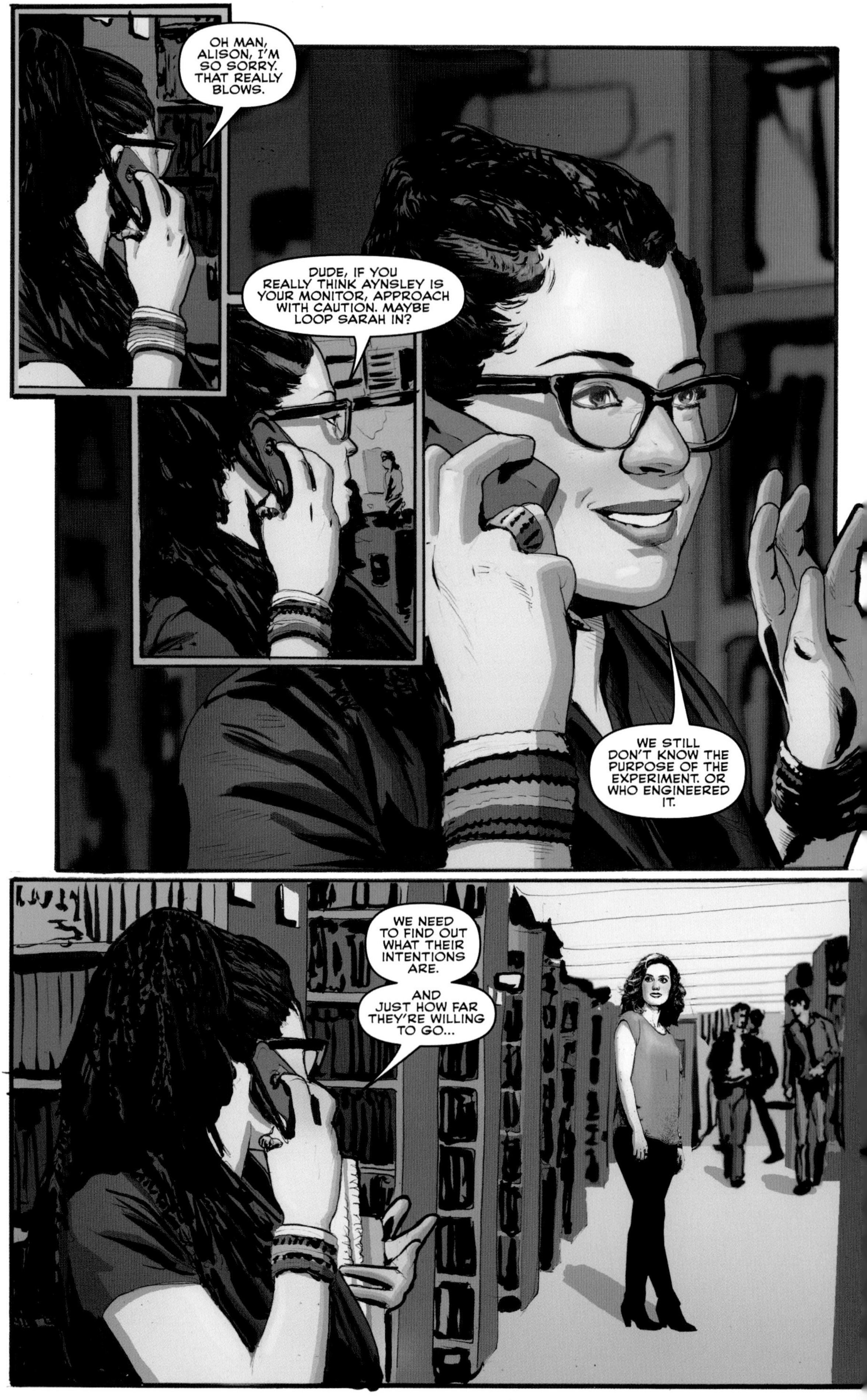
OH MAN, ALISON, I'M SO SORRY. THAT REALLY BLOWS.
DUDE, IF YOU REALLY THINK AYNSLEY IS YOUR MONITOR, APPROACH WITH CAUTION. MAYBE LOOP SARAH IN?
WE STILL DON'T KNOW THE PURPOSE OF THE EXPERIMENT. OR WHO ENGINEERED IT.
WE NEED TO FIND OUT WHAT THEIR INTENTIONS ARE.
AND JUST HOW FAR THEY'RE WILLING TO GO...

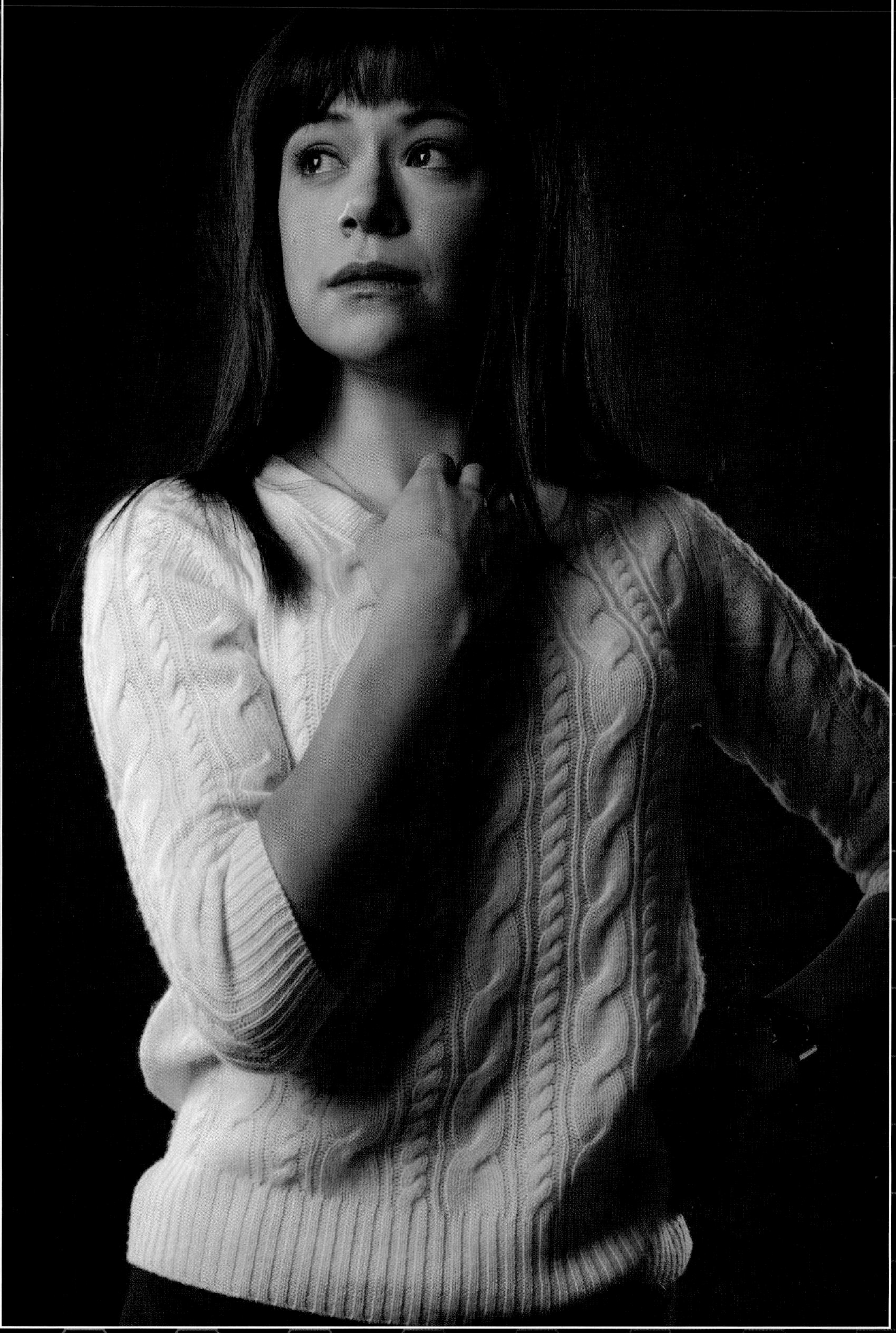

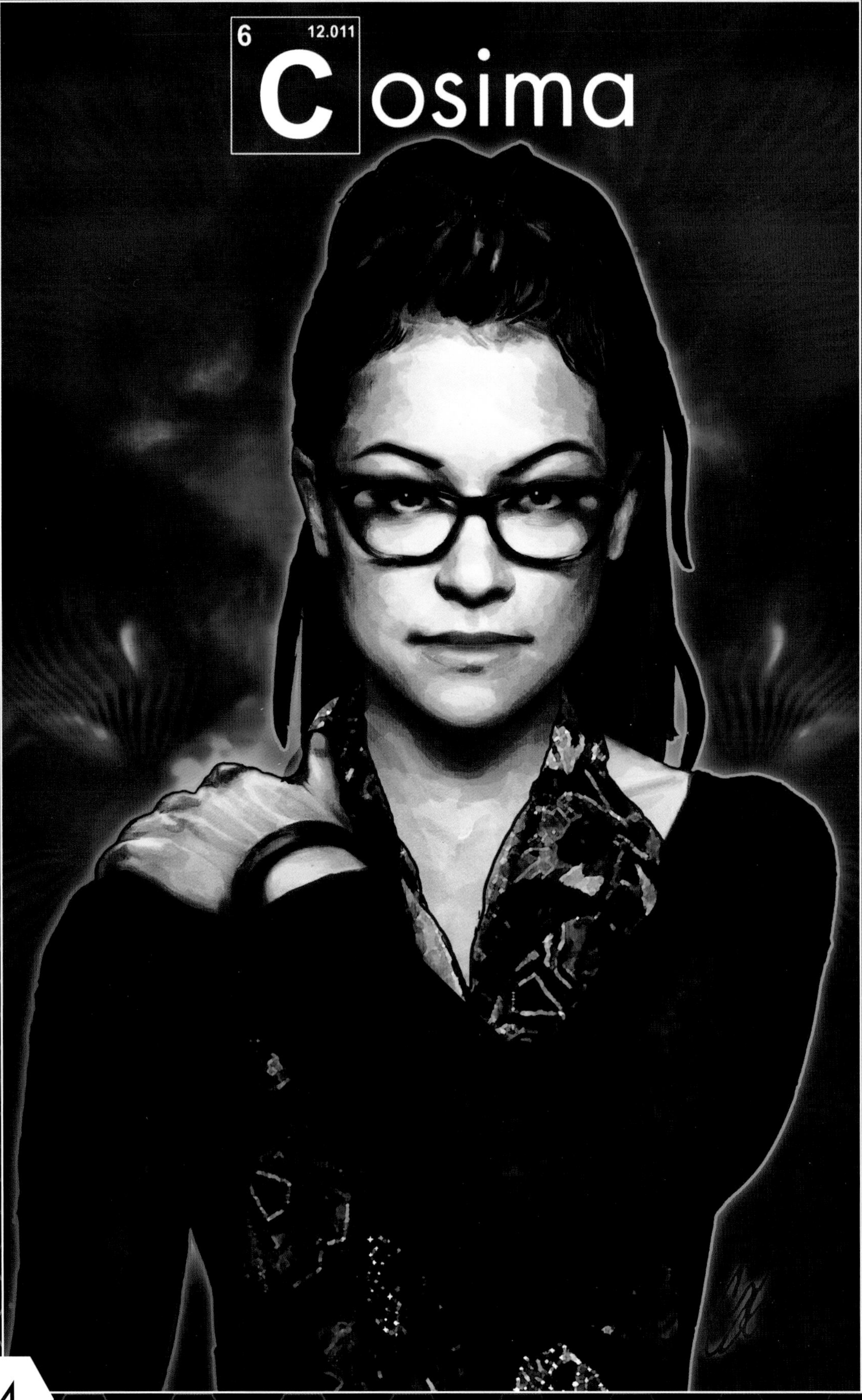
6
12.011
C
osima

BY **CAT STAGGS**

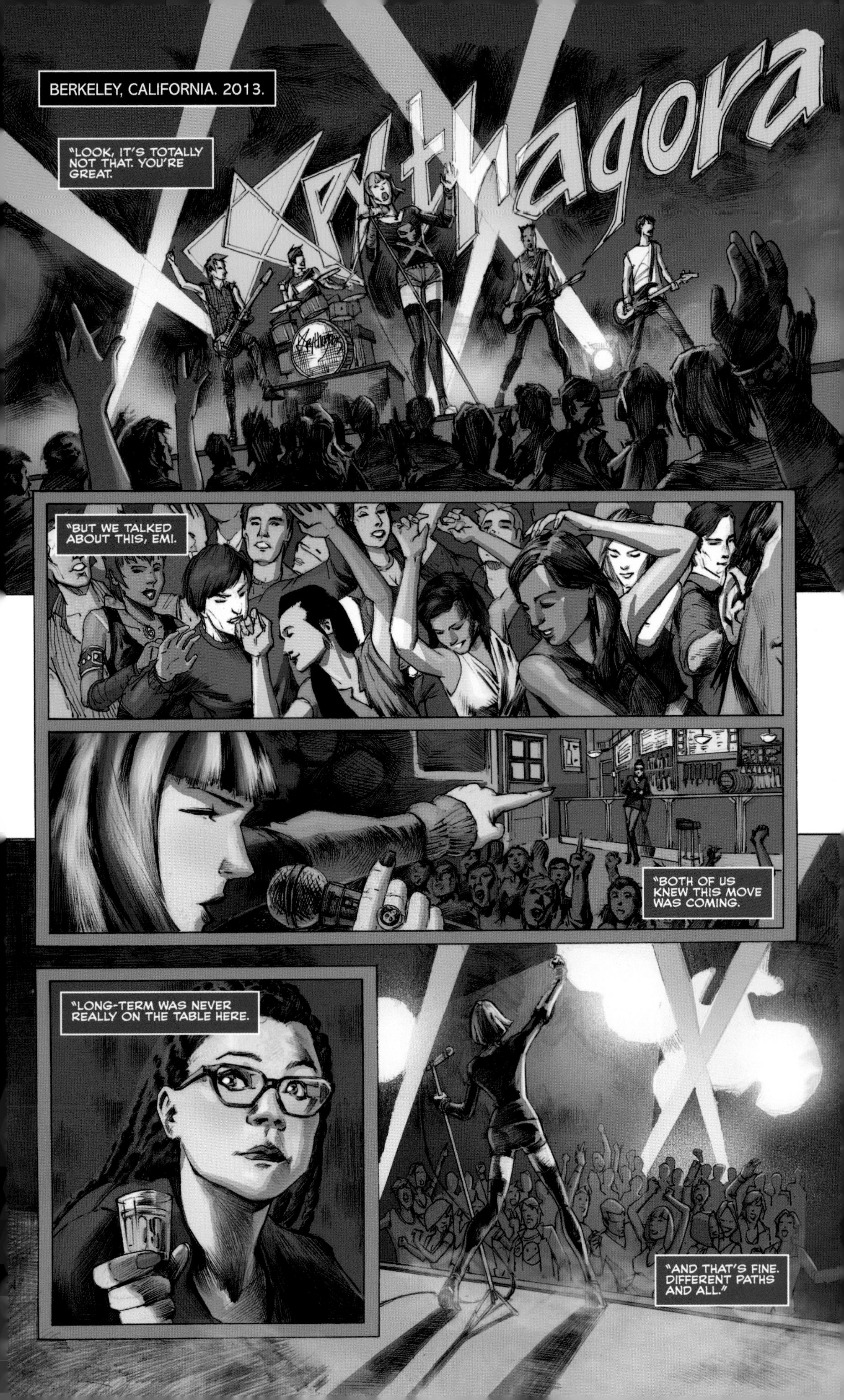
BERKELEY, CALIFORNIA. 2013.
"LOOK, IT'S TOTALLY NOT THAT. YOU'RE GREAT.
Pythagora
"BUT WE TALKED ABOUT THIS, EMI.
"BOTH OF US KNEW THIS MOVE WAS COMING.
"LONG-TERM WAS NEVER REALLY ON THE TABLE HERE.
"AND THAT'S FINE. DIFFERENT PATHS AND ALL."

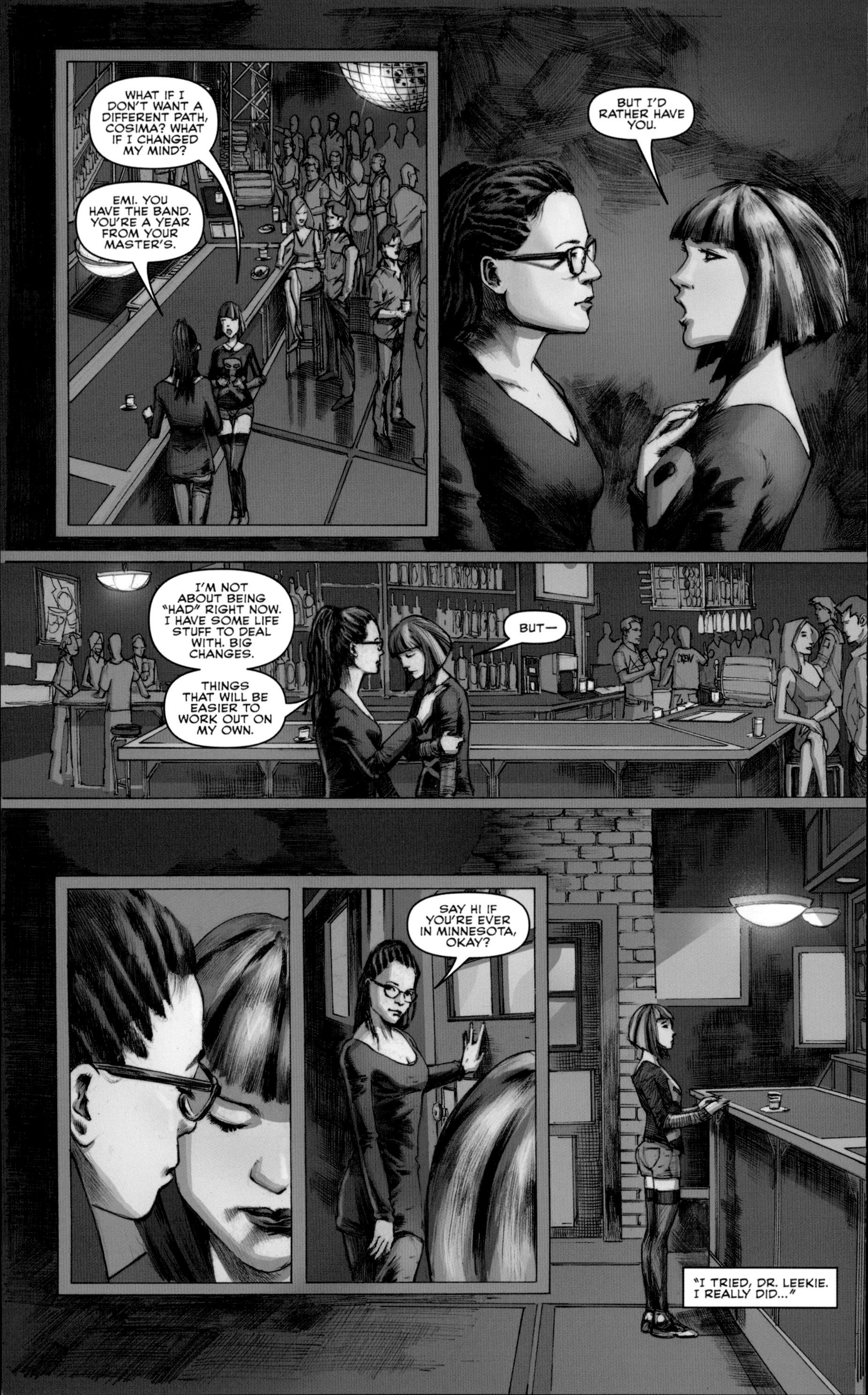
WHAT IF I DON'T WANT A DIFFERENT PATH, COSIMA? WHAT IF I CHANGED MY MIND?
EMI. YOU HAVE THE BAND. YOU'RE A YEAR FROM YOUR MASTER'S.
BUT I'D RATHER HAVE YOU.
I'M NOT ABOUT BEING "HAD" RIGHT NOW. I HAVE SOME LIFE STUFF TO DEAL WITH. BIG CHANGES.
THINGS THAT WILL BE EASIER TO WORK OUT ON MY OWN.
BUT—
SAY HI IF YOU'RE EVER IN MINNESOTA, OKAY?
"I TRIED, DR. LEEKIE. I REALLY DID..."

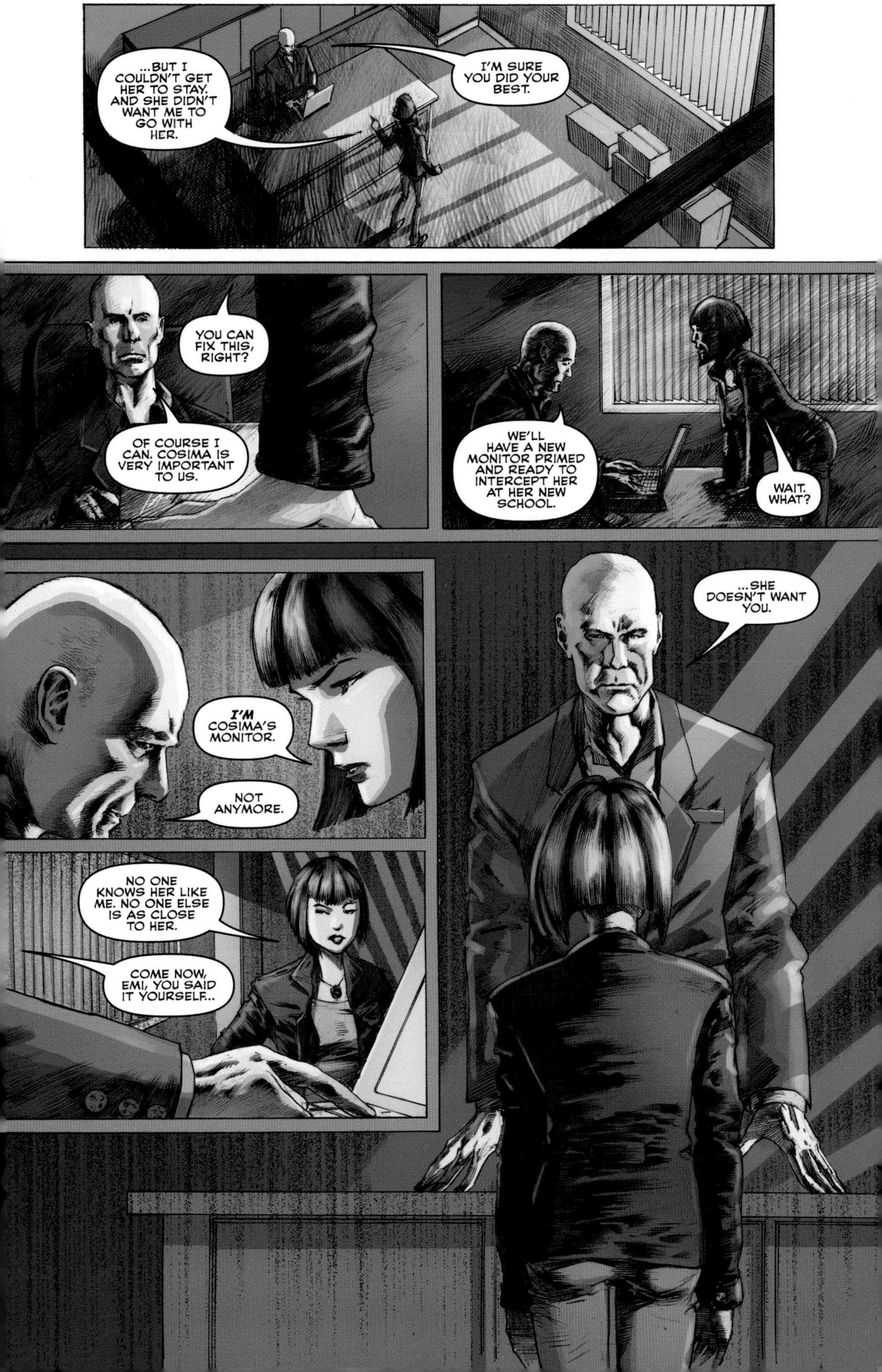
...BUT I COULDN'T GET HER TO STAY. AND SHE DIDN'T WANT ME TO GO WITH HER.
I'M SURE YOU DID YOUR BEST.
YOU CAN FIX THIS, RIGHT?
OF COURSE I CAN. COSIMA IS VERY IMPORTANT TO US.
WE'LL HAVE A NEW MONITOR PRIMED AND READY TO INTERCEPT HER AT HER NEW SCHOOL.
WAIT. WHAT?
I'M COSIMA'S MONITOR.
NOT ANYMORE.
NO ONE KNOWS HER LIKE ME. NO ONE ELSE IS AS CLOSE TO HER.
COME NOW, EMI, YOU SAID IT YOURSELF...
...SHE DOESN'T WANT YOU.

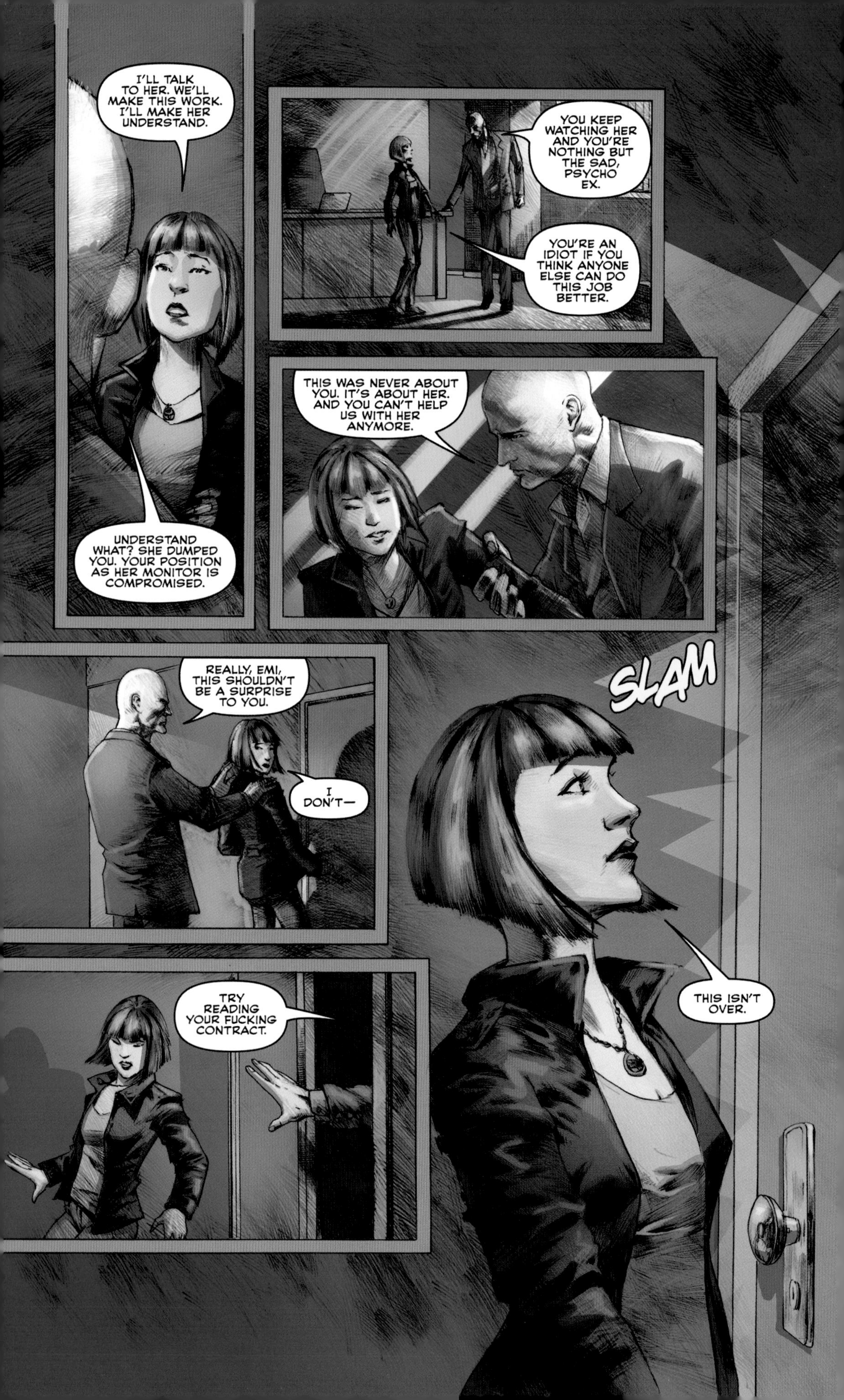
I'LL TALK TO HER. WE'LL MAKE THIS WORK. I'LL MAKE HER UNDERSTAND.
UNDERSTAND WHAT? SHE DUMPED YOU. YOUR POSITION AS HER MONITOR IS COMPROMISED.
YOU KEEP WATCHING HER AND YOU'RE NOTHING BUT THE SAD, PSYCHO EX.
YOU'RE AN IDIOT IF YOU THINK ANYONE ELSE CAN DO THIS JOB BETTER.
THIS WAS NEVER ABOUT YOU. IT'S ABOUT HER. AND YOU CAN'T HELP US WITH HER ANYMORE.
REALLY, EMI, THIS SHOULDN'T BE A SURPRISE TO YOU.
I DON'T—
TRY READING YOUR FUCKING CONTRACT.
SLAM
THIS ISN'T OVER.

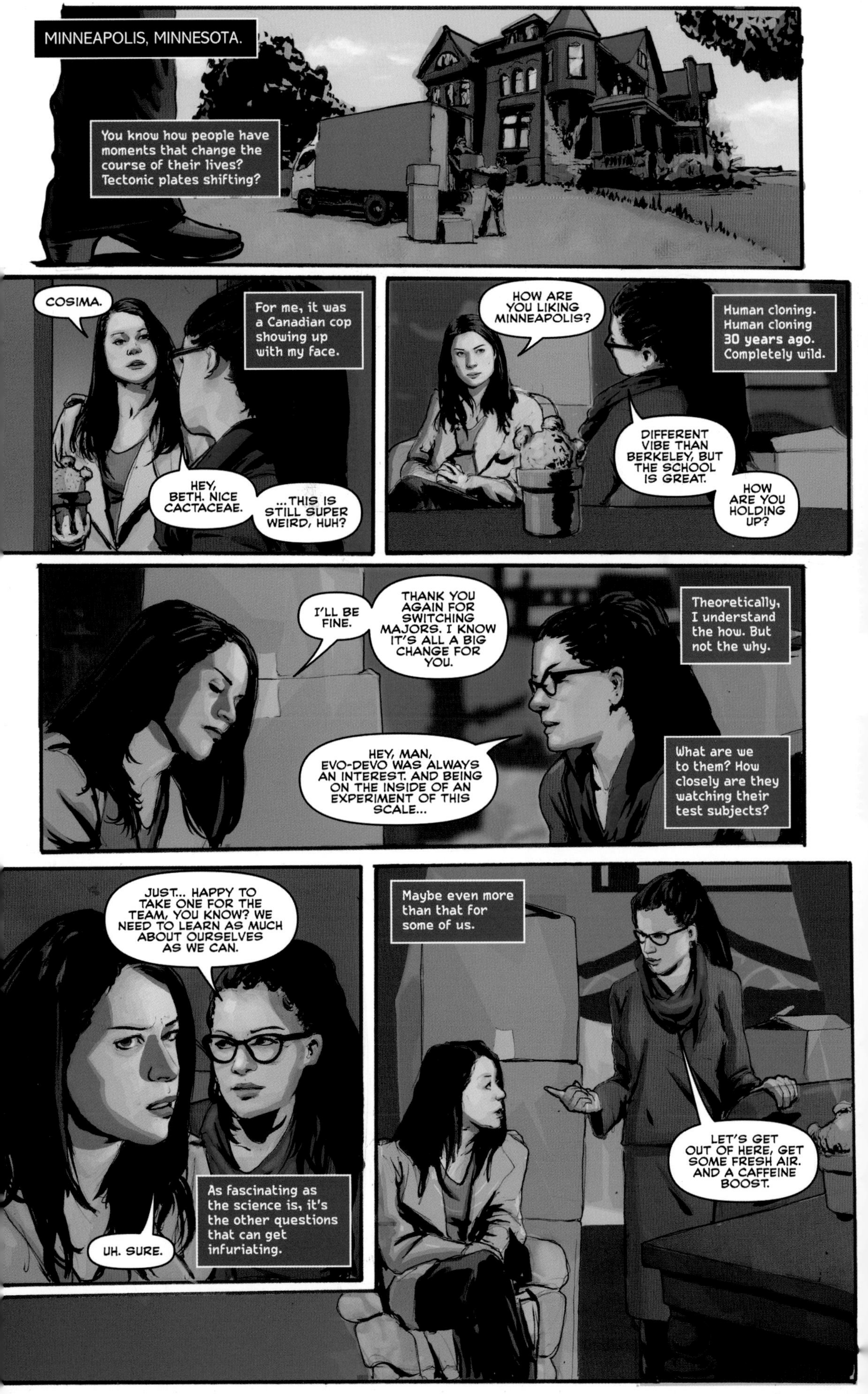
MINNEAPOLIS, MINNESOTA.
You know how people have moments that change the course of their lives? Tectonic plates shifting?
COSIMA.
For me, it was a Canadian cop showing up with my face.
HEY, BETH. NICE CACTACEAE.
...THIS IS STILL SUPER WEIRD, HUH?
HOW ARE YOU LIKING MINNEAPOLIS?
Human cloning. Human cloning 30 years ago. Completely wild.
DIFFERENT VIBE THAN BERKELEY, BUT THE SCHOOL IS GREAT.
HOW ARE YOU HOLDING UP?
I'LL BE FINE.
THANK YOU AGAIN FOR SWITCHING MAJORS. I KNOW IT'S ALL A BIG CHANGE FOR YOU.
Theoretically, I understand the how. But not the why.
HEY, MAN, EVO-DEVO WAS ALWAYS AN INTEREST. AND BEING ON THE INSIDE OF AN EXPERIMENT OF THIS SCALE...
What are we to them? How closely are they watching their test subjects?
JUST... HAPPY TO TAKE ONE FOR THE TEAM, YOU KNOW? WE NEED TO LEARN AS MUCH ABOUT OURSELVES AS WE CAN.
UH. SURE.
As fascinating as the science is, it's the other questions that can get infuriating.
Maybe even more than that for some of us.
LET'S GET OUT OF HERE, GET SOME FRESH AIR. AND A CAFFEINE BOOST.

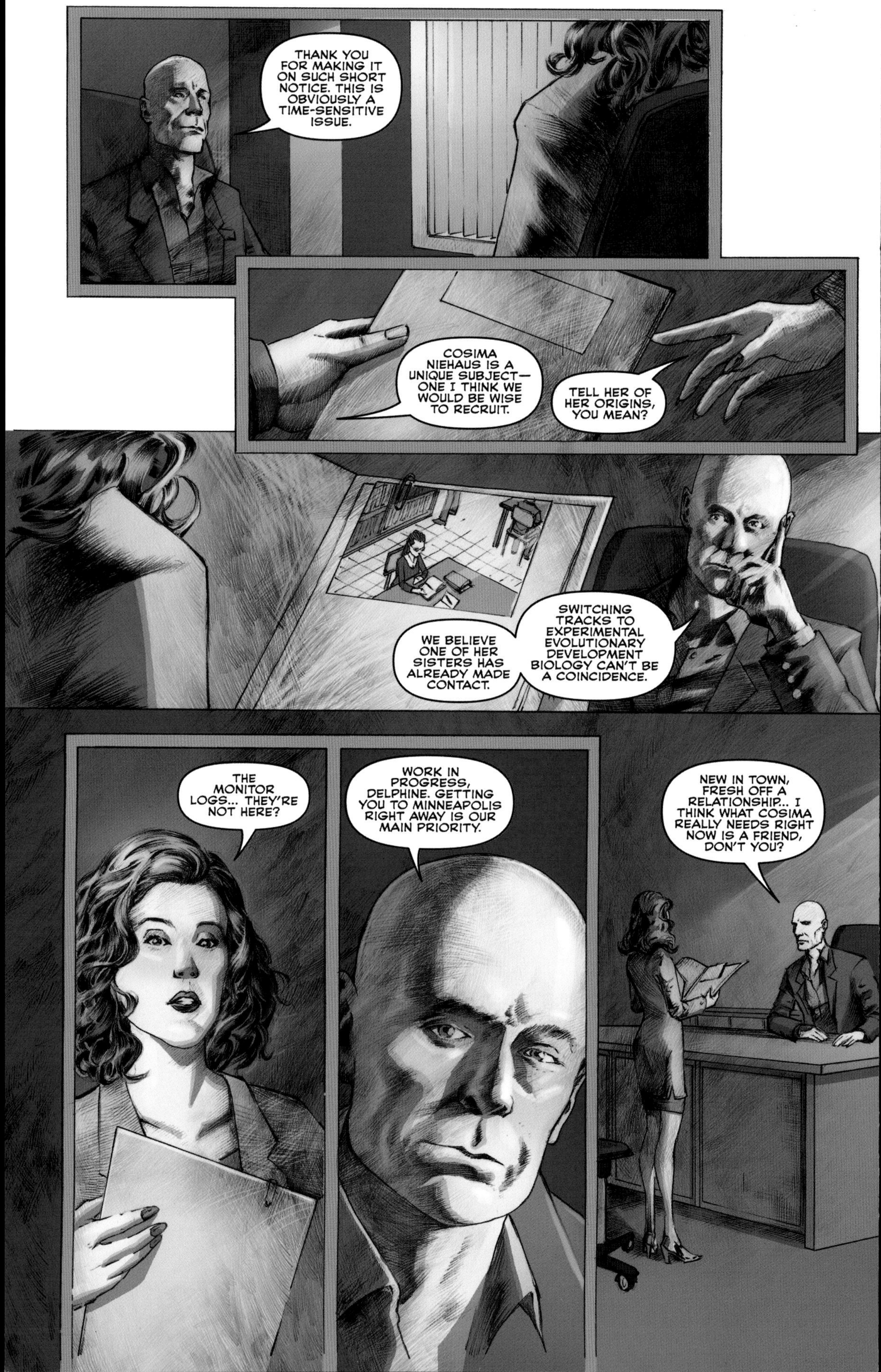
THANK YOU FOR MAKING IT ON SUCH SHORT NOTICE. THIS IS OBVIOUSLY A TIME-SENSITIVE ISSUE.
COSIMA NIEHAUS IS A UNIQUE SUBJECT— ONE I THINK WE WOULD BE WISE TO RECRUIT.
TELL HER OF HER ORIGINS, YOU MEAN?
SWITCHING TRACKS TO EXPERIMENTAL EVOLUTIONARY DEVELOPMENT BIOLOGY CAN'T BE A COINCIDENCE.
WE BELIEVE ONE OF HER SISTERS HAS ALREADY MADE CONTACT.
THE MONITOR LOGS... THEY'RE NOT HERE?
WORK IN PROGRESS, DELPHINE. GETTING YOU TO MINNEAPOLIS RIGHT AWAY IS OUR MAIN PRIORITY.
NEW IN TOWN, FRESH OFF A RELATIONSHIP... I THINK WHAT COSIMA REALLY NEEDS RIGHT NOW IS A FRIEND, DON'T YOU?

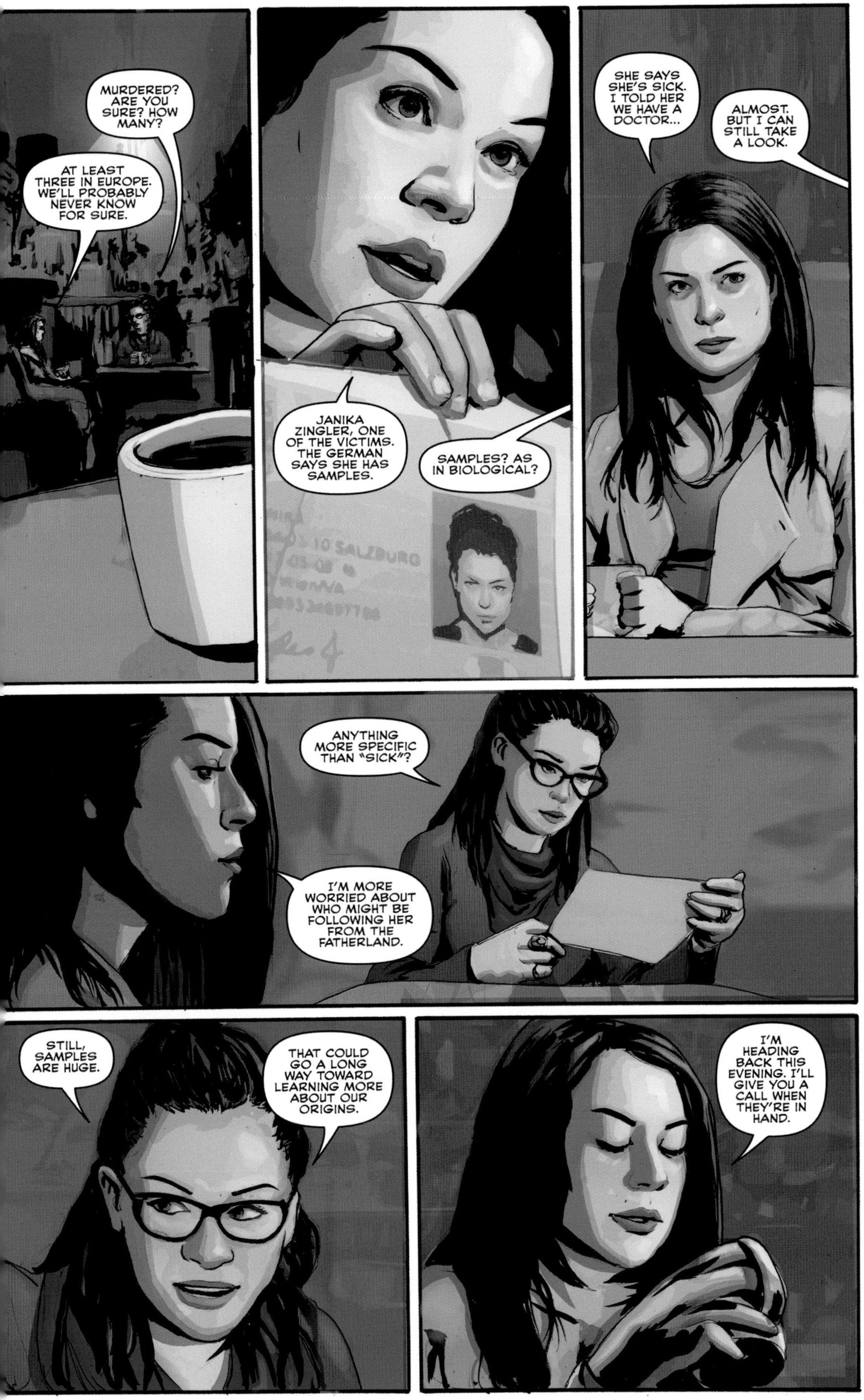
MURDERED? ARE YOU SURE? HOW MANY?
AT LEAST THREE IN EUROPE. WE'LL PROBABLY NEVER KNOW FOR SURE.
JANIKA ZINGLER, ONE OF THE VICTIMS. THE GERMAN SAYS SHE HAS SAMPLES.
SAMPLES? AS IN BIOLOGICAL?
SHE SAYS SHE'S SICK. I TOLD HER WE HAVE A DOCTOR...
ALMOST. BUT I CAN STILL TAKE A LOOK.
ANYTHING MORE SPECIFIC THAN "SICK"?
I'M MORE WORRIED ABOUT WHO MIGHT BE FOLLOWING HER FROM THE FATHERLAND.
STILL, SAMPLES ARE HUGE.
THAT COULD GO A LONG WAY TOWARD LEARNING MORE ABOUT OUR ORIGINS.
I'M HEADING BACK THIS EVENING. I'LL GIVE YOU A CALL WHEN THEY'RE IN HAND.

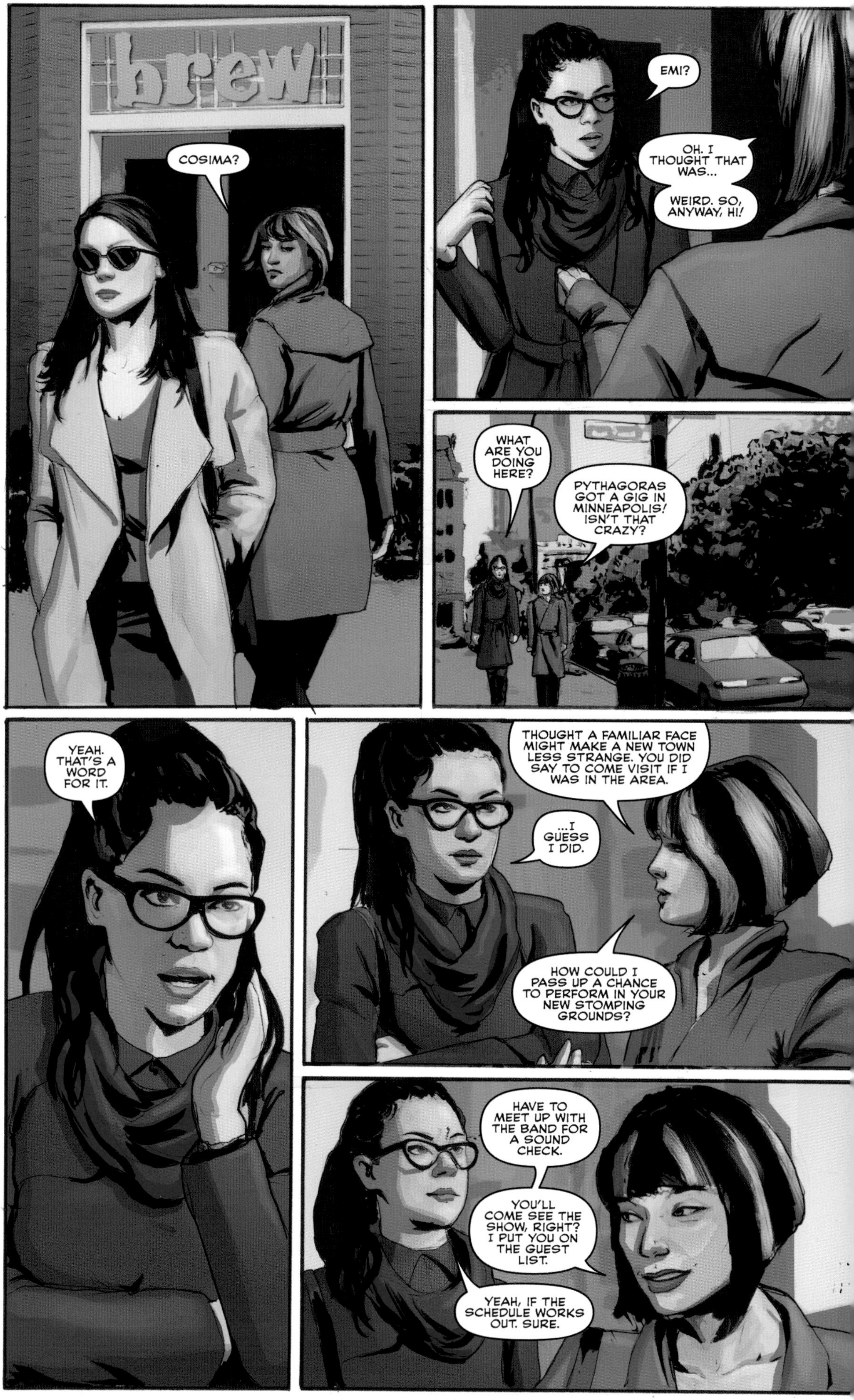
brew
COSIMA?
EMI?
OH. I THOUGHT THAT WAS...
WEIRD. SO, ANYWAY, HI!
WHAT ARE YOU DOING HERE?
PYTHAGORAS GOT A GIG IN MINNEAPOLIS! ISN'T THAT CRAZY?
YEAH. THAT'S A WORD FOR IT.
THOUGHT A FAMILIAR FACE MIGHT MAKE A NEW TOWN LESS STRANGE. YOU DID SAY TO COME VISIT IF I WAS IN THE AREA.
...I GUESS I DID.
HOW COULD I PASS UP A CHANCE TO PERFORM IN YOUR NEW STOMPING GROUNDS?
HAVE TO MEET UP WITH THE BAND FOR A SOUND CHECK.
YOU'LL COME SEE THE SHOW, RIGHT? I PUT YOU ON THE GUEST LIST.
YEAH, IF THE SCHEDULE WORKS OUT. SURE.

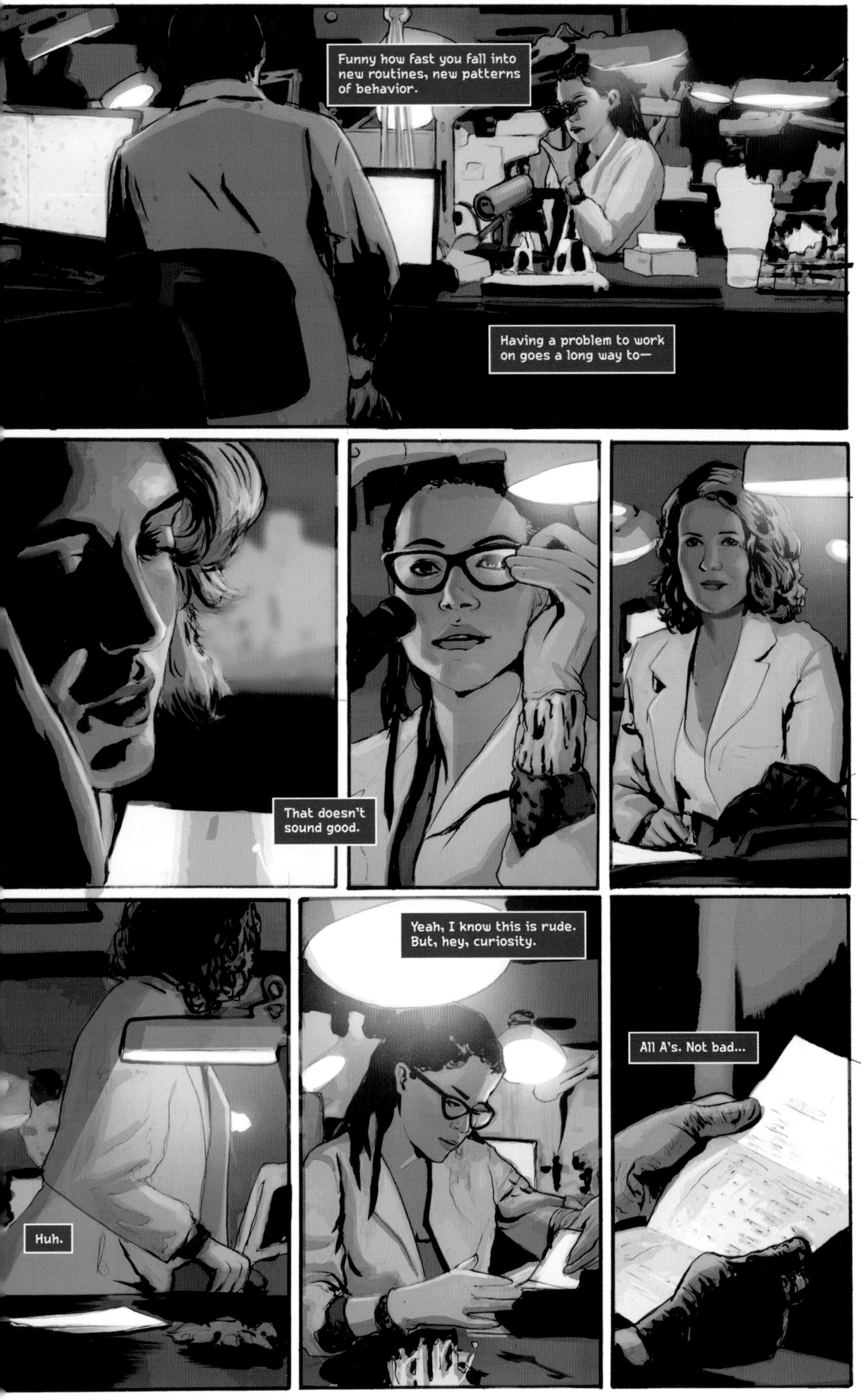
Funny how fast you fall into new routines, new patterns of behavior.
Having a problem to work on goes a long way to—
That doesn't sound good.
Huh.
Yeah, I know this is rude. But, hey, curiosity.
All A's. Not bad...

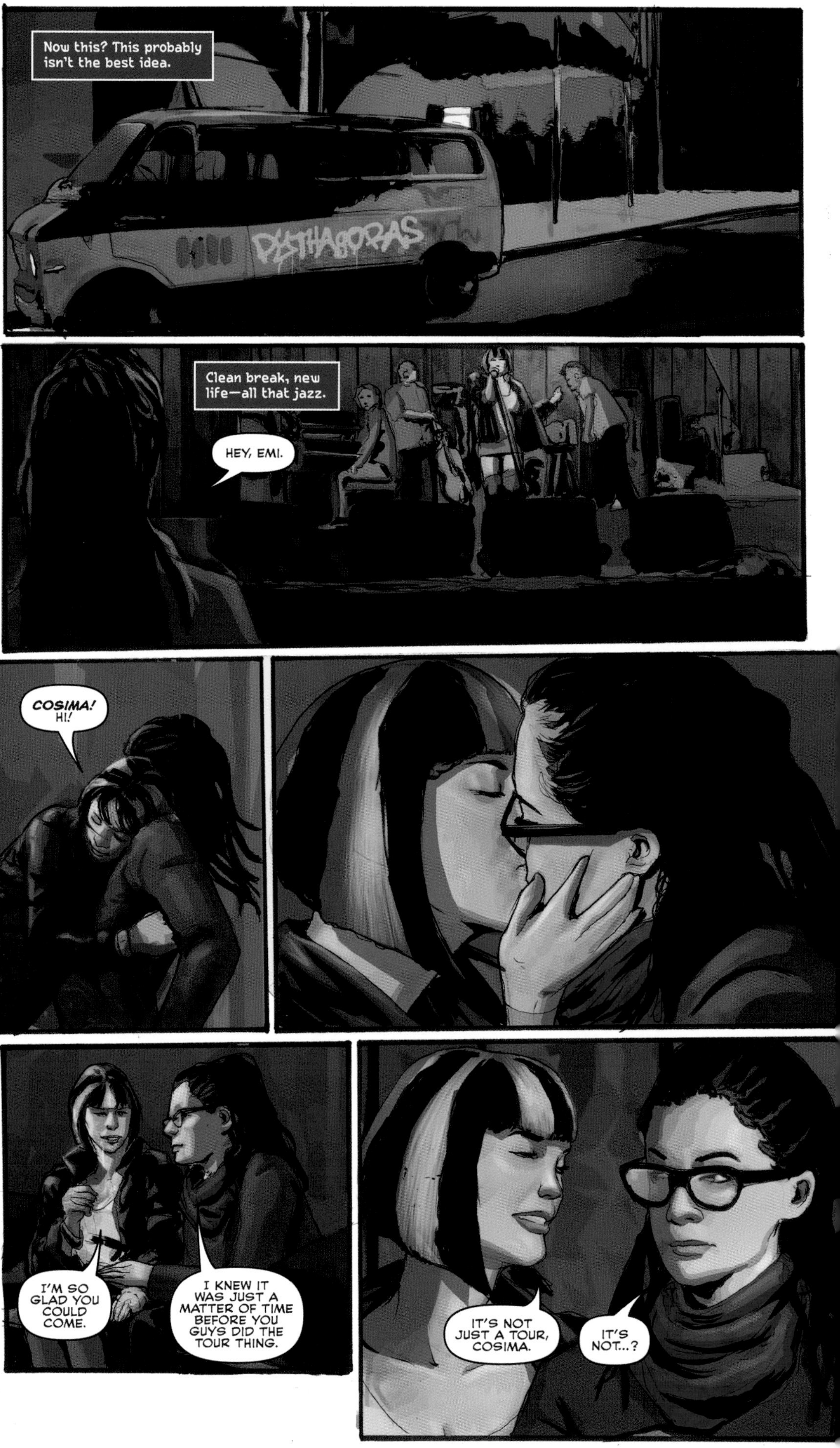

Now this? This probably isn't the best idea.
Clean break, new life—all that jazz.
HEY, EMI.
COSIMA! HI!
I'M SO GLAD YOU COULD COME.
I KNEW IT WAS JUST A MATTER OF TIME BEFORE YOU GUYS DID THE TOUR THING.
IT'S NOT JUST A TOUR, COSIMA.
IT'S NOT...?

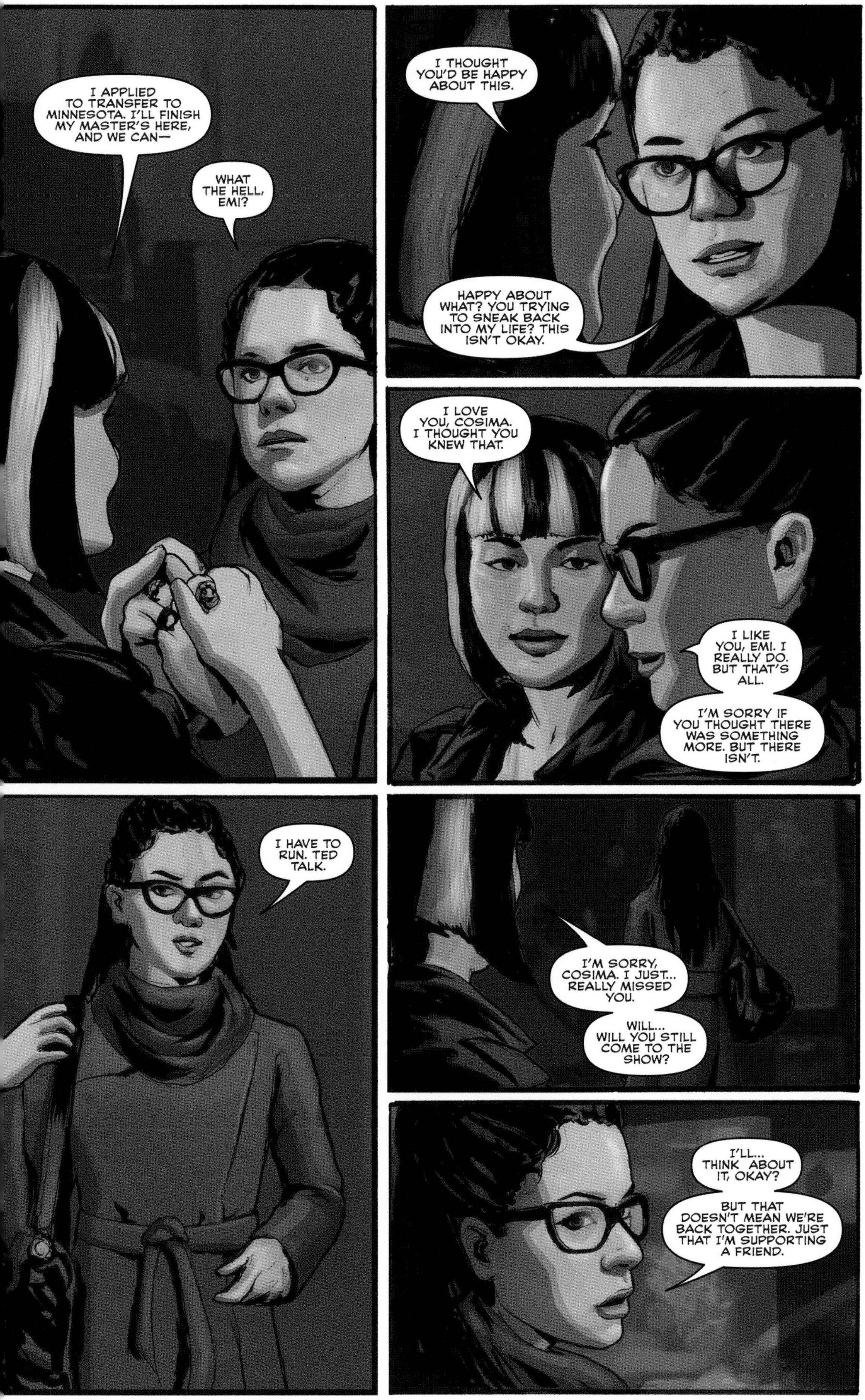

I APPLIED TO TRANSFER TO MINNESOTA. I'LL FINISH MY MASTER'S HERE, AND WE CAN—
WHAT THE HELL, EMI?
I THOUGHT YOU'D BE HAPPY ABOUT THIS.
HAPPY ABOUT WHAT? YOU TRYING TO SNEAK BACK INTO MY LIFE? THIS ISN'T OKAY.
I LOVE YOU, COSIMA. I THOUGHT YOU KNEW THAT.
I LIKE YOU, EMI. I REALLY DO. BUT THAT'S ALL.
I'M SORRY IF YOU THOUGHT THERE WAS SOMETHING MORE. BUT THERE ISN'T.
I HAVE TO RUN. TED TALK.
I'M SORRY, COSIMA. I JUST... REALLY MISSED YOU.
WILL... WILL YOU STILL COME TO THE SHOW?
I'LL... THINK ABOUT IT, OKAY?
BUT THAT DOESN'T MEAN WE'RE BACK TOGETHER. JUST THAT I'M SUPPORTING A FRIEND.

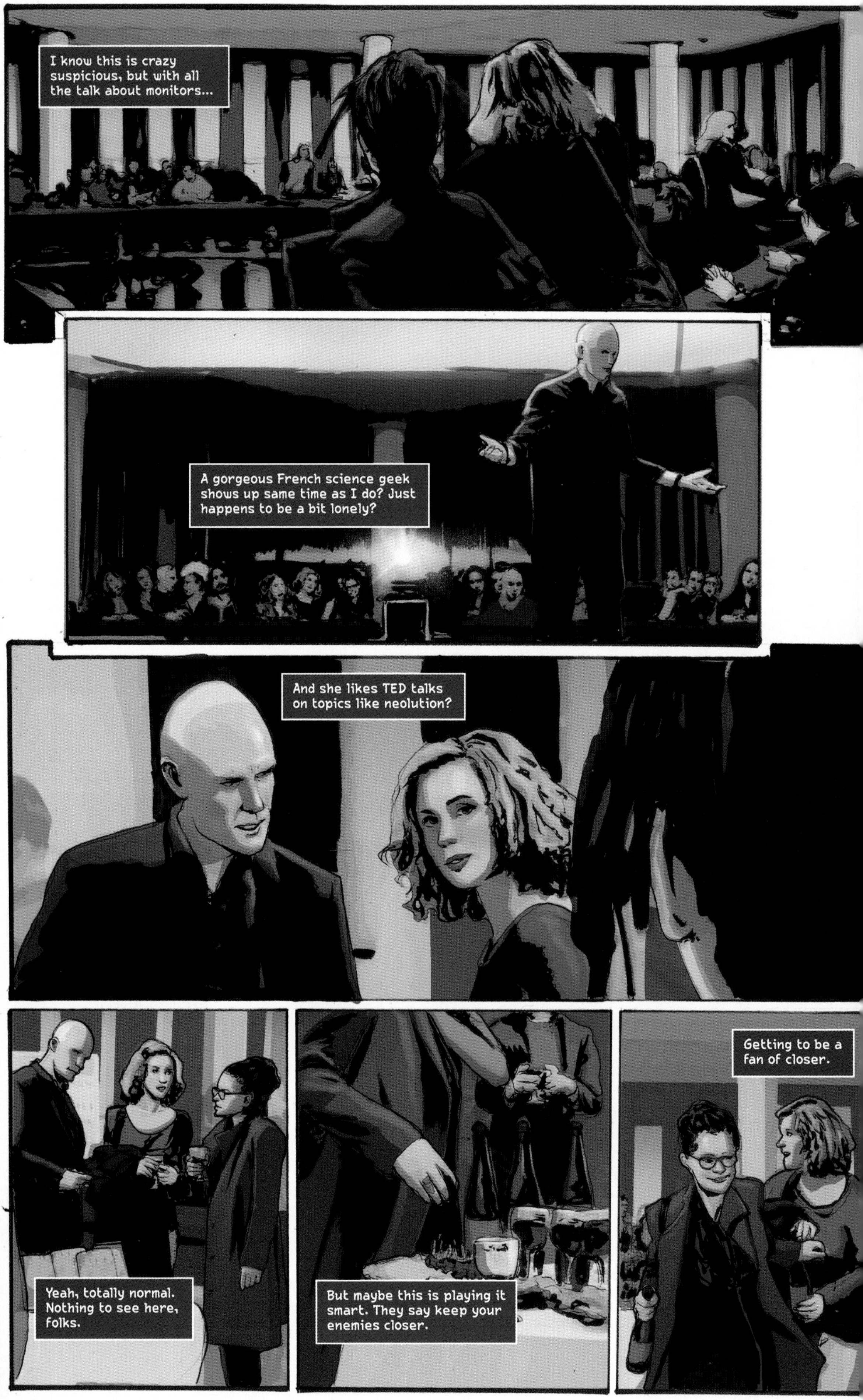
I know this is crazy suspicious, but with all the talk about monitors...
A gorgeous French science geek shows up same time as I do? Just happens to be a bit lonely?
And she likes TED talks on topics like neolution?
Yeah, totally normal. Nothing to see here, folks.
But maybe this is playing it smart. They say keep your enemies closer.
Getting to be a fan of closer.

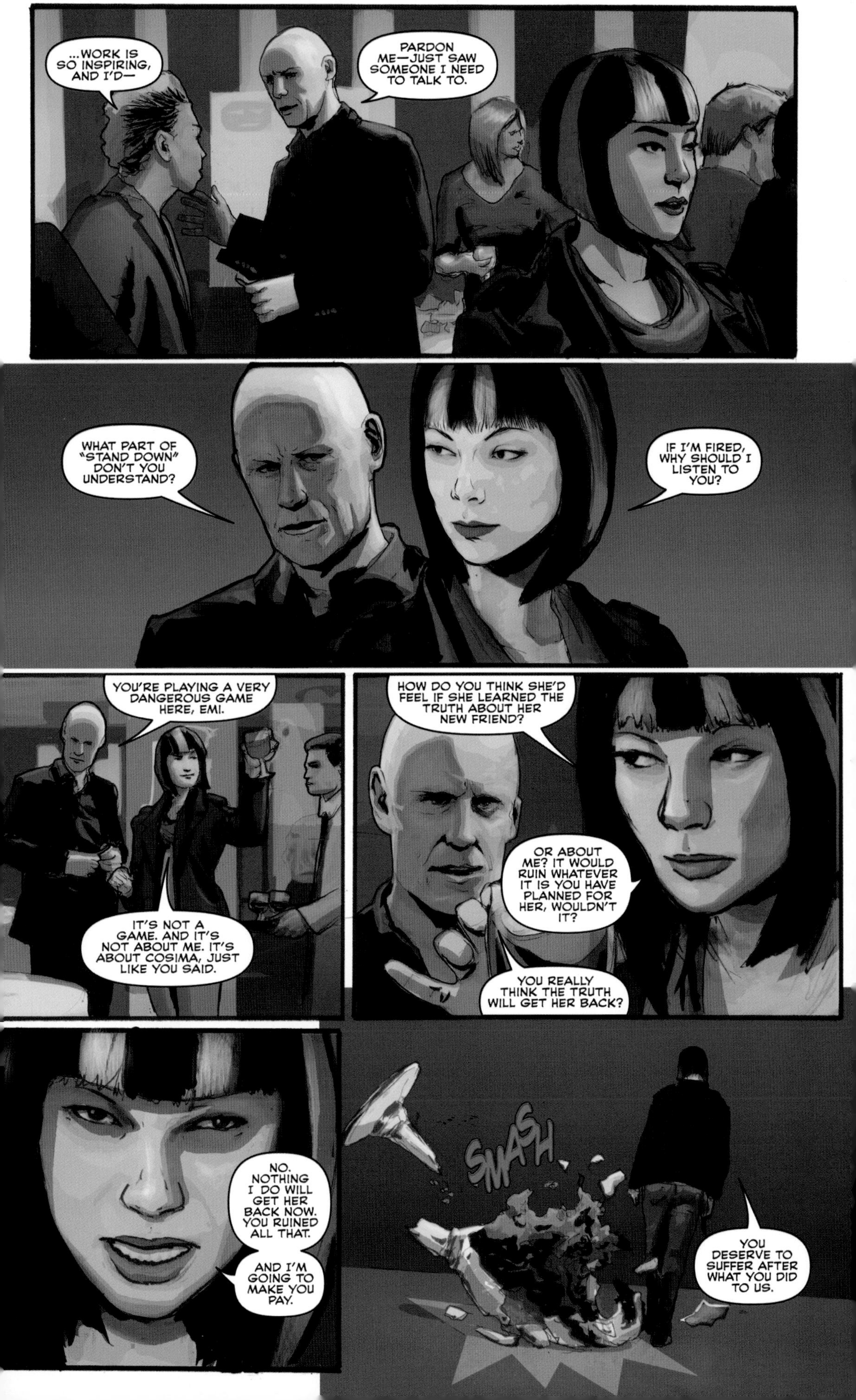
...WORK IS SO INSPIRING, AND I'D—
PARDON ME—JUST SAW SOMEONE I NEED TO TALK TO.
WHAT PART OF "STAND DOWN" DON'T YOU UNDERSTAND?
IF I'M FIRED, WHY SHOULD I LISTEN TO YOU?
YOU'RE PLAYING A VERY DANGEROUS GAME HERE, EMI.
IT'S NOT A GAME. AND IT'S NOT ABOUT ME. IT'S ABOUT COSIMA, JUST LIKE YOU SAID.
HOW DO YOU THINK SHE'D FEEL IF SHE LEARNED THE TRUTH ABOUT HER NEW FRIEND?
OR ABOUT ME? IT WOULD RUIN WHATEVER IT IS YOU HAVE PLANNED FOR HER, WOULDN'T IT?
YOU REALLY THINK THE TRUTH WILL GET HER BACK?
NO. NOTHING I DO WILL GET HER BACK NOW. YOU RUINED ALL THAT.
AND I'M GOING TO MAKE YOU PAY.
SMASH
YOU DESERVE TO SUFFER AFTER WHAT YOU DID TO US.

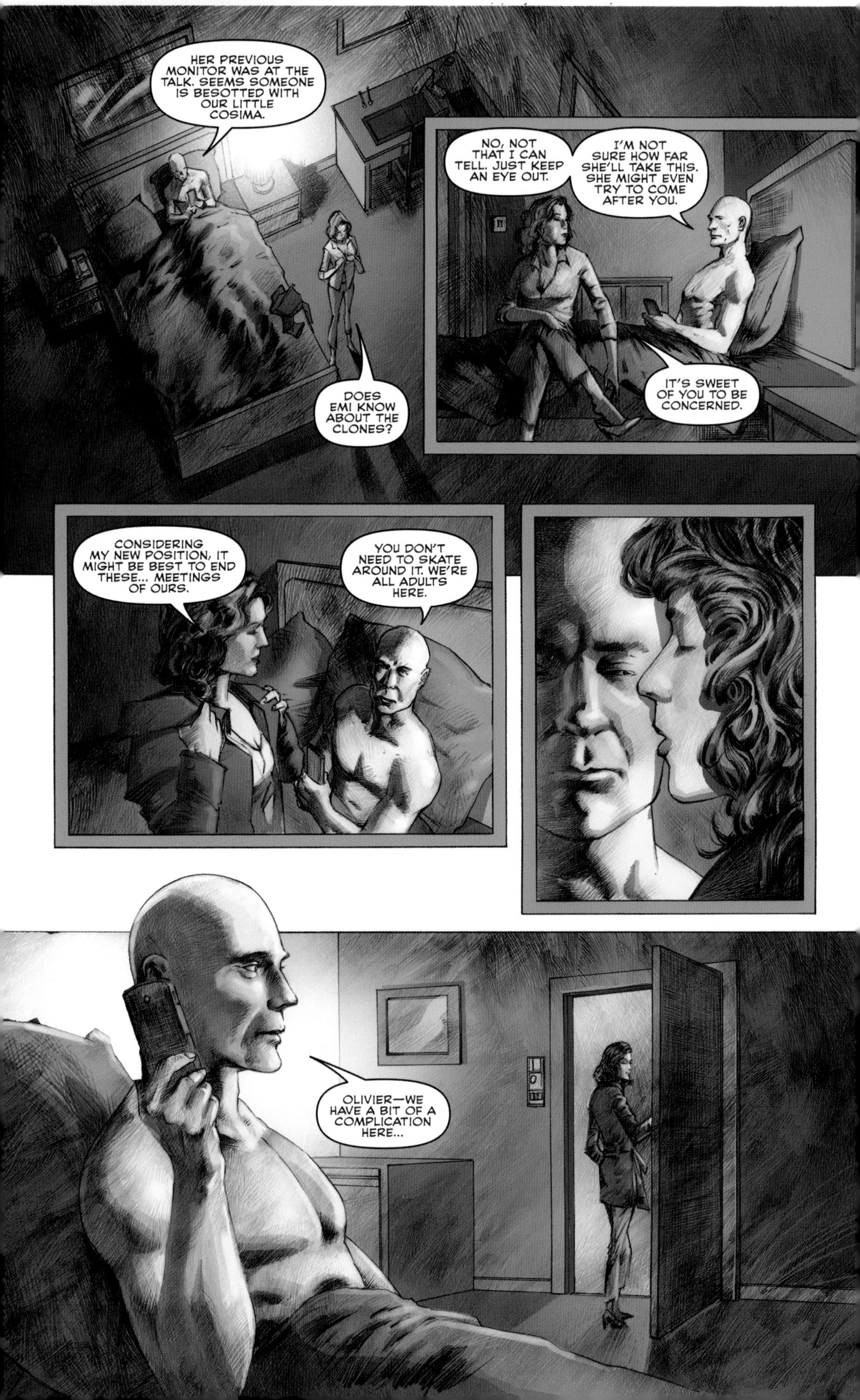
HER PREVIOUS MONITOR WAS AT THE TALK. SEEMS SOMEONE IS BESOTTED WITH OUR LITTLE COSIMA.
DOES EMI KNOW ABOUT THE CLONES?
NO, NOT THAT I CAN TELL. JUST KEEP AN EYE OUT.
I'M NOT SURE HOW FAR SHE'LL TAKE THIS. SHE MIGHT EVEN TRY TO COME AFTER YOU.
IT'S SWEET OF YOU TO BE CONCERNED.
CONSIDERING MY NEW POSITION, IT MIGHT BE BEST TO END THESE... MEETINGS OF OURS.
YOU DON'T NEED TO SKATE AROUND IT. WE'RE ALL ADULTS HERE.
OLIVIER—WE HAVE A BIT OF A COMPLICATION HERE...

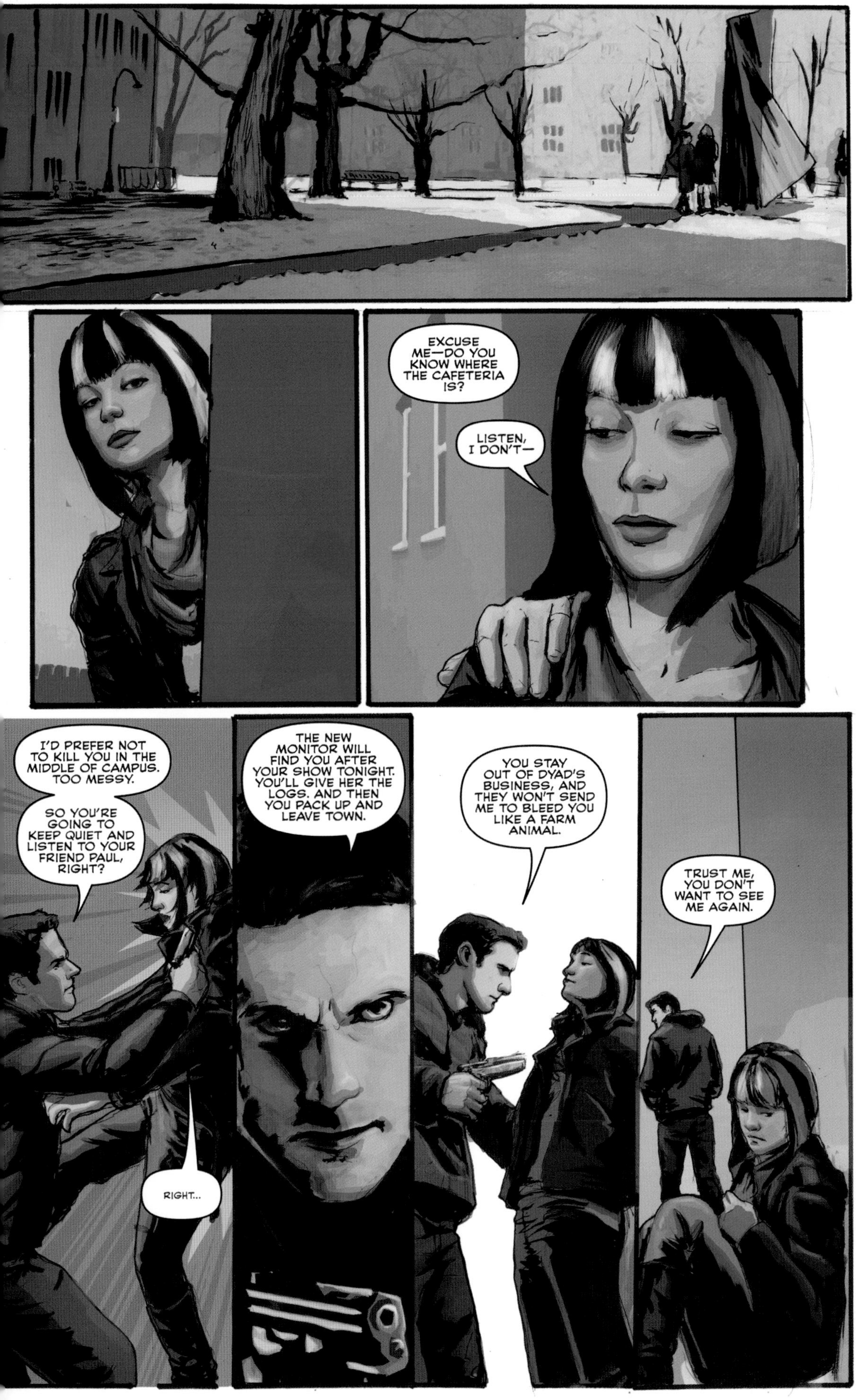
EXCUSE ME—DO YOU KNOW WHERE THE CAFETERIA IS?
LISTEN, I DON'T—
I'D PREFER NOT TO KILL YOU IN THE MIDDLE OF CAMPUS. TOO MESSY.
SO YOU'RE GOING TO KEEP QUIET AND LISTEN TO YOUR FRIEND PAUL, RIGHT?
RIGHT...
THE NEW MONITOR WILL FIND YOU AFTER YOUR SHOW TONIGHT. YOU'LL GIVE HER THE LOGS. AND THEN YOU PACK UP AND LEAVE TOWN.
YOU STAY OUT OF DYAD'S BUSINESS, AND THEY WON'T SEND ME TO BLEED YOU LIKE A FARM ANIMAL.
TRUST ME, YOU DON'T WANT TO SEE ME AGAIN.

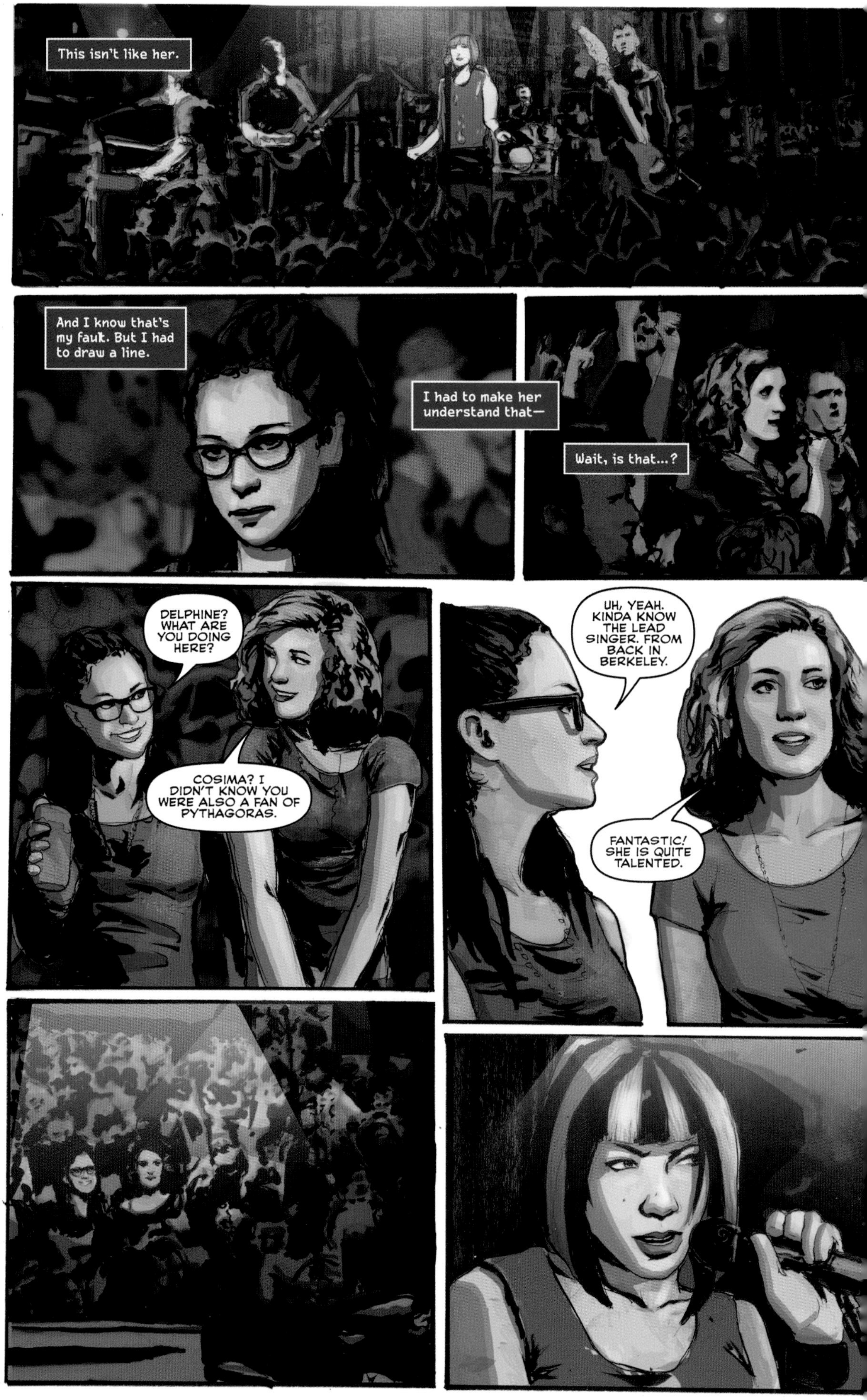
This isn't like her.
And I know that's my fault. But I had to draw a line.
I had to make her understand that—
Wait, is that...?
DELPHINE? WHAT ARE YOU DOING HERE?
COSIMA? I DIDN'T KNOW YOU WERE ALSO A FAN OF PYTHAGORAS.
UH, YEAH. KINDA KNOW THE LEAD SINGER. FROM BACK IN BERKELEY.
FANTASTIC! SHE IS QUITE TALENTED.

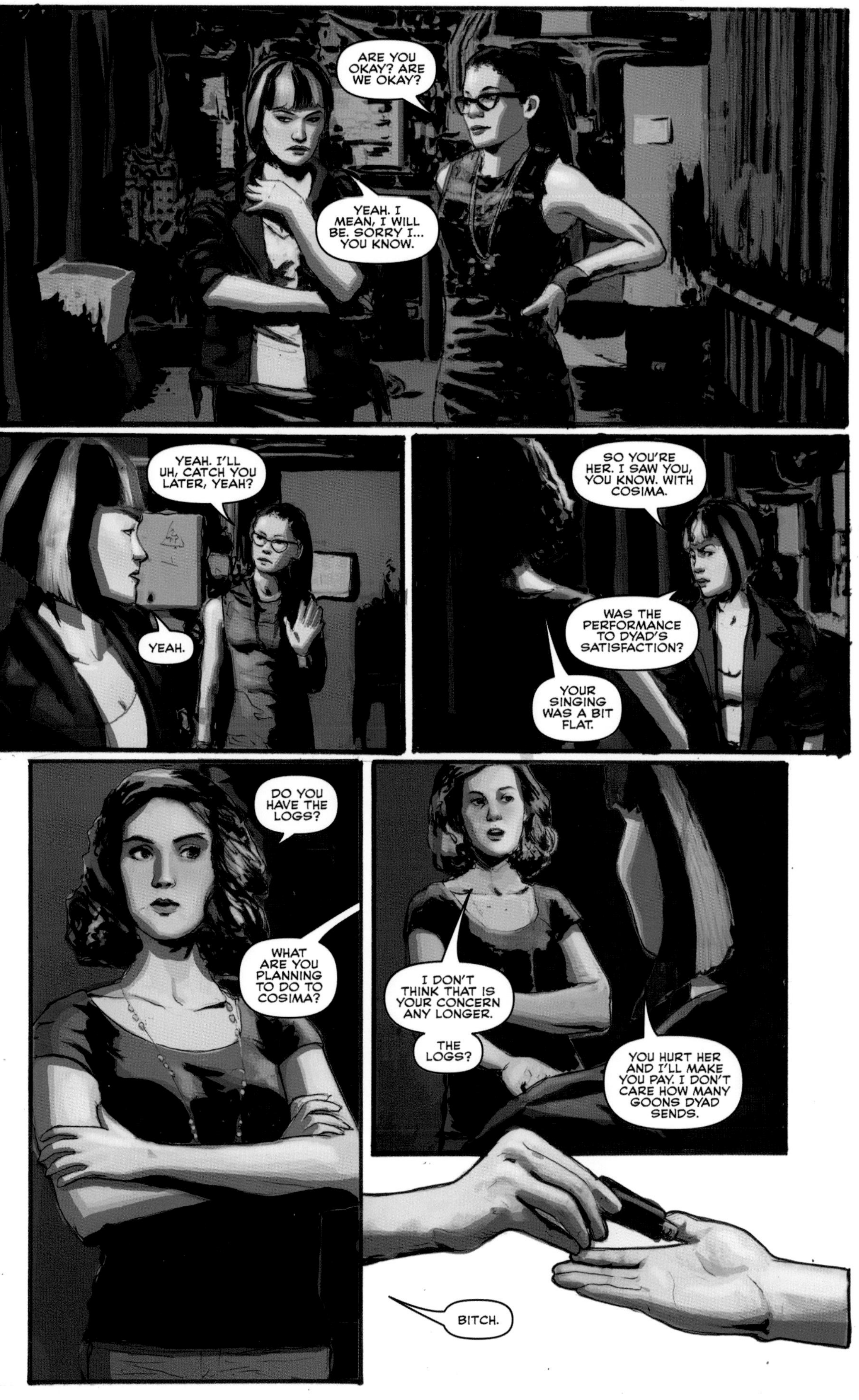
ARE YOU OKAY? ARE WE OKAY?
YEAH. I MEAN, I WILL BE. SORRY I... YOU KNOW.
YEAH. I'LL UH, CATCH YOU LATER, YEAH?
YEAH.
SO YOU'RE HER. I SAW YOU, YOU KNOW. WITH COSIMA.
WAS THE PERFORMANCE TO DYAD'S SATISFACTION?
YOUR SINGING WAS A BIT FLAT.
DO YOU HAVE THE LOGS?
WHAT ARE YOU PLANNING TO DO TO COSIMA?
I DON'T THINK THAT IS YOUR CONCERN ANY LONGER.
THE LOGS?
YOU HURT HER AND I'LL MAKE YOU PAY. I DON'T CARE HOW MANY GOONS DYAD SENDS.
BITCH.

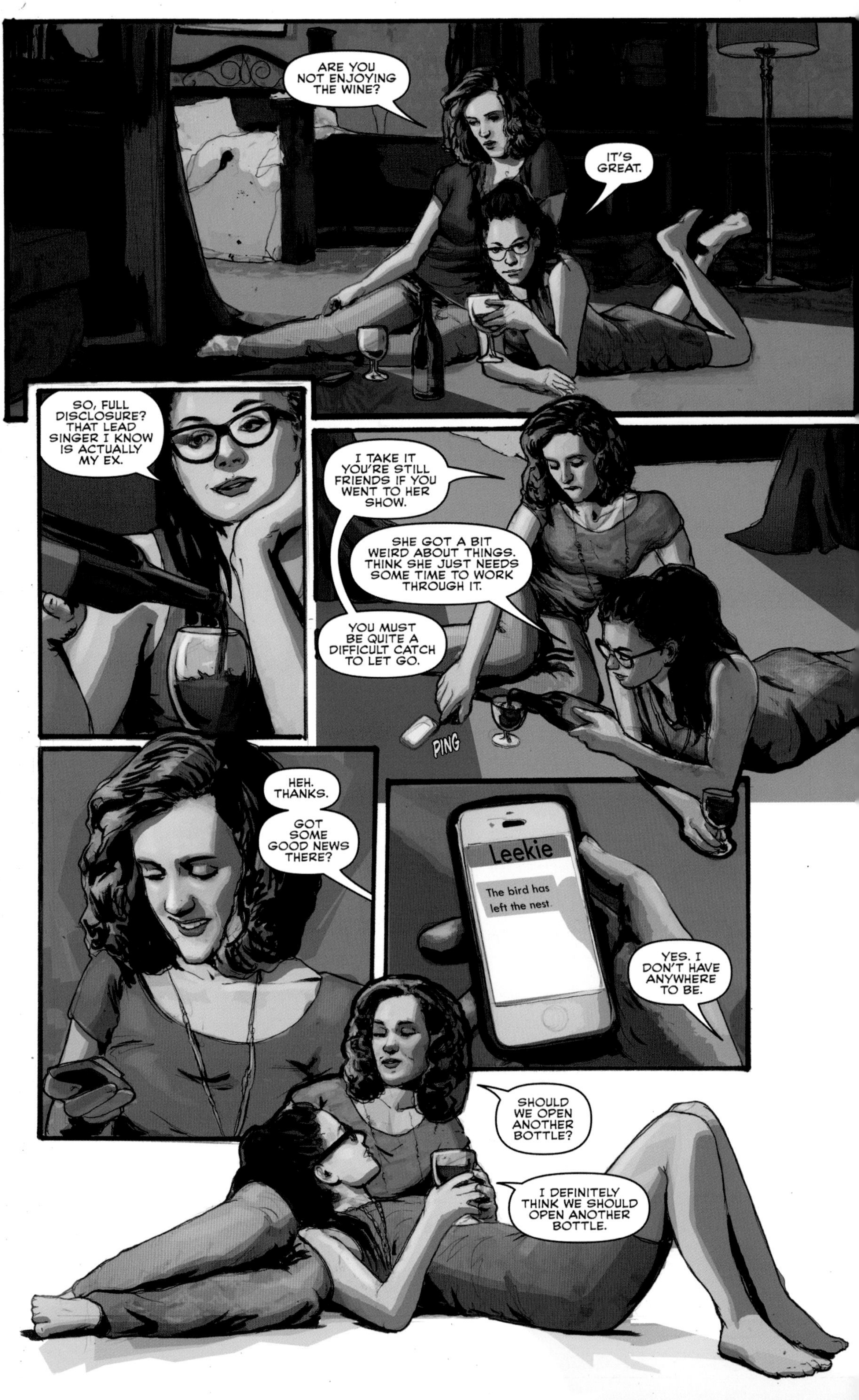

ARE YOU NOT ENJOYING THE WINE?
IT'S GREAT.
SO, FULL DISCLOSURE? THAT LEAD SINGER I KNOW IS ACTUALLY MY EX.
I TAKE IT YOU'RE STILL FRIENDS IF YOU WENT TO HER SHOW.
SHE GOT A BIT WEIRD ABOUT THINGS. THINK SHE JUST NEEDS SOME TIME TO WORK THROUGH IT.
YOU MUST BE QUITE A DIFFICULT CATCH TO LET GO.
PING
HEH. THANKS.
GOT SOME GOOD NEWS THERE?
Leekie
The bird has left the nest.
YES. I DON'T HAVE ANYWHERE TO BE.
SHOULD WE OPEN ANOTHER BOTTLE?
I DEFINITELY THINK WE SHOULD OPEN ANOTHER BOTTLE.

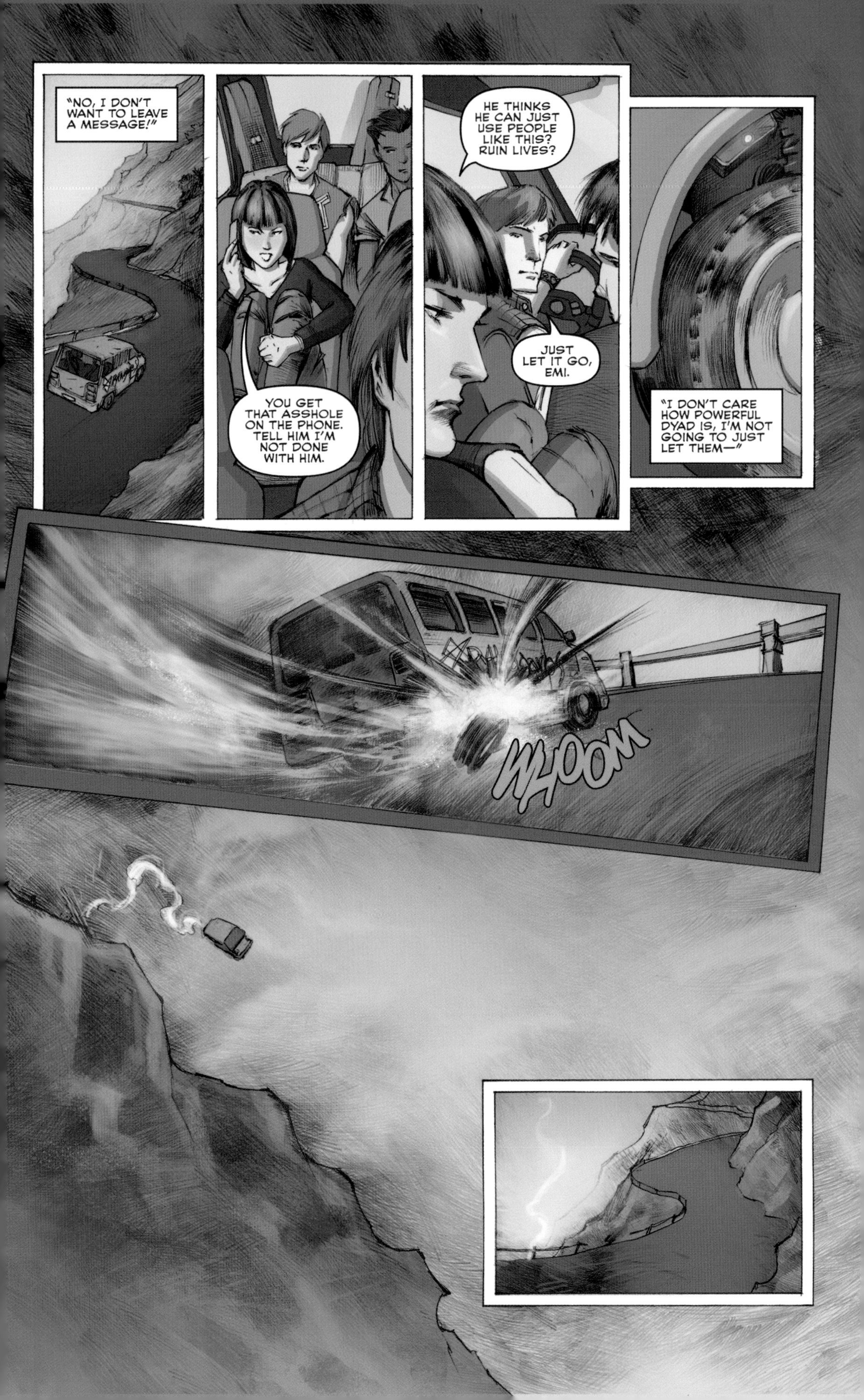
"NO, I DON'T WANT TO LEAVE A MESSAGE!"
YOU GET THAT ASSHOLE ON THE PHONE. TELL HIM I'M NOT DONE WITH HIM.
HE THINKS HE CAN JUST USE PEOPLE LIKE THIS? RUIN LIVES?
JUST LET IT GO, EMI.
"I DON'T CARE HOW POWERFUL DYAD IS, I'M NOT GOING TO JUST LET THEM—"
WHOOM

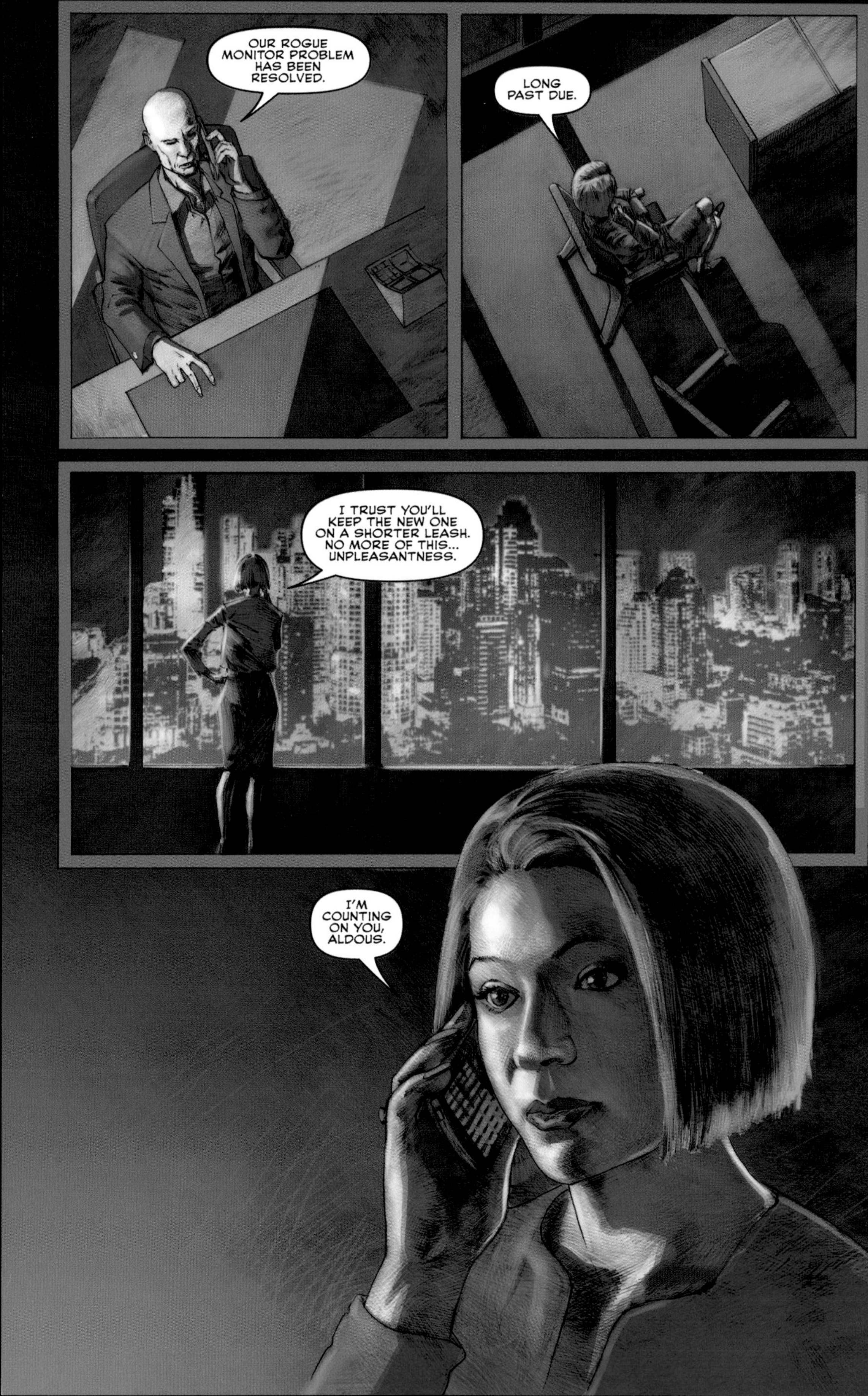
OUR ROGUE MONITOR PROBLEM HAS BEEN RESOLVED.
LONG PAST DUE.
I TRUST YOU'LL KEEP THE NEW ONE ON A SHORTER LEASH. NO MORE OF THIS... UNPLEASANTNESS.
I'M COUNTING ON YOU, ALDOUS.

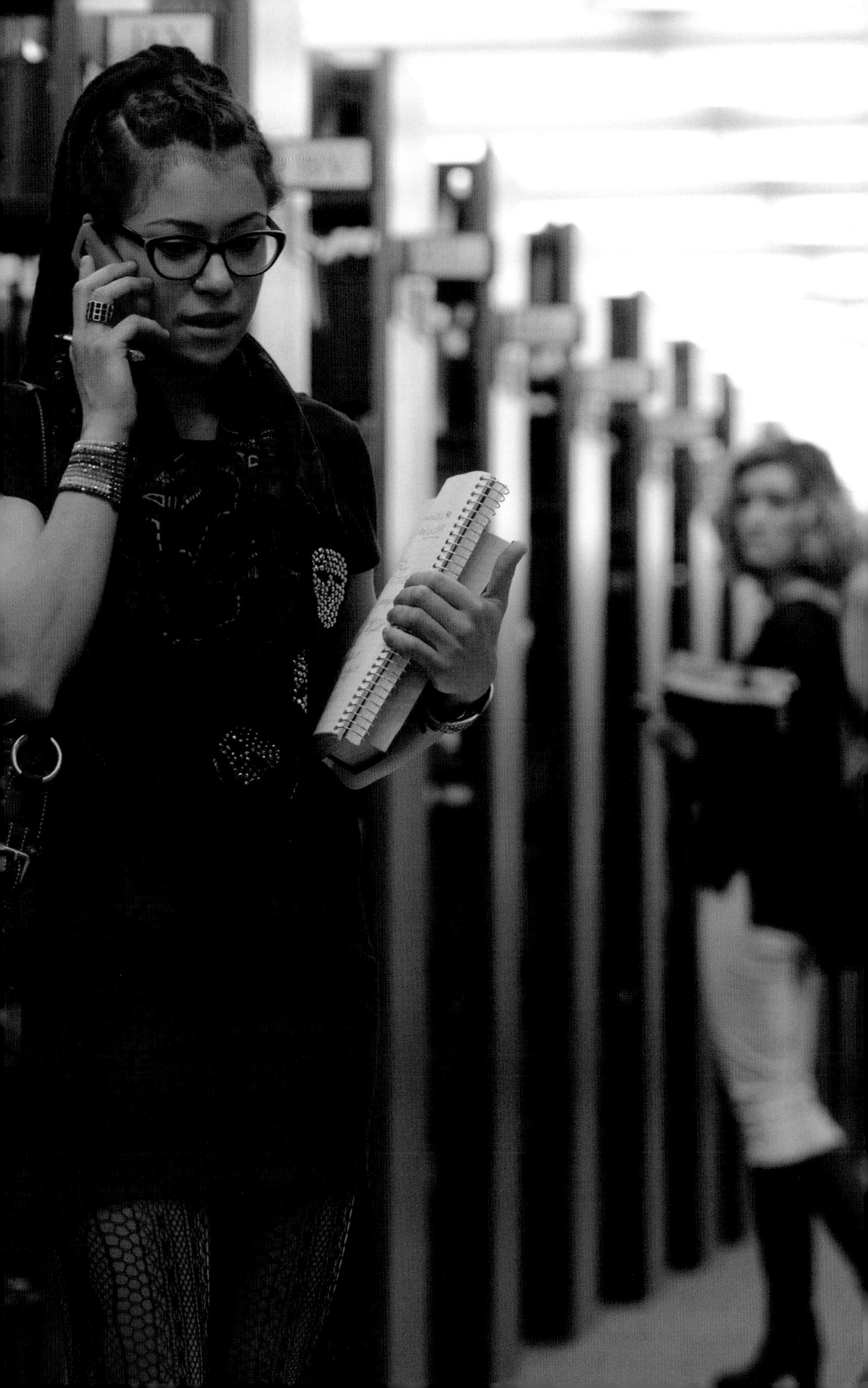

RACHEL

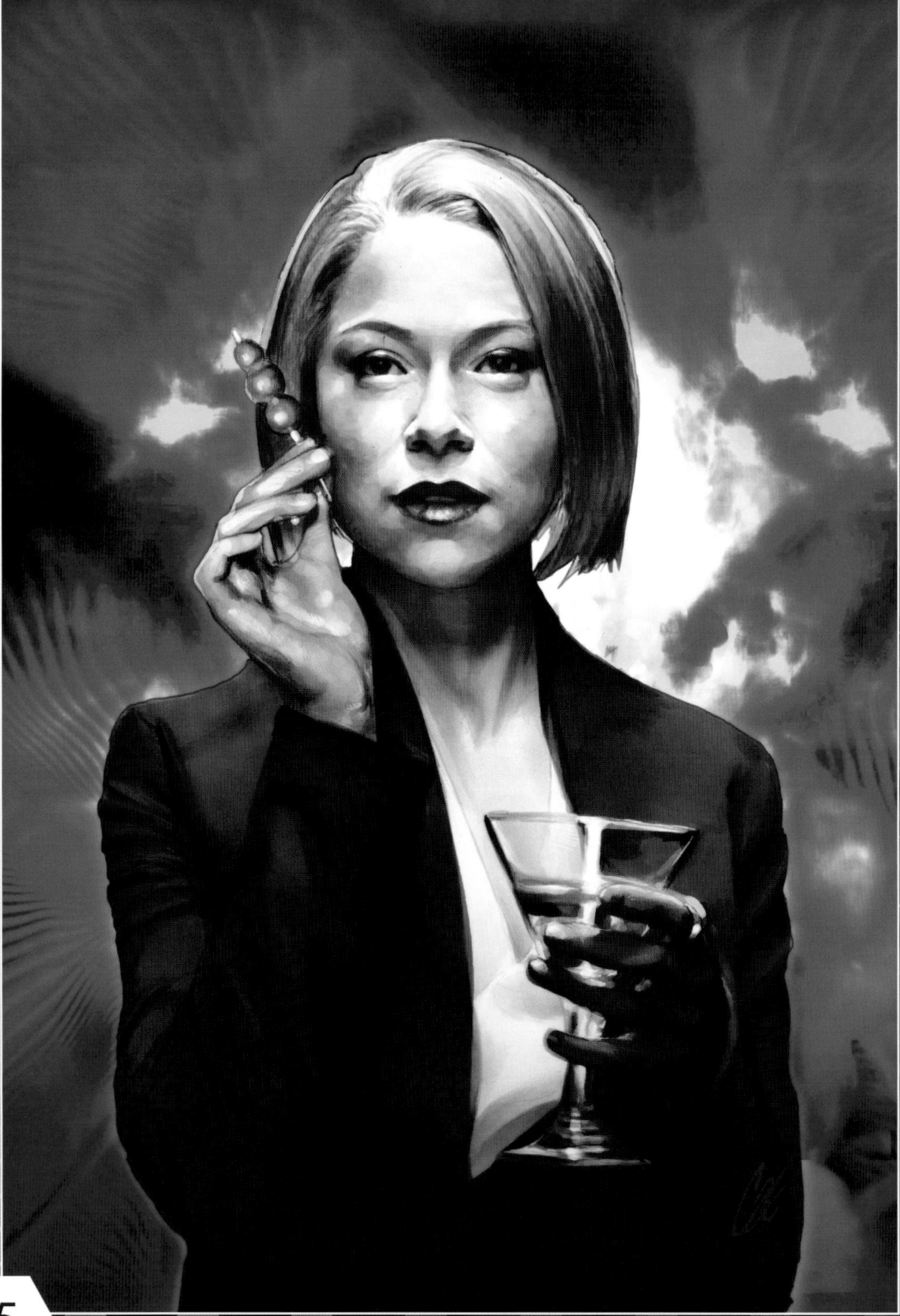

BY **CAT STAGGS**

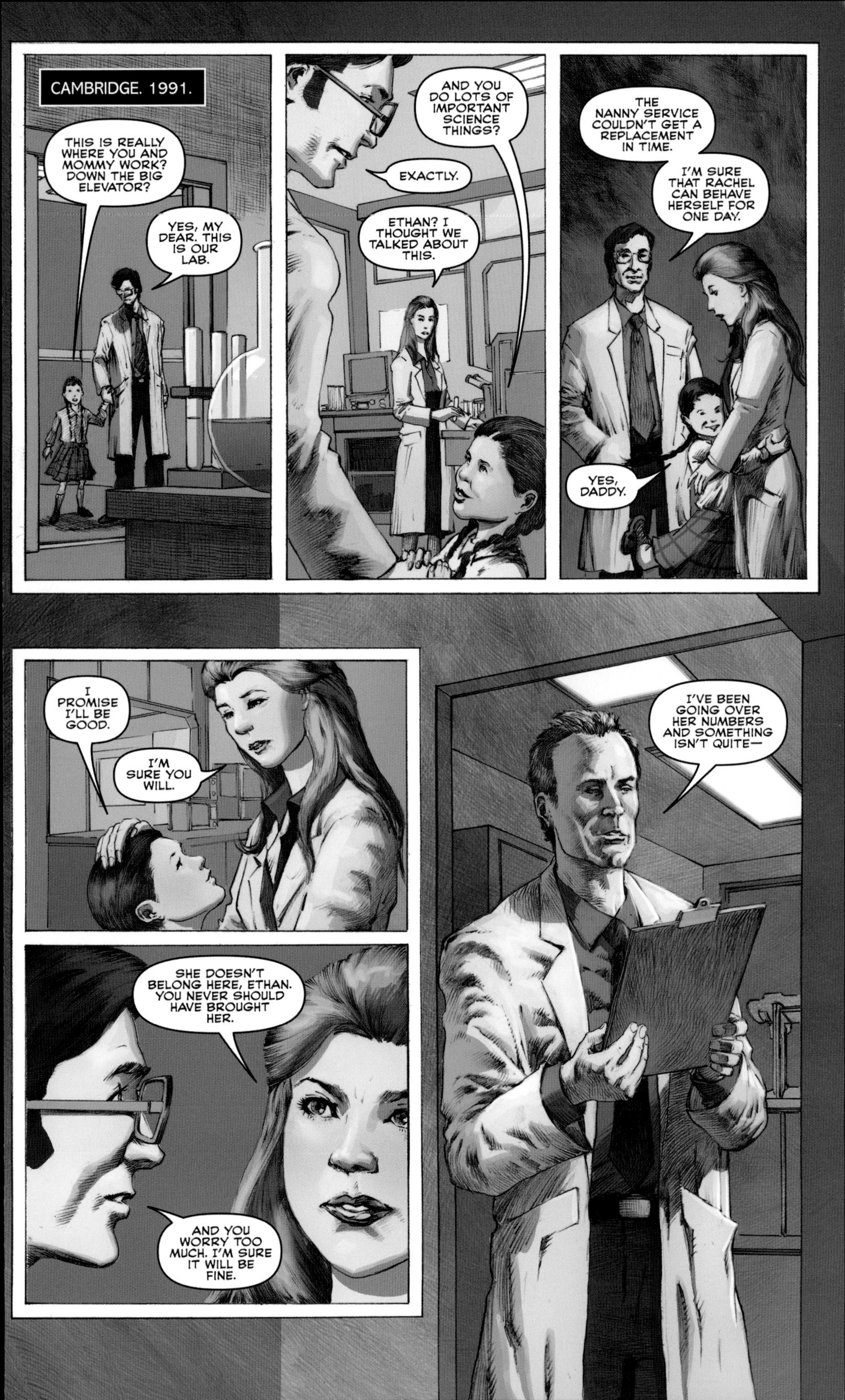
CAMBRIDGE. 1991.
THIS IS REALLY WHERE YOU AND MOMMY WORK? DOWN THE BIG ELEVATOR?
YES, MY DEAR. THIS IS OUR LAB.
AND YOU DO LOTS OF IMPORTANT SCIENCE THINGS?
EXACTLY.
ETHAN? I THOUGHT WE TALKED ABOUT THIS.
THE NANNY SERVICE COULDN'T GET A REPLACEMENT IN TIME.
I'M SURE THAT RACHEL CAN BEHAVE HERSELF FOR ONE DAY.
YES, DADDY.
I PROMISE I'LL BE GOOD.
I'M SURE YOU WILL.
SHE DOESN'T BELONG HERE, ETHAN. YOU NEVER SHOULD HAVE BROUGHT HER.
AND YOU WORRY TOO MUCH. I'M SURE IT WILL BE FINE.
I'VE BEEN GOING OVER HER NUMBERS AND SOMETHING ISN'T QUITE—

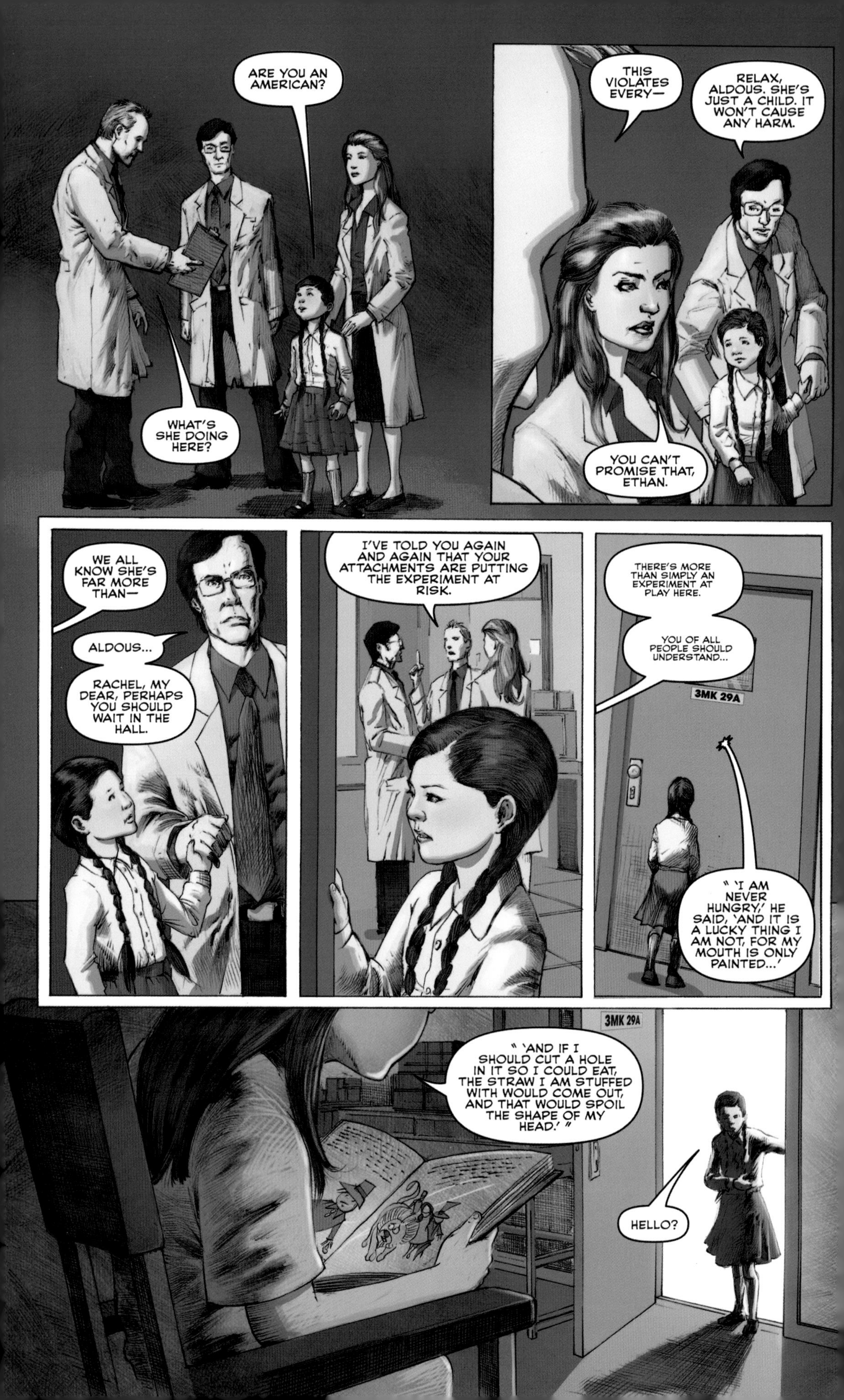
ARE YOU AN AMERICAN?
WHAT'S SHE DOING HERE?
THIS VIOLATES EVERY—
RELAX, ALDOUS. SHE'S JUST A CHILD. IT WON'T CAUSE ANY HARM.
YOU CAN'T PROMISE THAT, ETHAN.
WE ALL KNOW SHE'S FAR MORE THAN—
ALDOUS...
RACHEL, MY DEAR, PERHAPS YOU SHOULD WAIT IN THE HALL.
I'VE TOLD YOU AGAIN AND AGAIN THAT YOUR ATTACHMENTS ARE PUTTING THE EXPERIMENT AT RISK.
THERE'S MORE THAN SIMPLY AN EXPERIMENT AT PLAY HERE.
YOU OF ALL PEOPLE SHOULD UNDERSTAND...
3MK 29A
" 'I AM NEVER HUNGRY,' HE SAID, 'AND IT IS A LUCKY THING I AM NOT, FOR MY MOUTH IS ONLY PAINTED...'
3MK 29A
" 'AND IF I SHOULD CUT A HOLE IN IT SO I COULD EAT, THE STRAW I AM STUFFED WITH WOULD COME OUT, AND THAT WOULD SPOIL THE SHAPE OF MY HEAD.' "
HELLO?

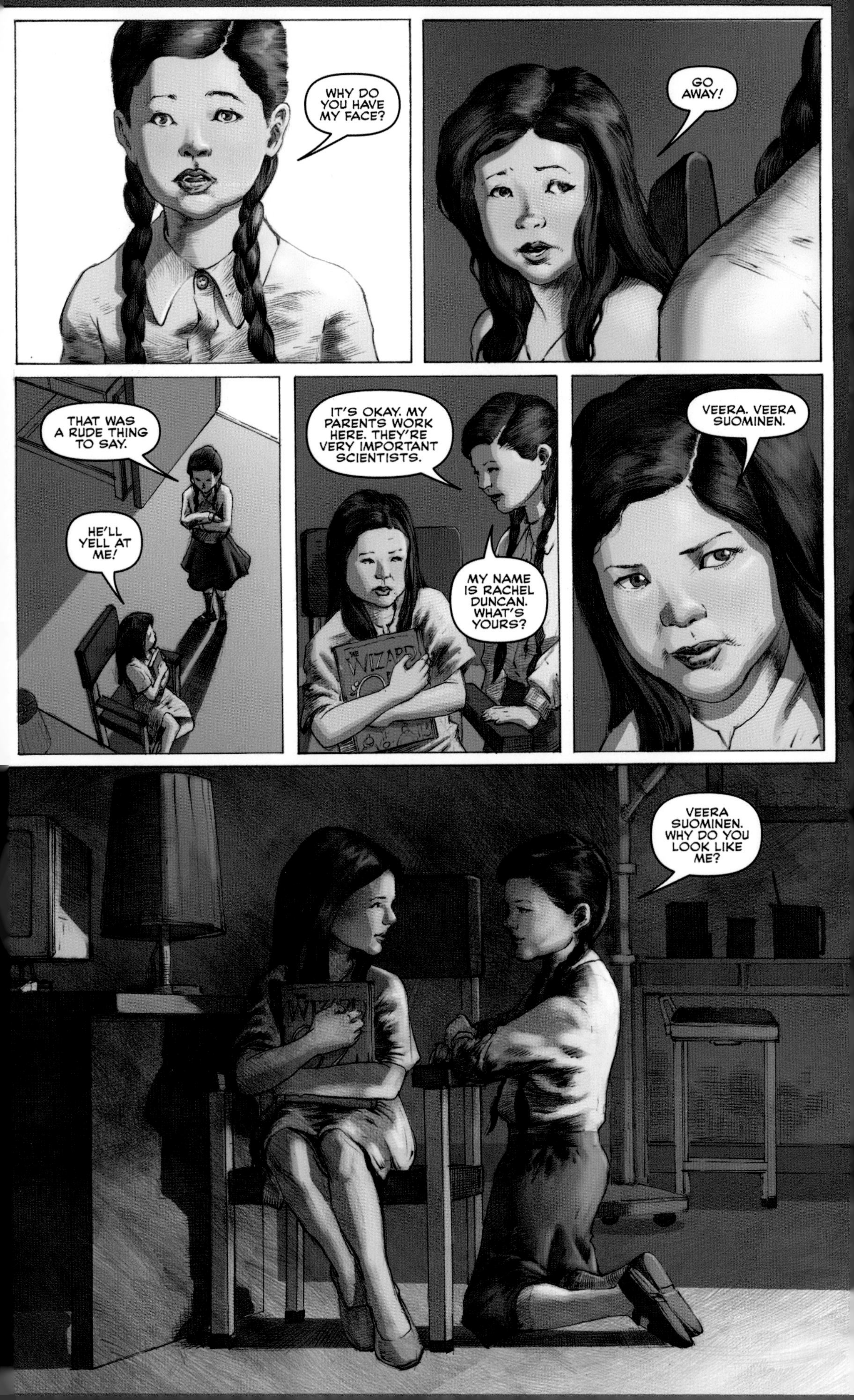
WHY DO YOU HAVE MY FACE?
GO AWAY!
THAT WAS A RUDE THING TO SAY.
HE'LL YELL AT ME!
IT'S OKAY. MY PARENTS WORK HERE. THEY'RE VERY IMPORTANT SCIENTISTS.
MY NAME IS RACHEL DUNCAN. WHAT'S YOURS?
VEERA. VEERA SUOMINEN.
VEERA SUOMINEN. WHY DO YOU LOOK LIKE ME?

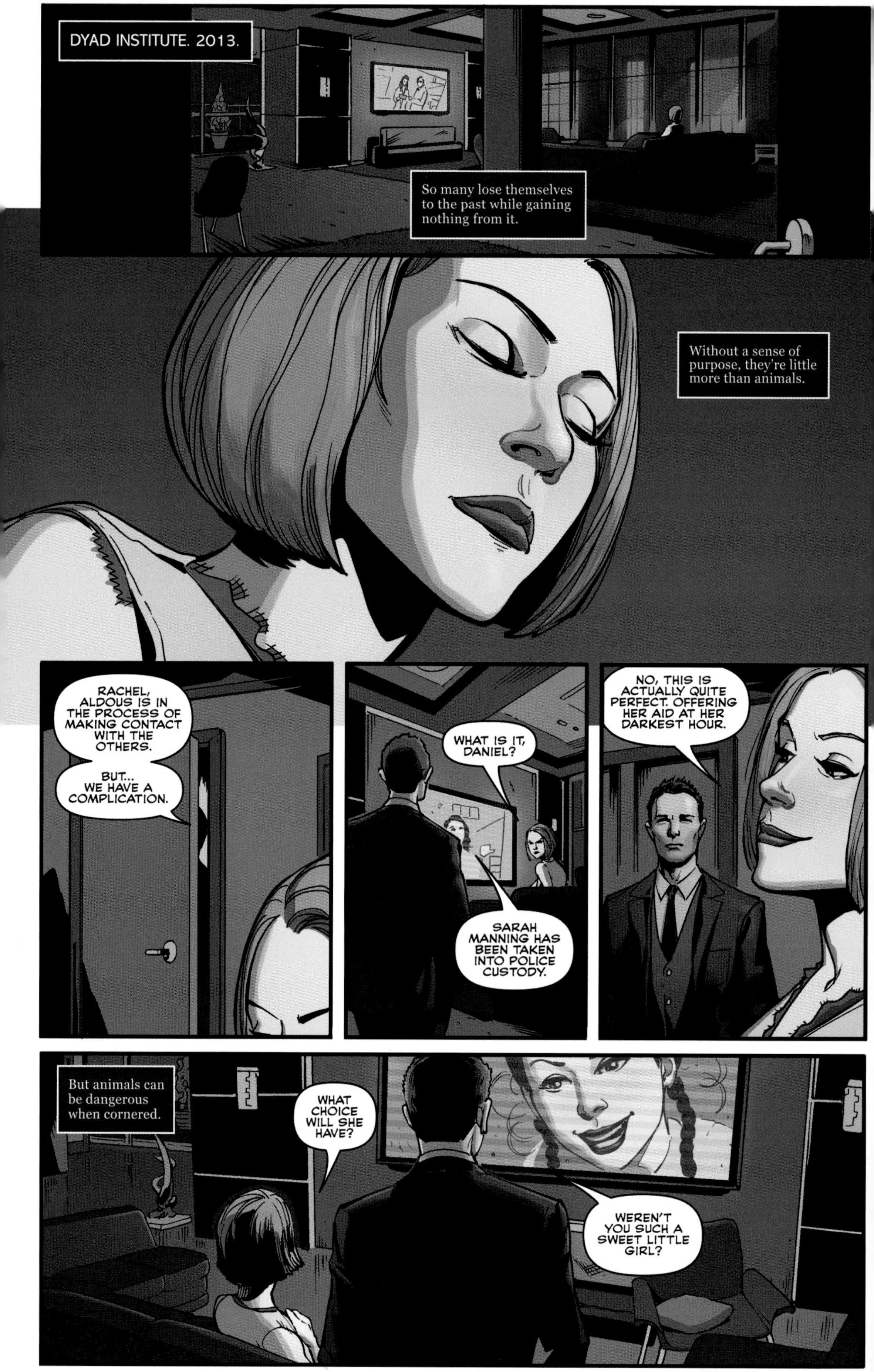
DYAD INSTITUTE. 2013.
So many lose themselves to the past while gaining nothing from it.
Without a sense of purpose, they're little more than animals.
RACHEL, ALDOUS IS IN THE PROCESS OF MAKING CONTACT WITH THE OTHERS.
BUT... WE HAVE A COMPLICATION.
WHAT IS IT, DANIEL?
SARAH MANNING HAS BEEN TAKEN INTO POLICE CUSTODY.
NO, THIS IS ACTUALLY QUITE PERFECT. OFFERING HER AID AT HER DARKEST HOUR.
But animals can be dangerous when cornered.
WHAT CHOICE WILL SHE HAVE?
WEREN'T YOU SUCH A SWEET LITTLE GIRL?

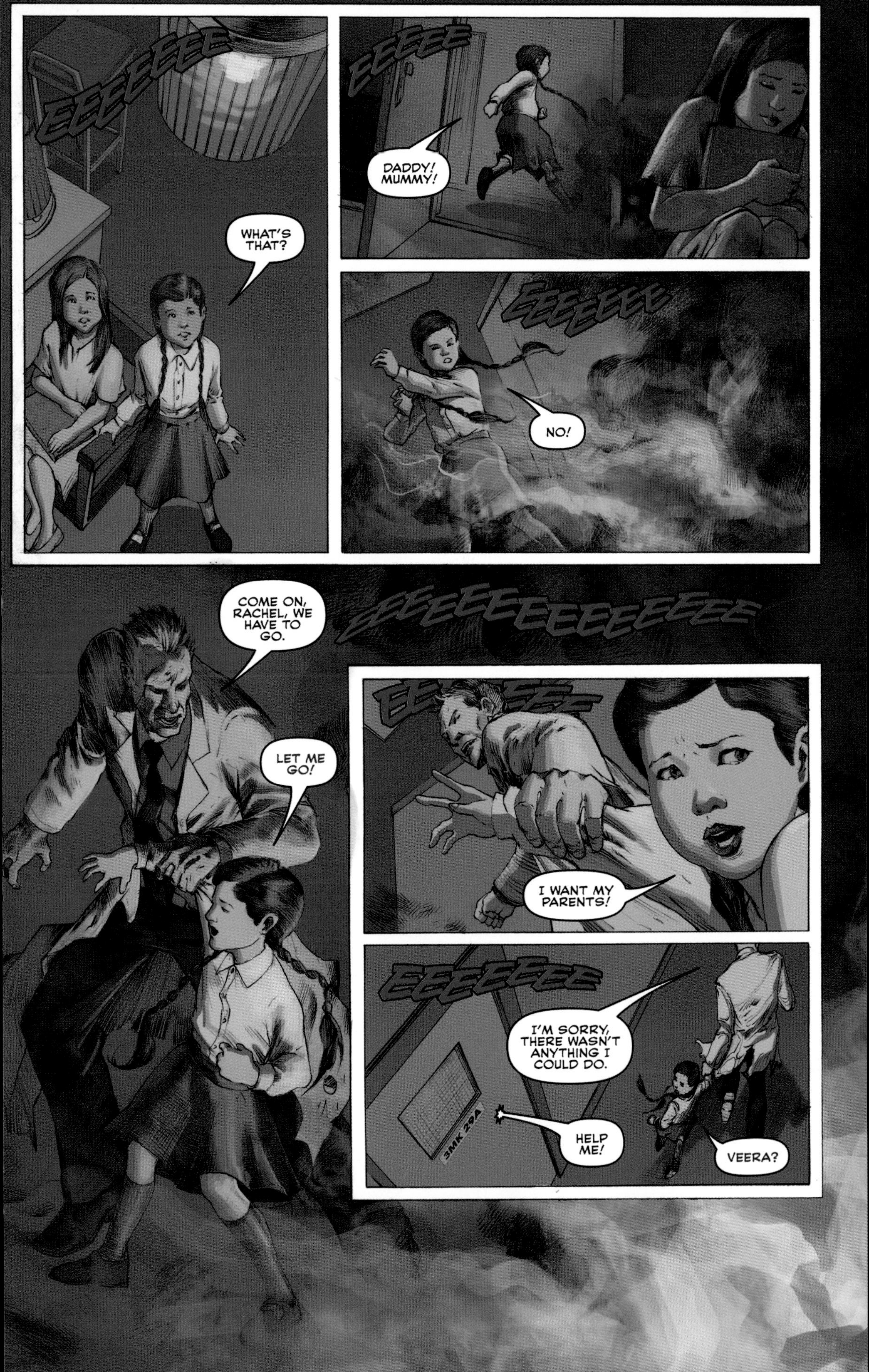
EEEEEEEE
WHAT'S THAT?
EEEEE
DADDY! MUMMY!
EEEEEEE
NO!
COME ON, RACHEL, WE HAVE TO GO.
EEEEEEEEEEEEEEE
LET ME GO!
I WANT MY PARENTS!
EEEEEEE
I'M SORRY, THERE WASN'T ANYTHING I COULD DO.
3MK 29A
HELP ME!
VEERA?

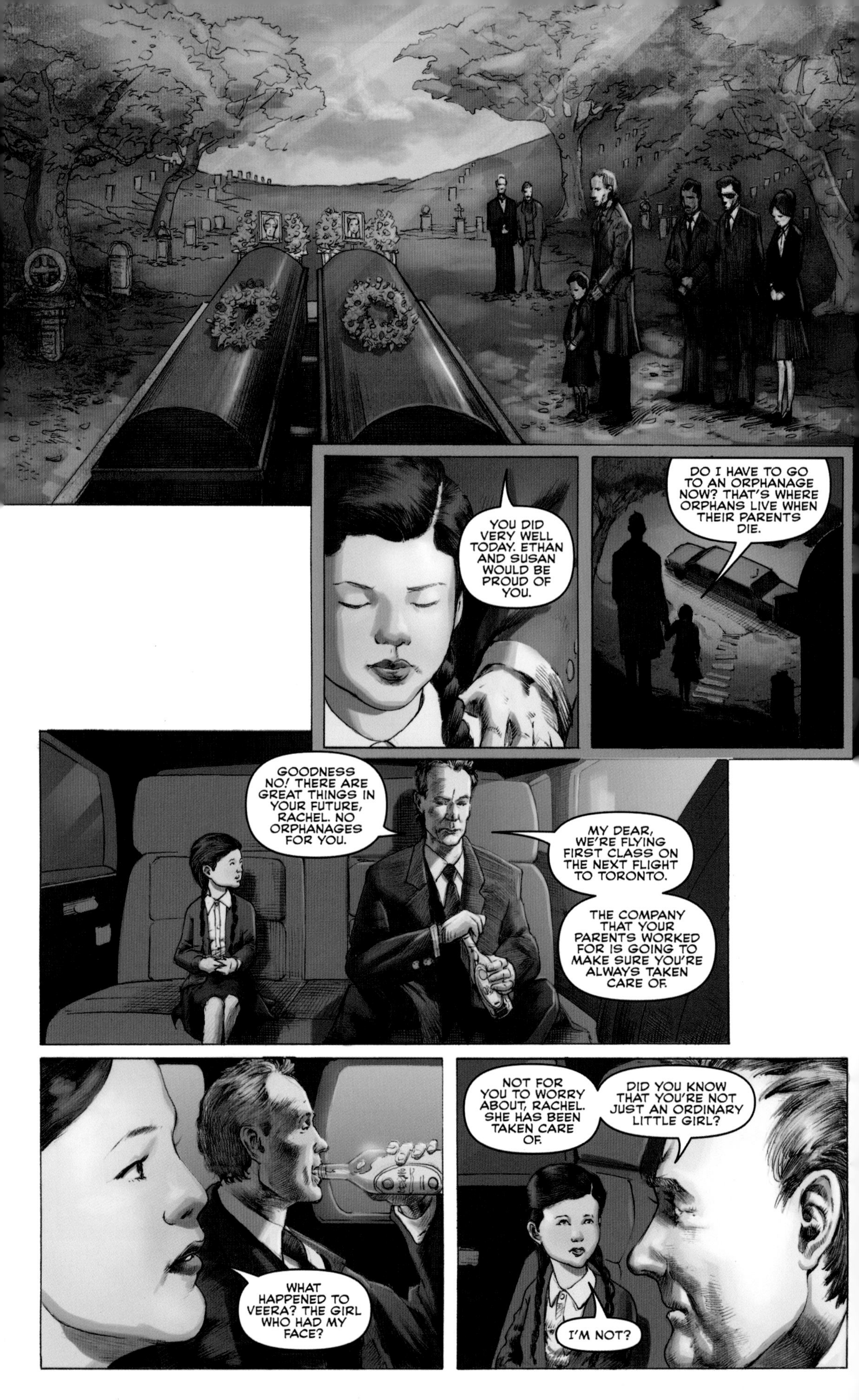
YOU DID VERY WELL TODAY. ETHAN AND SUSAN WOULD BE PROUD OF YOU.
DO I HAVE TO GO TO AN ORPHANAGE NOW? THAT'S WHERE ORPHANS LIVE WHEN THEIR PARENTS DIE.
GOODNESS NO! THERE ARE GREAT THINGS IN YOUR FUTURE, RACHEL. NO ORPHANAGES FOR YOU.
MY DEAR, WE'RE FLYING FIRST CLASS ON THE NEXT FLIGHT TO TORONTO.
THE COMPANY THAT YOUR PARENTS WORKED FOR IS GOING TO MAKE SURE YOU'RE ALWAYS TAKEN CARE OF.
WHAT HAPPENED TO VEERA? THE GIRL WHO HAD MY FACE?
NOT FOR YOU TO WORRY ABOUT, RACHEL. SHE HAS BEEN TAKEN CARE OF.
DID YOU KNOW THAT YOU'RE NOT JUST AN ORDINARY LITTLE GIRL?
I'M NOT?

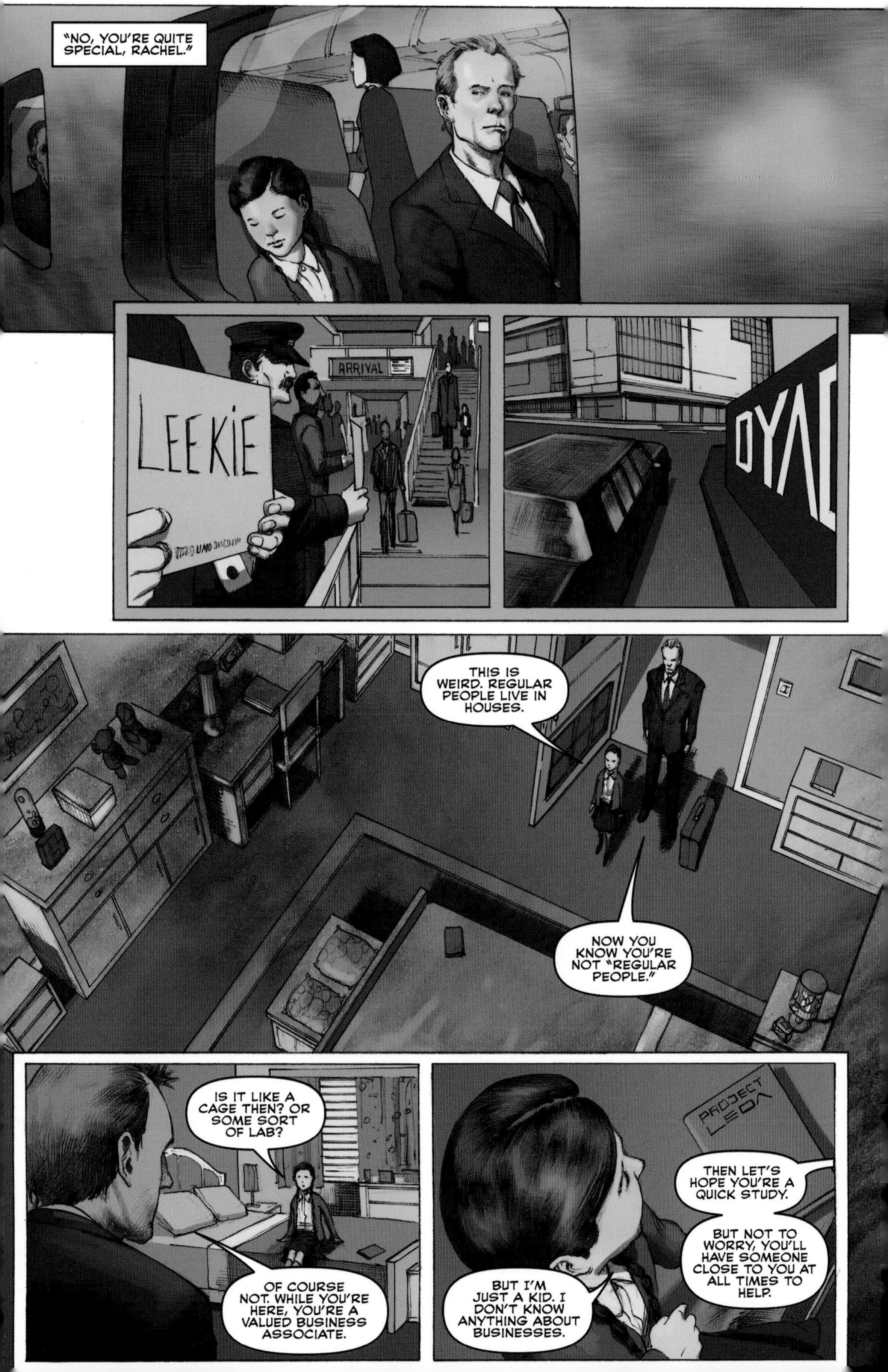
"NO, YOU'RE QUITE SPECIAL, RACHEL."
ARRIVAL
LEEKIE
THIS IS WEIRD. REGULAR PEOPLE LIVE IN HOUSES.
NOW YOU KNOW YOU'RE NOT "REGULAR PEOPLE."
IS IT LIKE A CAGE THEN? OR SOME SORT OF LAB?
OF COURSE NOT. WHILE YOU'RE HERE, YOU'RE A VALUED BUSINESS ASSOCIATE.
PROJECT LEDA
BUT I'M JUST A KID. I DON'T KNOW ANYTHING ABOUT BUSINESSES.
THEN LET'S HOPE YOU'RE A QUICK STUDY.
BUT NOT TO WORRY, YOU'LL HAVE SOMEONE CLOSE TO YOU AT ALL TIMES TO HELP.

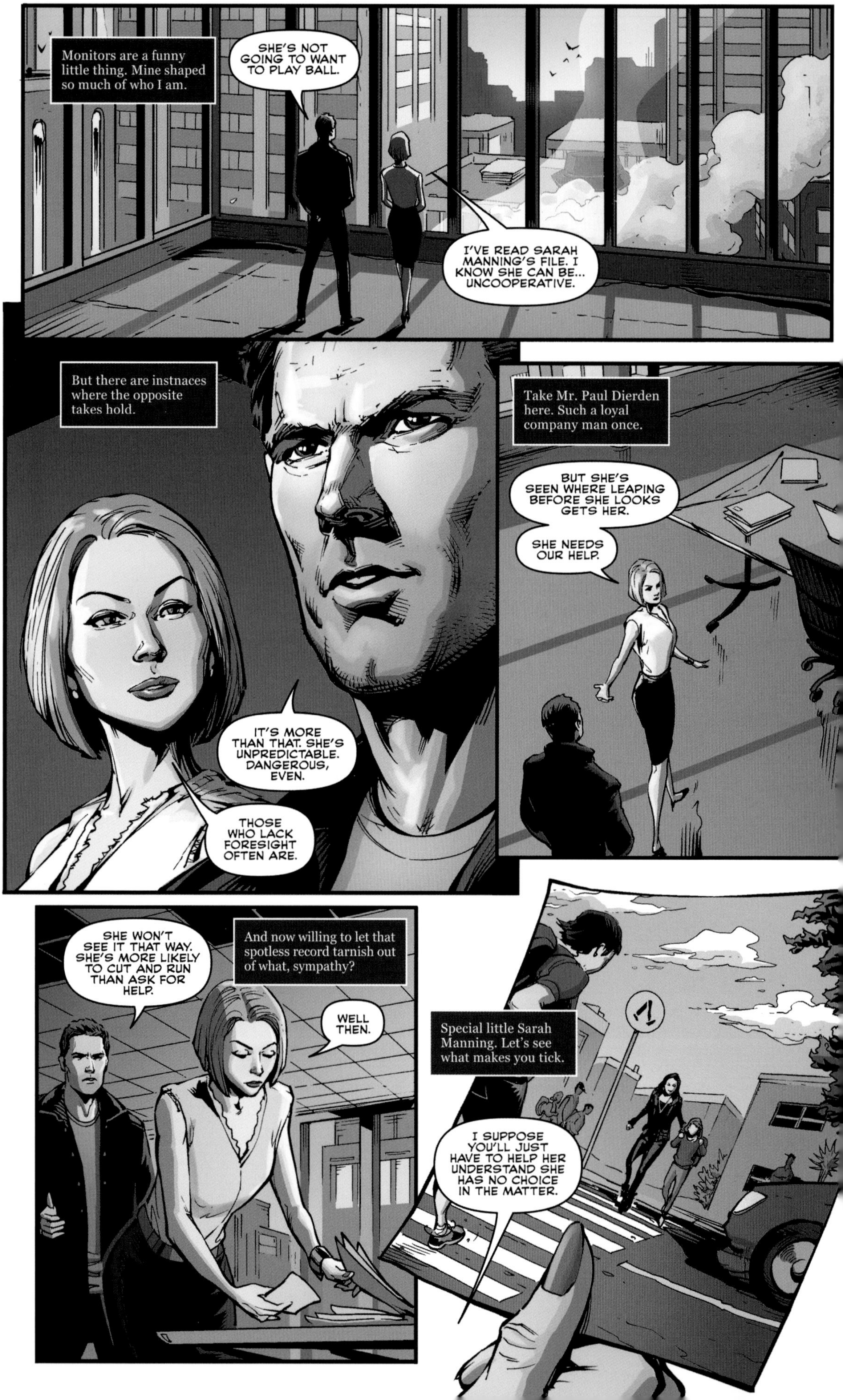
Monitors are a funny little thing. Mine shaped so much of who I am.
SHE'S NOT GOING TO WANT TO PLAY BALL.
I'VE READ SARAH MANNING'S FILE. I KNOW SHE CAN BE... UNCOOPERATIVE.
But there are instnaces where the opposite takes hold.
IT'S MORE THAN THAT. SHE'S UNPREDICTABLE. DANGEROUS, EVEN.
THOSE WHO LACK FORESIGHT OFTEN ARE.
Take Mr. Paul Dierden here. Such a loyal company man once.
BUT SHE'S SEEN WHERE LEAPING BEFORE SHE LOOKS GETS HER.
SHE NEEDS OUR HELP.
SHE WON'T SEE IT THAT WAY. SHE'S MORE LIKELY TO CUT AND RUN THAN ASK FOR HELP.
And now willing to let that spotless record tarnish out of what, sympathy?
WELL THEN.
Special little Sarah Manning. Let's see what makes you tick.
I SUPPOSE YOU'LL JUST HAVE TO HELP HER UNDERSTAND SHE HAS NO CHOICE IN THE MATTER.

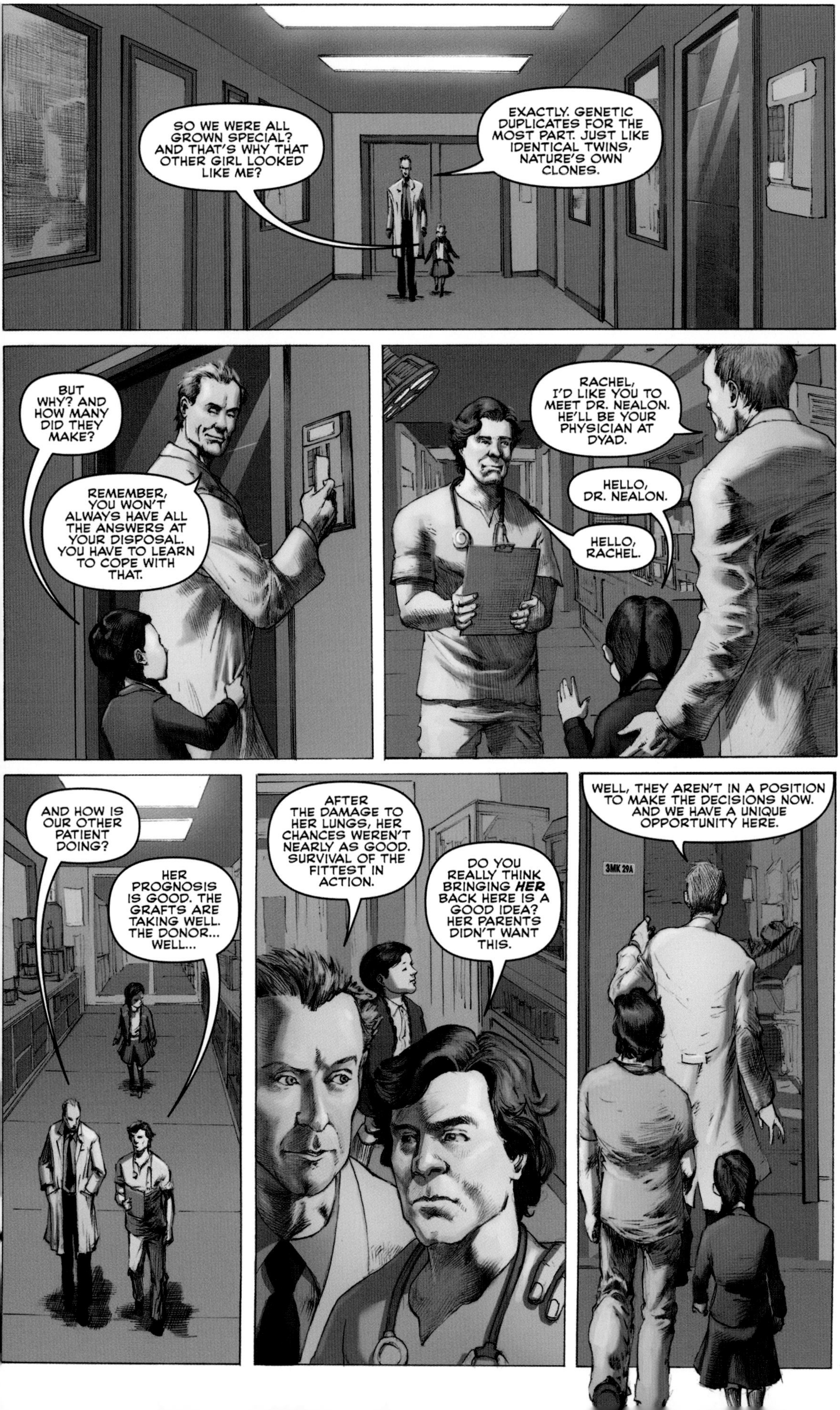
SO WE WERE ALL GROWN SPECIAL? AND THAT'S WHY THAT OTHER GIRL LOOKED LIKE ME?
EXACTLY. GENETIC DUPLICATES FOR THE MOST PART. JUST LIKE IDENTICAL TWINS, NATURE'S OWN CLONES.
BUT WHY? AND HOW MANY DID THEY MAKE?
REMEMBER, YOU WON'T ALWAYS HAVE ALL THE ANSWERS AT YOUR DISPOSAL. YOU HAVE TO LEARN TO COPE WITH THAT.
RACHEL, I'D LIKE YOU TO MEET DR. NEALON. HE'LL BE YOUR PHYSICIAN AT DYAD.
HELLO, DR. NEALON.
HELLO, RACHEL.
AND HOW IS OUR OTHER PATIENT DOING?
HER PROGNOSIS IS GOOD. THE GRAFTS ARE TAKING WELL. THE DONOR... WELL...
AFTER THE DAMAGE TO HER LUNGS, HER CHANCES WEREN'T NEARLY AS GOOD. SURVIVAL OF THE FITTEST IN ACTION.
DO YOU REALLY THINK BRINGING *HER* BACK HERE IS A GOOD IDEA? HER PARENTS DIDN'T WANT THIS.
WELL, THEY AREN'T IN A POSITION TO MAKE THE DECISIONS NOW. AND WE HAVE A UNIQUE OPPORTUNITY HERE.
3MK 29A

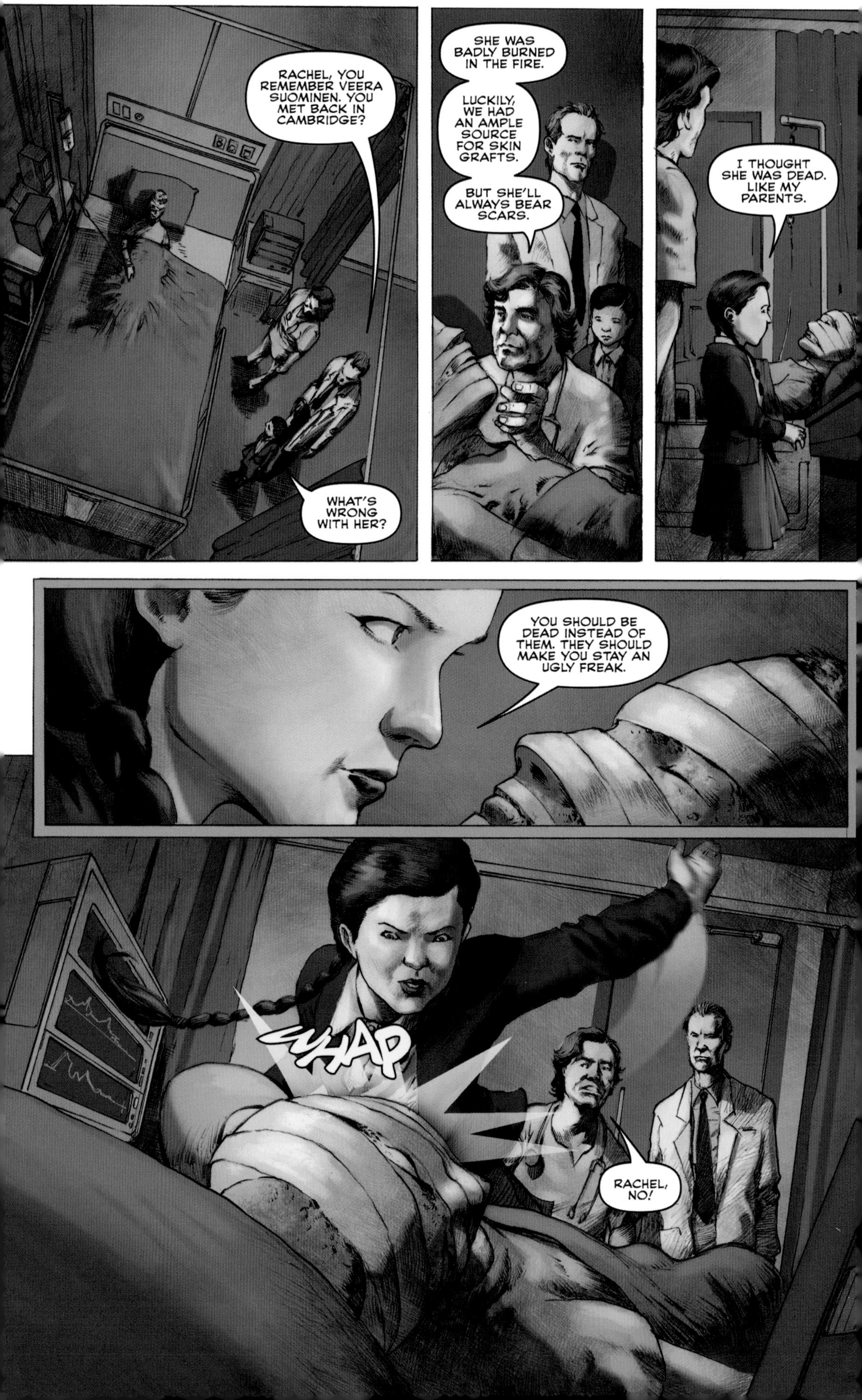
RACHEL, YOU REMEMBER VEERA SUOMINEN. YOU MET BACK IN CAMBRIDGE?
WHAT'S WRONG WITH HER?
SHE WAS BADLY BURNED IN THE FIRE.
LUCKILY, WE HAD AN AMPLE SOURCE FOR SKIN GRAFTS.
BUT SHE'LL ALWAYS BEAR SCARS.
I THOUGHT SHE WAS DEAD. LIKE MY PARENTS.
YOU SHOULD BE DEAD INSTEAD OF THEM. THEY SHOULD MAKE YOU STAY AN UGLY FREAK.
WHAP
RACHEL, NO!

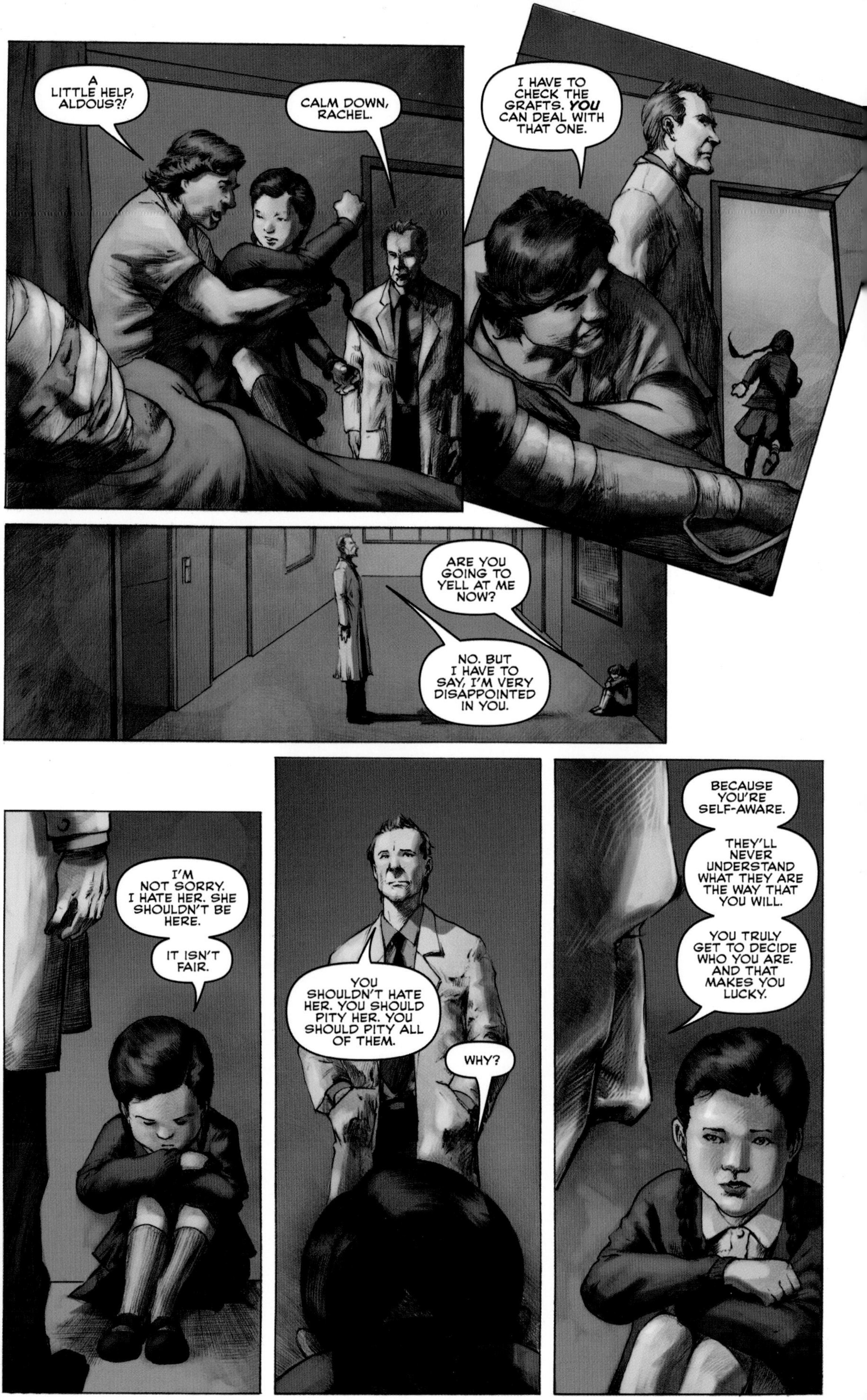
A LITTLE HELP, ALDOUS?!
CALM DOWN, RACHEL.
I HAVE TO CHECK THE GRAFTS. *YOU* CAN DEAL WITH THAT ONE.
ARE YOU GOING TO YELL AT ME NOW?
NO. BUT I HAVE TO SAY, I'M VERY DISAPPOINTED IN YOU.
I'M NOT SORRY. I HATE HER. SHE SHOULDN'T BE HERE.
IT ISN'T FAIR.
YOU SHOULDN'T HATE HER. YOU SHOULD PITY HER. YOU SHOULD PITY ALL OF THEM.
WHY?
BECAUSE YOU'RE SELF-AWARE.
THEY'LL NEVER UNDERSTAND WHAT THEY ARE THE WAY THAT YOU WILL.
YOU TRULY GET TO DECIDE WHO YOU ARE. AND THAT MAKES YOU LUCKY.

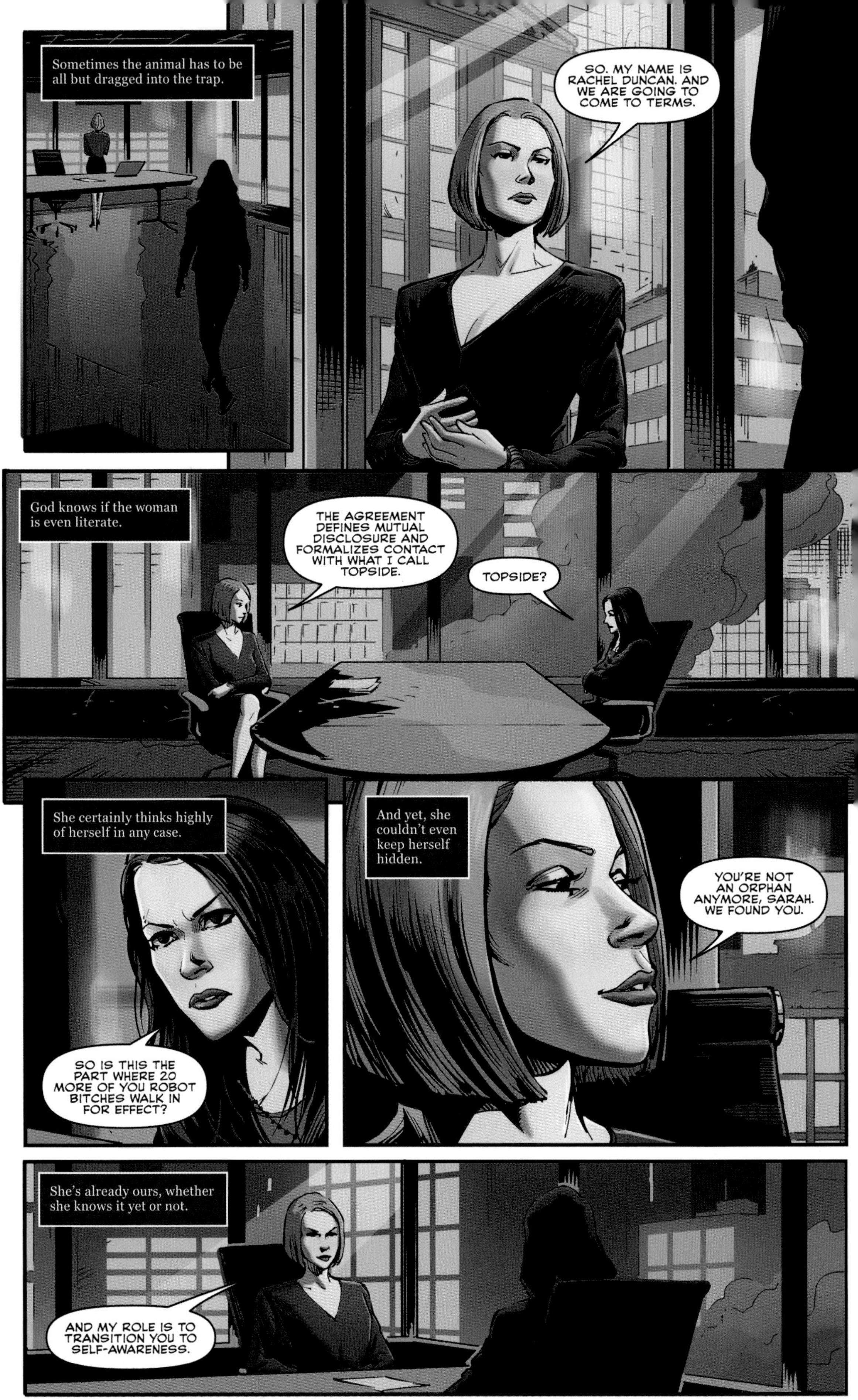
Sometimes the animal has to be all but dragged into the trap.
SO. MY NAME IS RACHEL DUNCAN. AND WE ARE GOING TO COME TO TERMS.
God knows if the woman is even literate.
THE AGREEMENT DEFINES MUTUAL DISCLOSURE AND FORMALIZES CONTACT WITH WHAT I CALL TOPSIDE.
TOPSIDE?
She certainly thinks highly of herself in any case.
SO IS THIS THE PART WHERE 20 MORE OF YOU ROBOT BITCHES WALK IN FOR EFFECT?
And yet, she couldn't even keep herself hidden.
YOU'RE NOT AN ORPHAN ANYMORE, SARAH. WE FOUND YOU.
She's already ours, whether she knows it yet or not.
AND MY ROLE IS TO TRANSITION YOU TO SELF-AWARENESS.

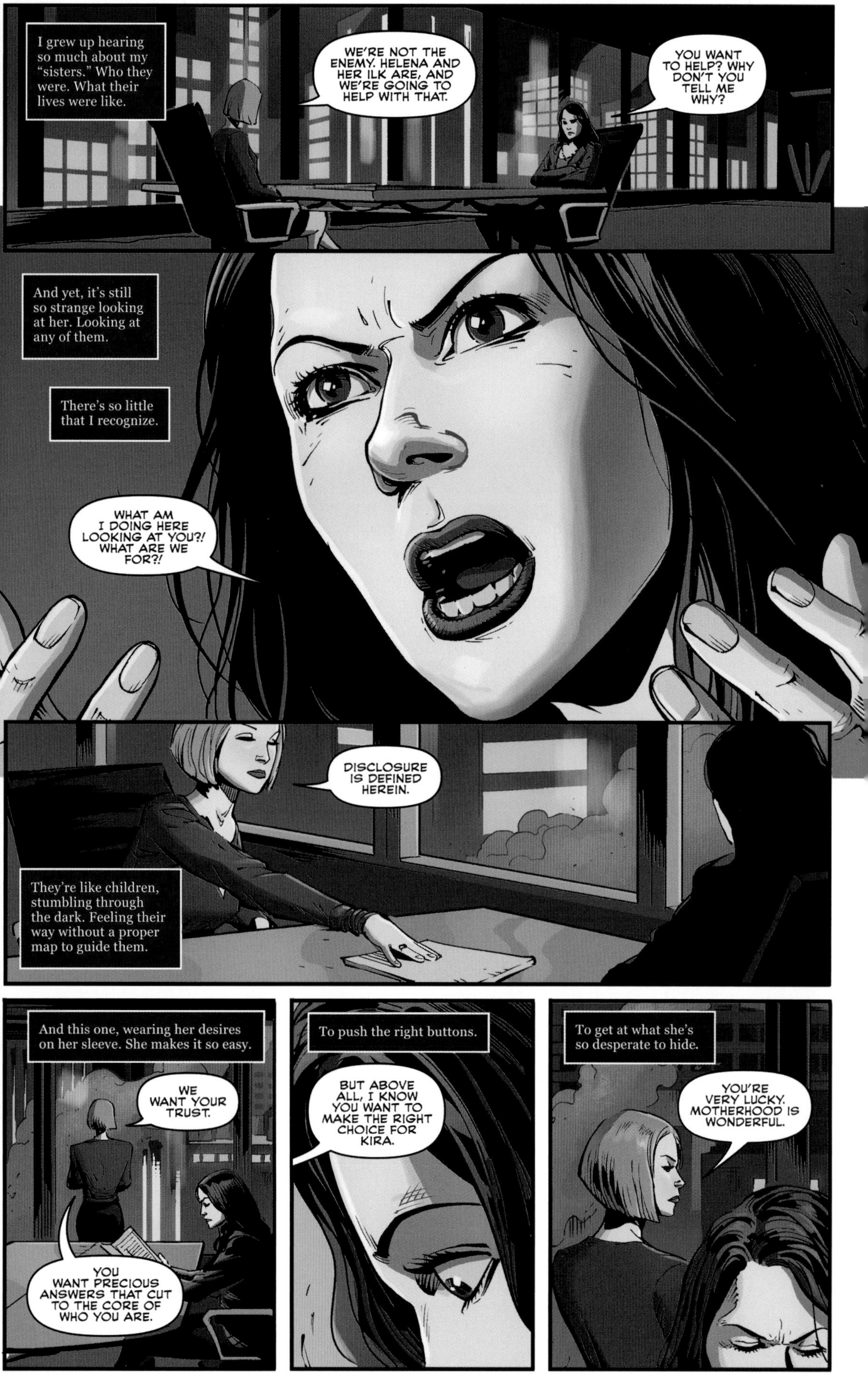

I grew up hearing so much about my "sisters." Who they were. What their lives were like.
WE'RE NOT THE ENEMY. HELENA AND HER ILK ARE, AND WE'RE GOING TO HELP WITH THAT.
YOU WANT TO HELP? WHY DON'T YOU TELL ME WHY?
And yet, it's still so strange looking at her. Looking at any of them.
There's so little that I recognize.
WHAT AM I DOING HERE LOOKING AT YOU?! WHAT ARE WE FOR?!
DISCLOSURE IS DEFINED HEREIN.
They're like children, stumbling through the dark. Feeling their way without a proper map to guide them.
And this one, wearing her desires on her sleeve. She makes it so easy.
WE WANT YOUR TRUST.
YOU WANT PRECIOUS ANSWERS THAT CUT TO THE CORE OF WHO YOU ARE.
To push the right buttons.
BUT ABOVE ALL, I KNOW YOU WANT TO MAKE THE RIGHT CHOICE FOR KIRA.
To get at what she's so desperate to hide.
YOU'RE VERY LUCKY. MOTHERHOOD IS WONDERFUL.

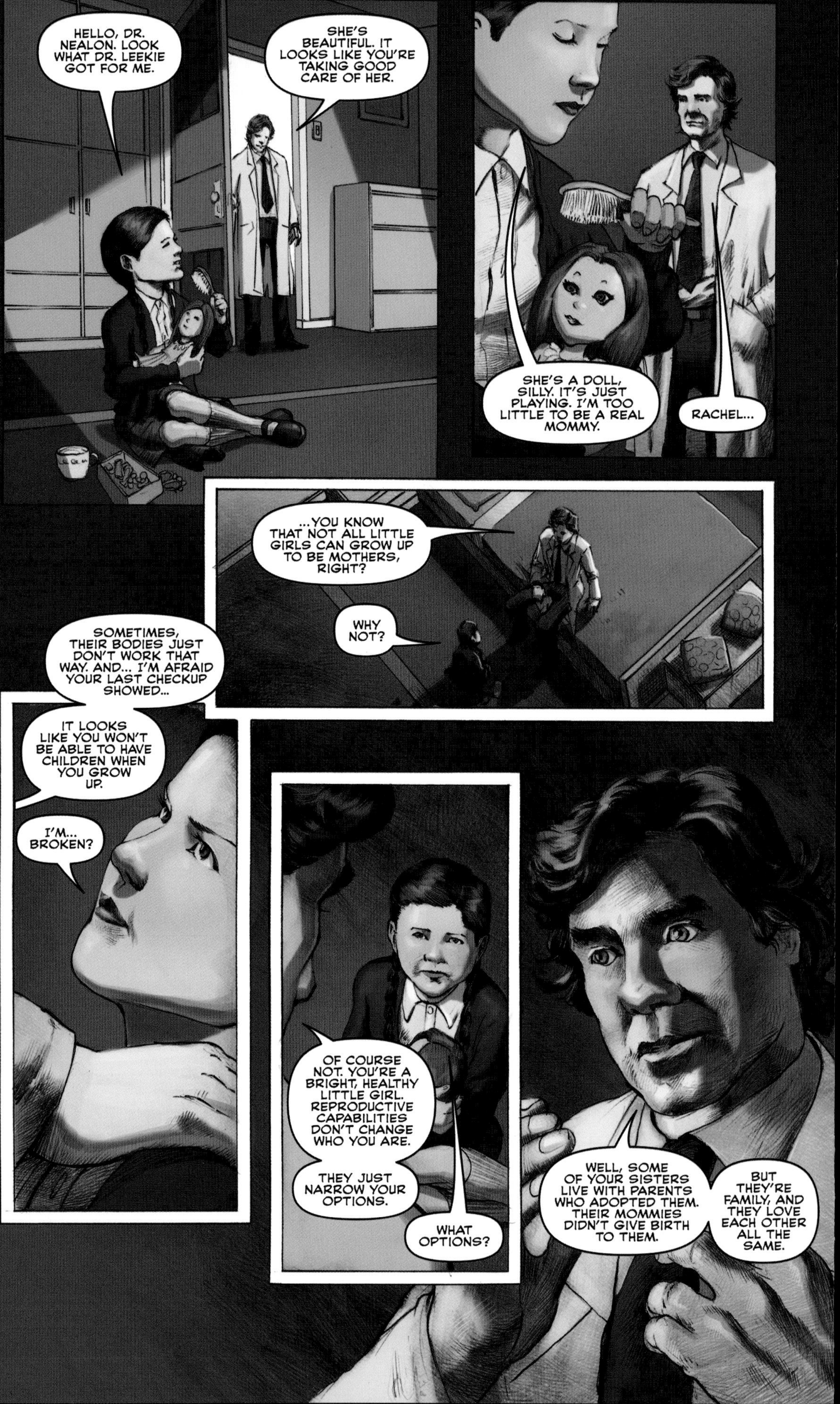
HELLO, DR. NEALON. LOOK WHAT DR. LEEKIE GOT FOR ME.
SHE'S BEAUTIFUL. IT LOOKS LIKE YOU'RE TAKING GOOD CARE OF HER.
SHE'S A DOLL, SILLY. IT'S JUST PLAYING. I'M TOO LITTLE TO BE A REAL MOMMY.
RACHEL...
...YOU KNOW THAT NOT ALL LITTLE GIRLS CAN GROW UP TO BE MOTHERS, RIGHT?
WHY NOT?
SOMETIMES, THEIR BODIES JUST DON'T WORK THAT WAY. AND... I'M AFRAID YOUR LAST CHECKUP SHOWED...
IT LOOKS LIKE YOU WON'T BE ABLE TO HAVE CHILDREN WHEN YOU GROW UP.
I'M... BROKEN?
OF COURSE NOT. YOU'RE A BRIGHT, HEALTHY LITTLE GIRL. REPRODUCTIVE CAPABILITIES DON'T CHANGE WHO YOU ARE.
THEY JUST NARROW YOUR OPTIONS.
WHAT OPTIONS?
WELL, SOME OF YOUR SISTERS LIVE WITH PARENTS WHO ADOPTED THEM. THEIR MOMMIES DIDN'T GIVE BIRTH TO THEM.
BUT THEY'RE FAMILY, AND THEY LOVE EACH OTHER ALL THE SAME.

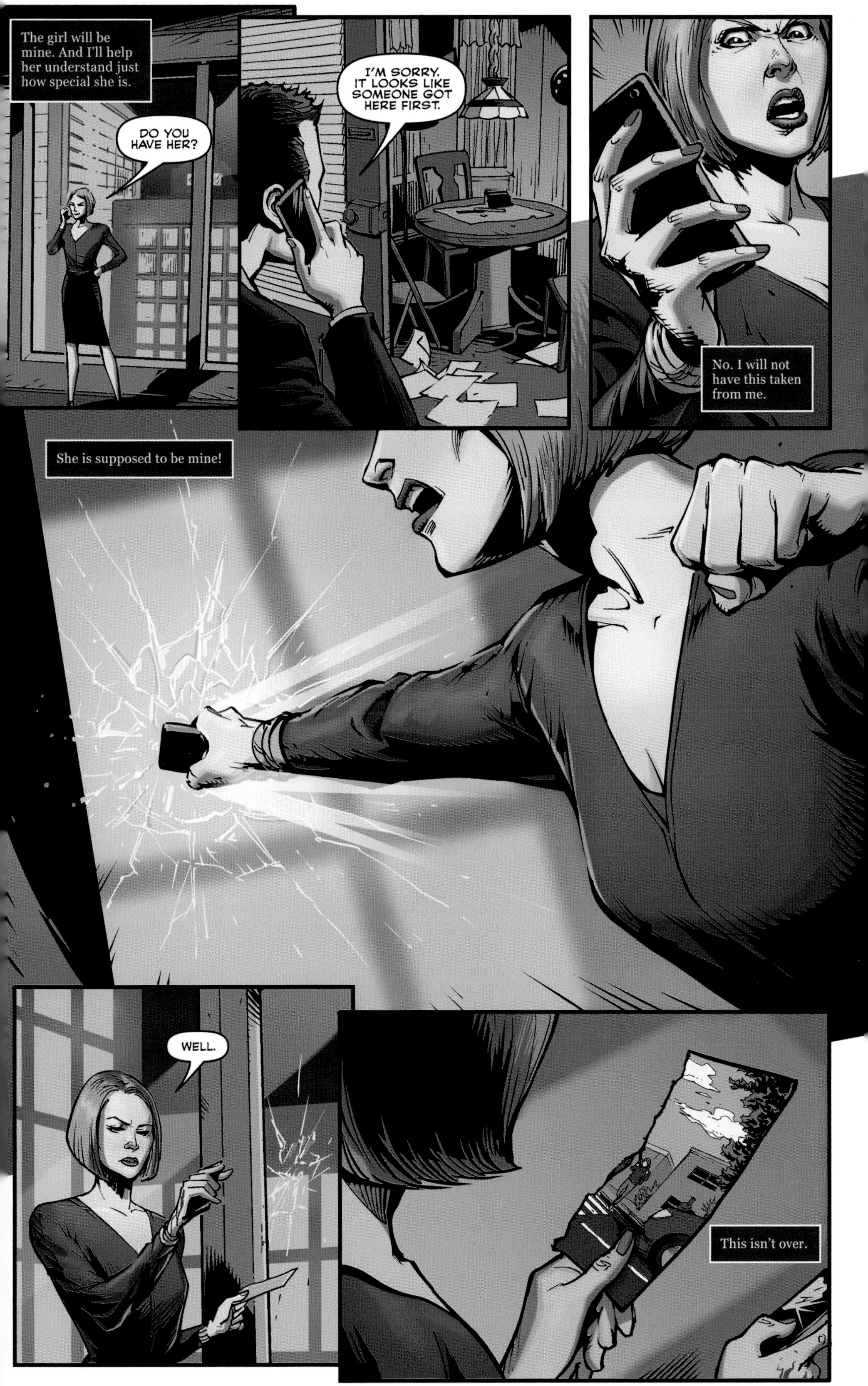

The girl will be mine. And I'll help her understand just how special she is.
DO YOU HAVE HER?
I'M SORRY. IT LOOKS LIKE SOMEONE GOT HERE FIRST.
No. I will not have this taken from me.
She is supposed to be mine!
WELL.
This isn't over.

Aldous always told me that I was the fortunate one. That I had knowledge and power my "sisters" never would.

That they were mere rats in a cage. But lately, I've begun to wonder if that's truly the case.

They have love; they have family. The very things that were denied to me.

What right do they have to that sort of happiness? They're little more than corporate property.

I'll take what is rightfully mine. And blind as they are, they'll never see me coming.

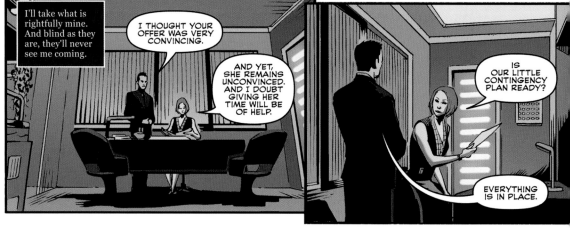

I THOUGHT YOUR OFFER WAS VERY CONVINCING.

AND YET, SHE REMAINS UNCONVINCED. AND I DOUBT GIVING HER TIME WILL BE OF HELP.

IS OUR LITTLE CONTINGENCY PLAN READY?

EVERYTHING IS IN PLACE.

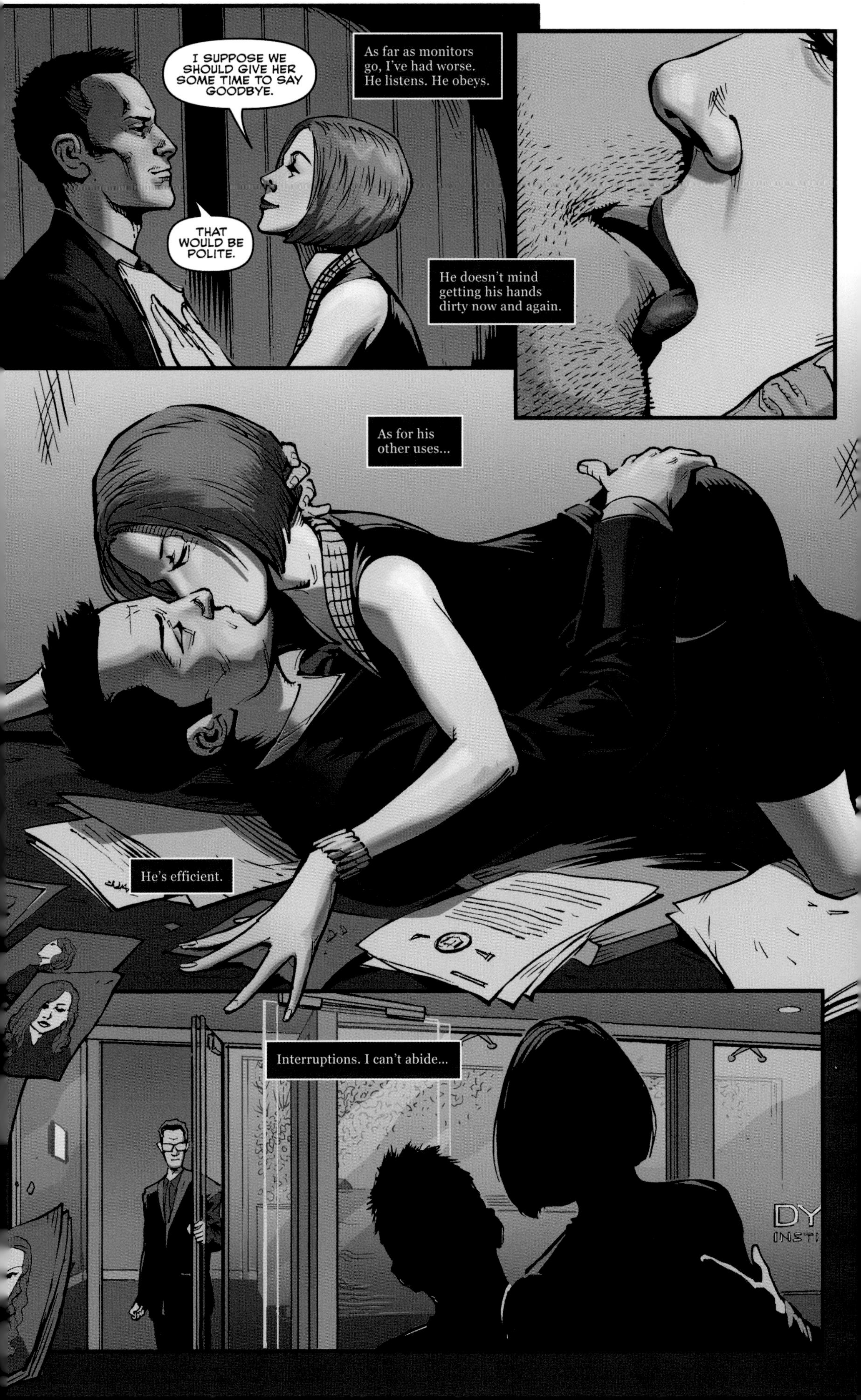
I SUPPOSE WE SHOULD GIVE HER SOME TIME TO SAY GOODBYE.
THAT WOULD BE POLITE.
As far as monitors go, I've had worse. He listens. He obeys.
He doesn't mind getting his hands dirty now and again.
As for his other uses...
He's efficient.
Interruptions. I can't abide...
DY
INSTI

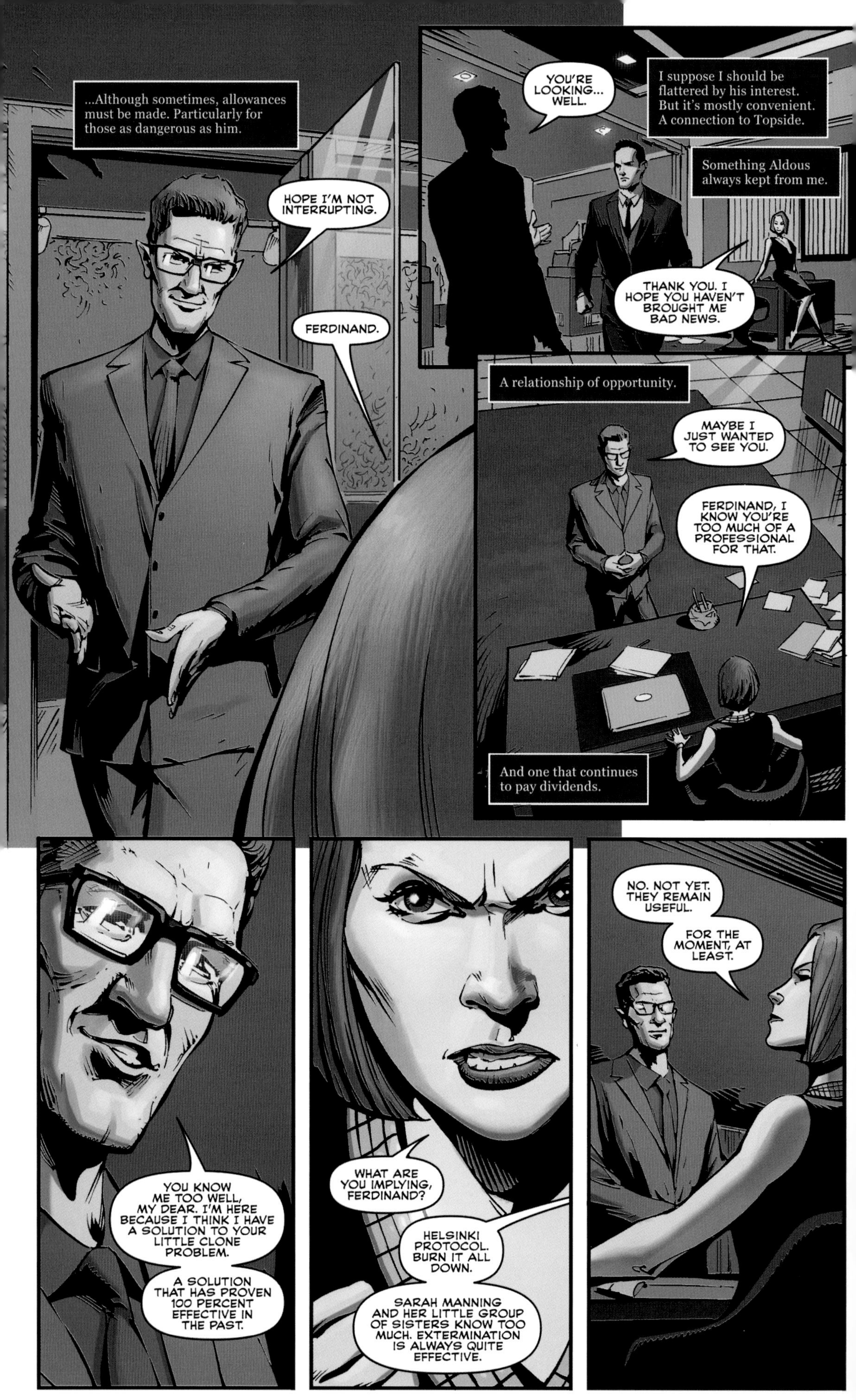
...Although sometimes, allowances must be made. Particularly for those as dangerous as him.
HOPE I'M NOT INTERRUPTING.
FERDINAND.
YOU'RE LOOKING... WELL.
I suppose I should be flattered by his interest. But it's mostly convenient. A connection to Topside.
Something Aldous always kept from me.
THANK YOU. I HOPE YOU HAVEN'T BROUGHT ME BAD NEWS.
A relationship of opportunity.
MAYBE I JUST WANTED TO SEE YOU.
FERDINAND, I KNOW YOU'RE TOO MUCH OF A PROFESSIONAL FOR THAT.
And one that continues to pay dividends.
YOU KNOW ME TOO WELL, MY DEAR. I'M HERE BECAUSE I THINK I HAVE A SOLUTION TO YOUR LITTLE CLONE PROBLEM.
A SOLUTION THAT HAS PROVEN 100 PERCENT EFFECTIVE IN THE PAST.
WHAT ARE YOU IMPLYING, FERDINAND?
HELSINKI PROTOCOL. BURN IT ALL DOWN.
SARAH MANNING AND HER LITTLE GROUP OF SISTERS KNOW TOO MUCH. EXTERMINATION IS ALWAYS QUITE EFFECTIVE.
NO. NOT YET. THEY REMAIN USEFUL.
FOR THE MOMENT, AT LEAST.

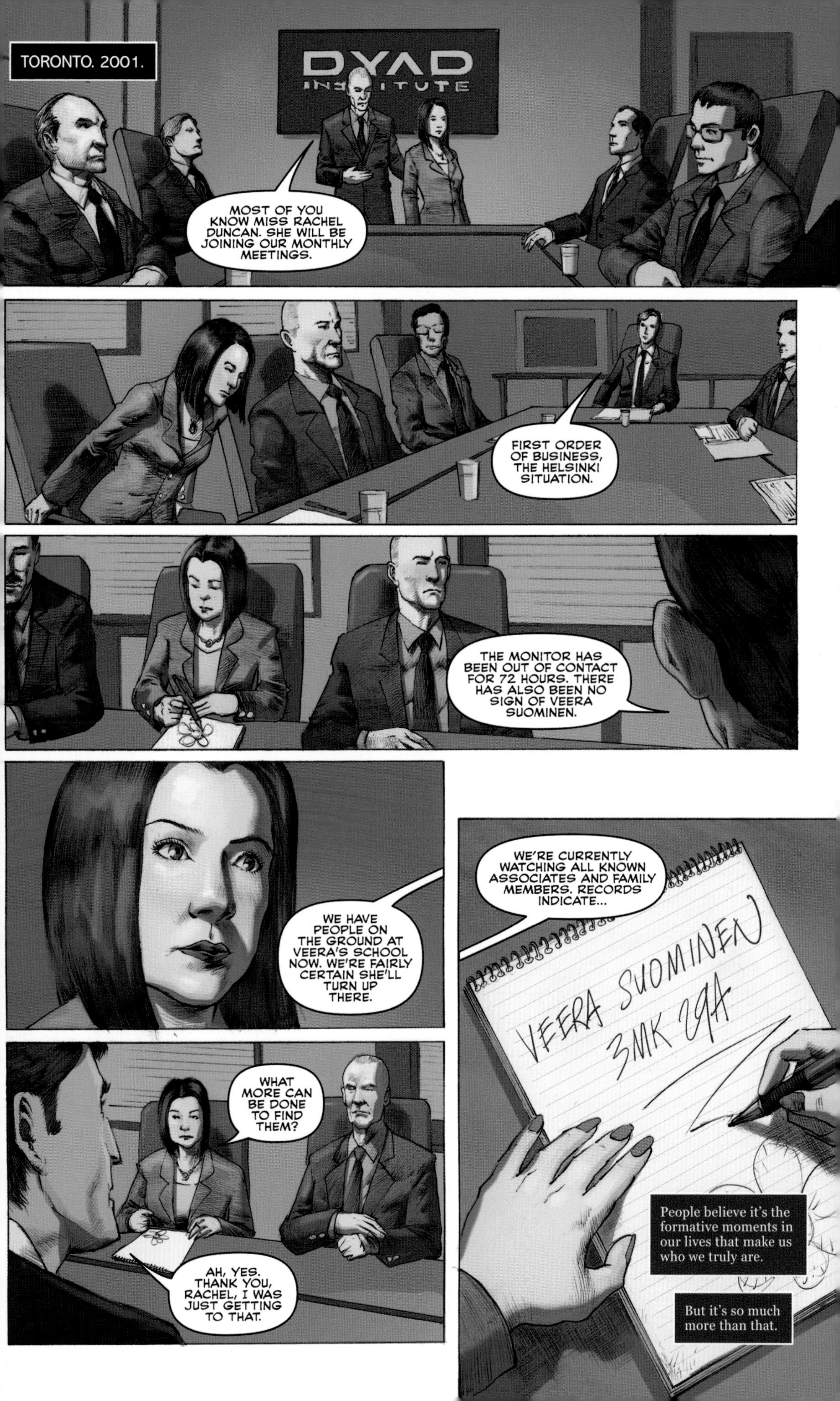
TORONTO. 2001.
DYAD INSTITUTE
MOST OF YOU KNOW MISS RACHEL DUNCAN. SHE WILL BE JOINING OUR MONTHLY MEETINGS.
FIRST ORDER OF BUSINESS, THE HELSINKI SITUATION.
THE MONITOR HAS BEEN OUT OF CONTACT FOR 72 HOURS. THERE HAS ALSO BEEN NO SIGN OF VEERA SUOMINEN.
WE HAVE PEOPLE ON THE GROUND AT VEERA'S SCHOOL NOW. WE'RE FAIRLY CERTAIN SHE'LL TURN UP THERE.
WE'RE CURRENTLY WATCHING ALL KNOWN ASSOCIATES AND FAMILY MEMBERS. RECORDS INDICATE...
VEERA SUOMINEN
3MK 29A
WHAT MORE CAN BE DONE TO FIND THEM?
AH, YES. THANK YOU, RACHEL, I WAS JUST GETTING TO THAT.
People believe it's the formative moments in our lives that make us who we truly are.
But it's so much more than that.

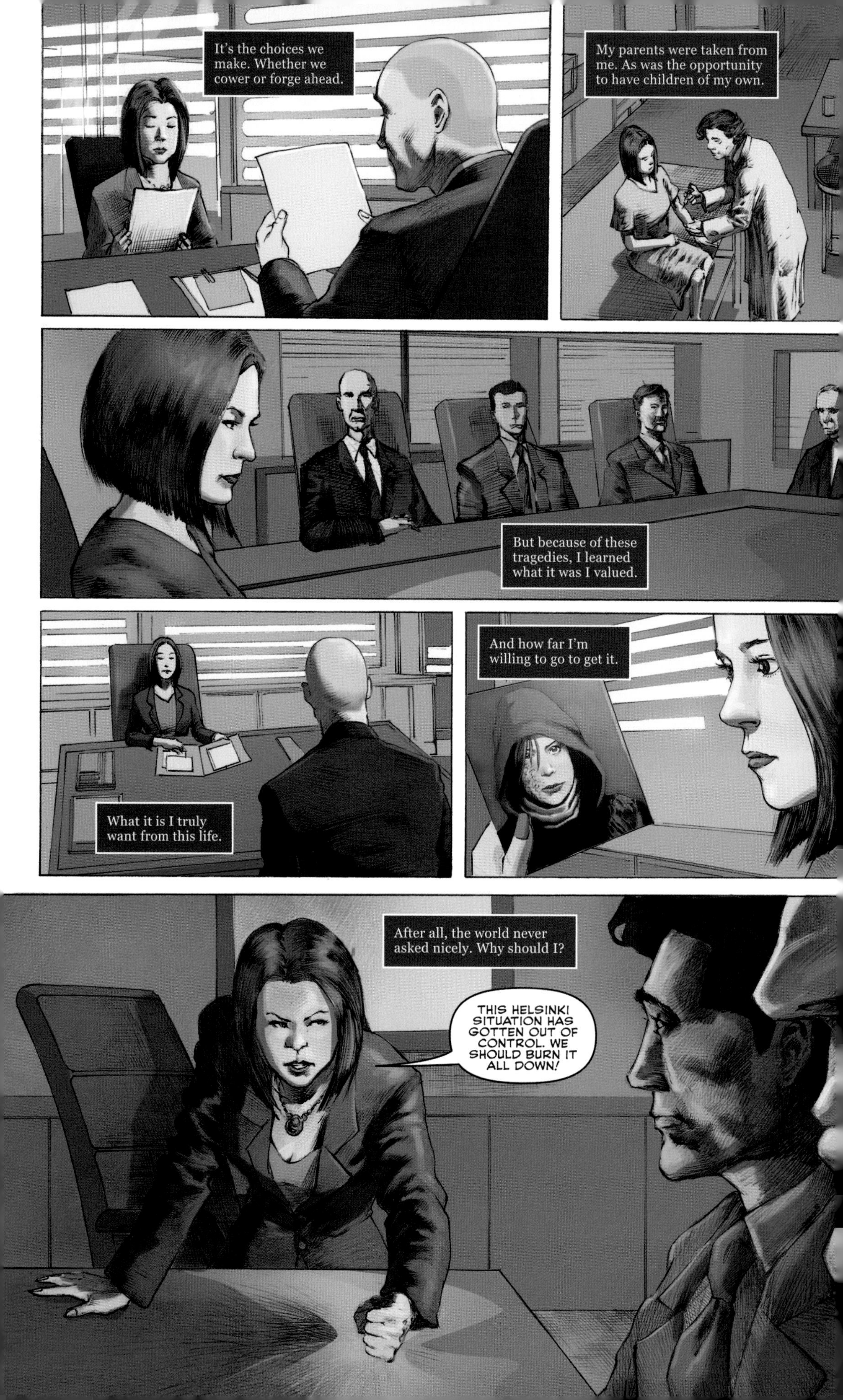
It's the choices we make. Whether we cower or forge ahead.
My parents were taken from me. As was the opportunity to have children of my own.
But because of these tragedies, I learned what it was I valued.
What it is I truly want from this life.
And how far I'm willing to go to get it.
After all, the world never asked nicely. Why should I?
THIS HELSINKI SITUATION HAS GOTTEN OUT OF CONTROL. WE SHOULD BURN IT ALL DOWN!

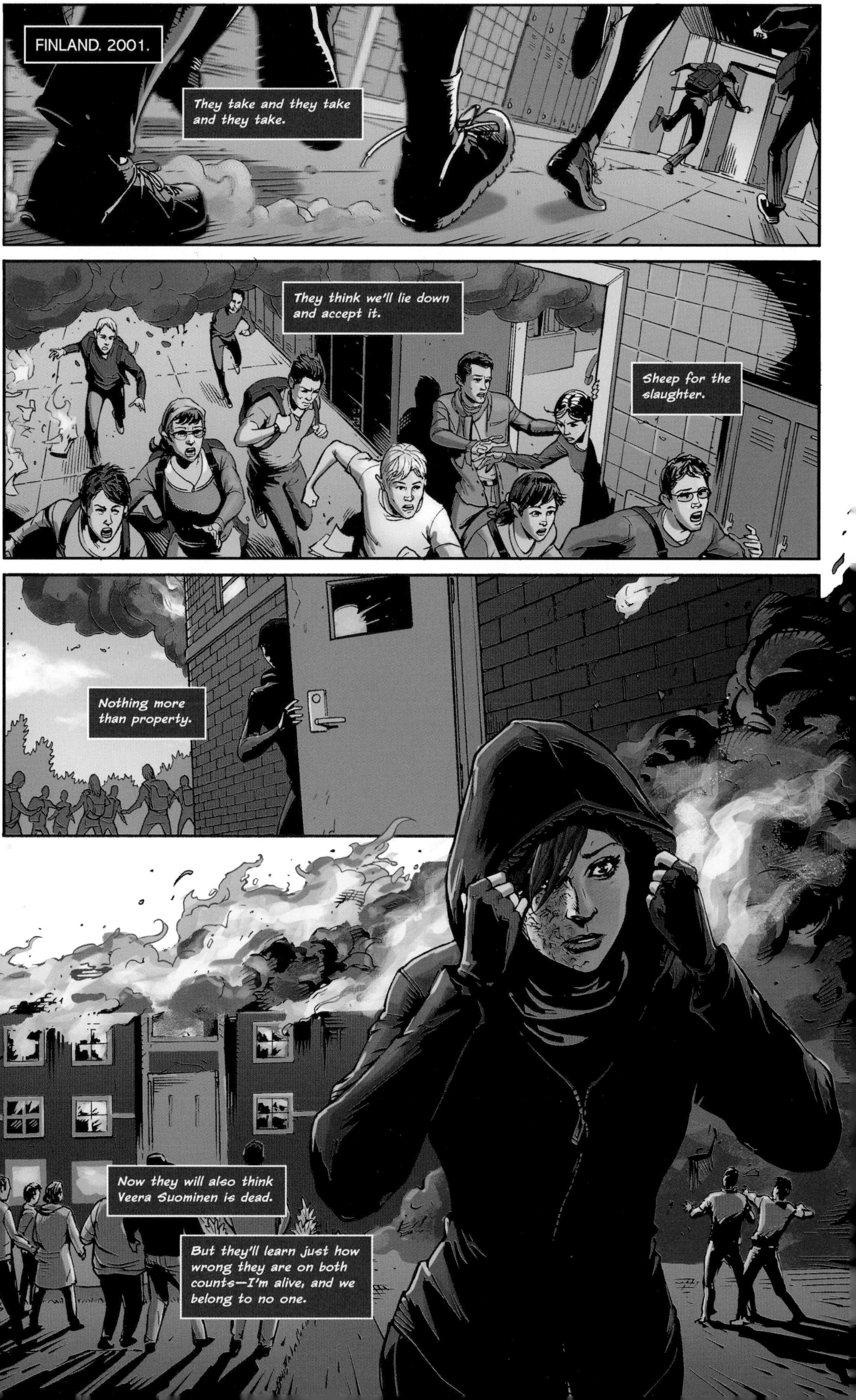
FINLAND. 2001.
They take and they take and they take.
They think we'll lie down and accept it.
Sheep for the slaughter.
Nothing more than property.
Now they will also think Veera Suominen is dead.
But they'll learn just how wrong they are on both counts—I'm alive, and we belong to no one.

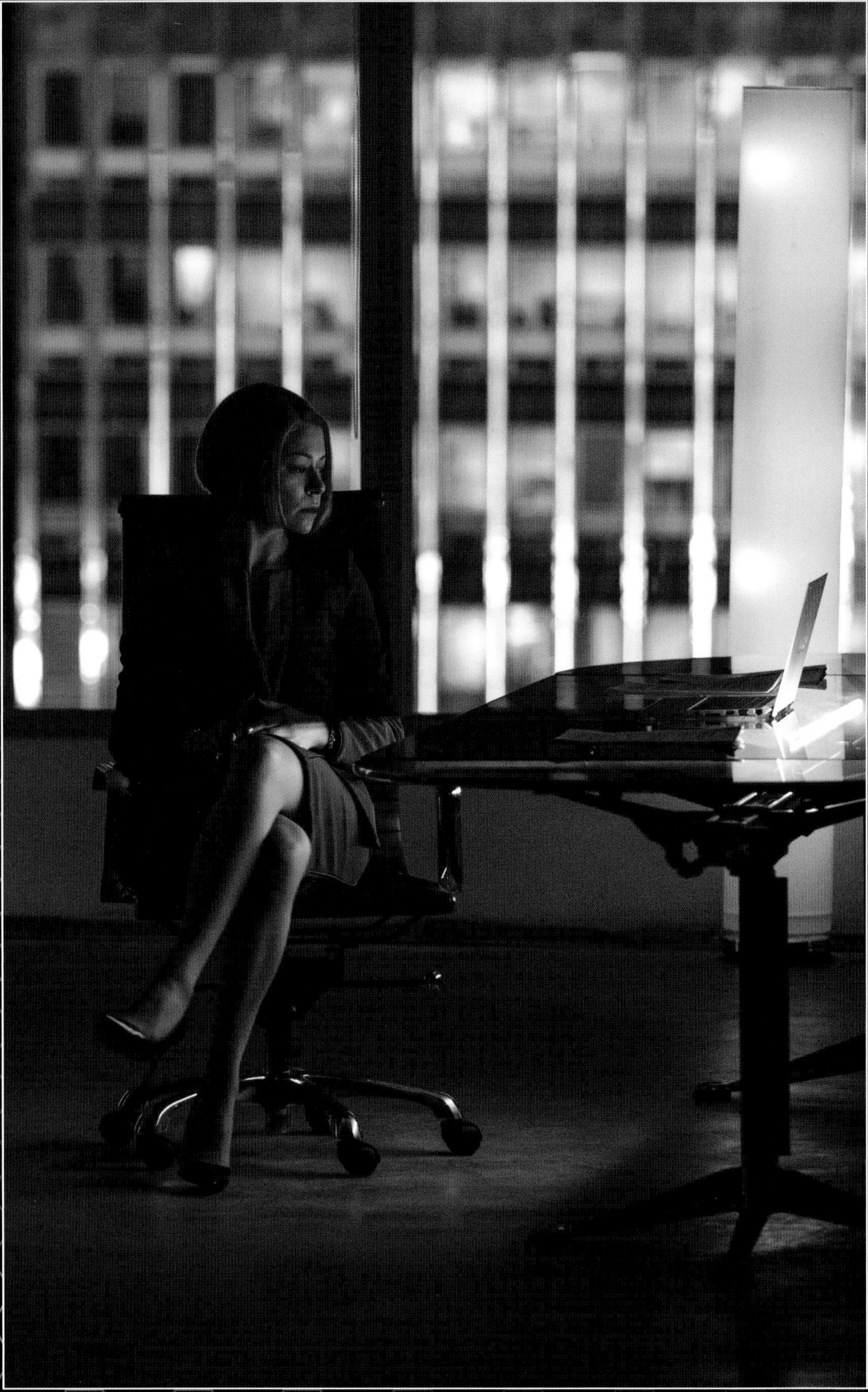

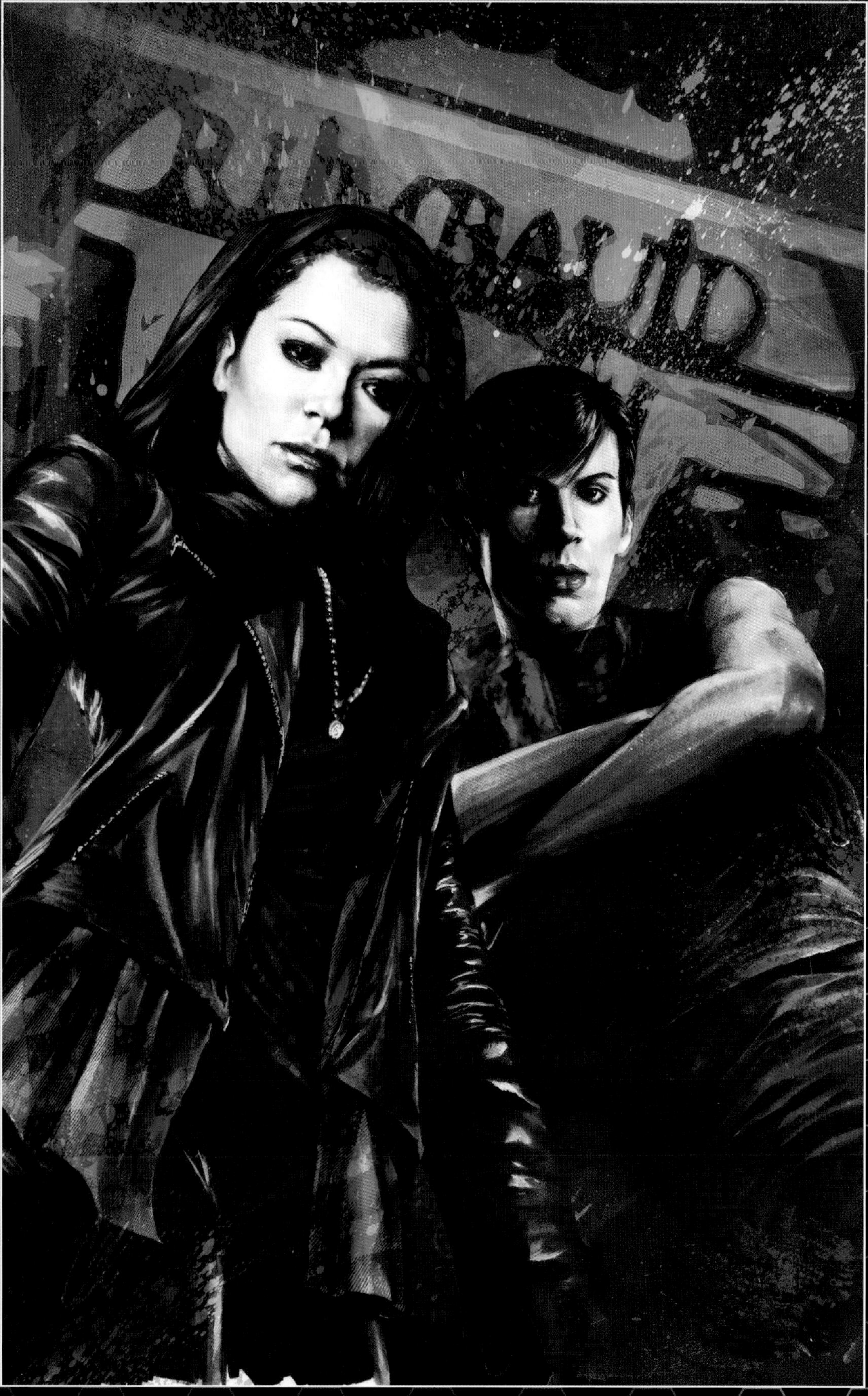

BY **CAT STAGGS**

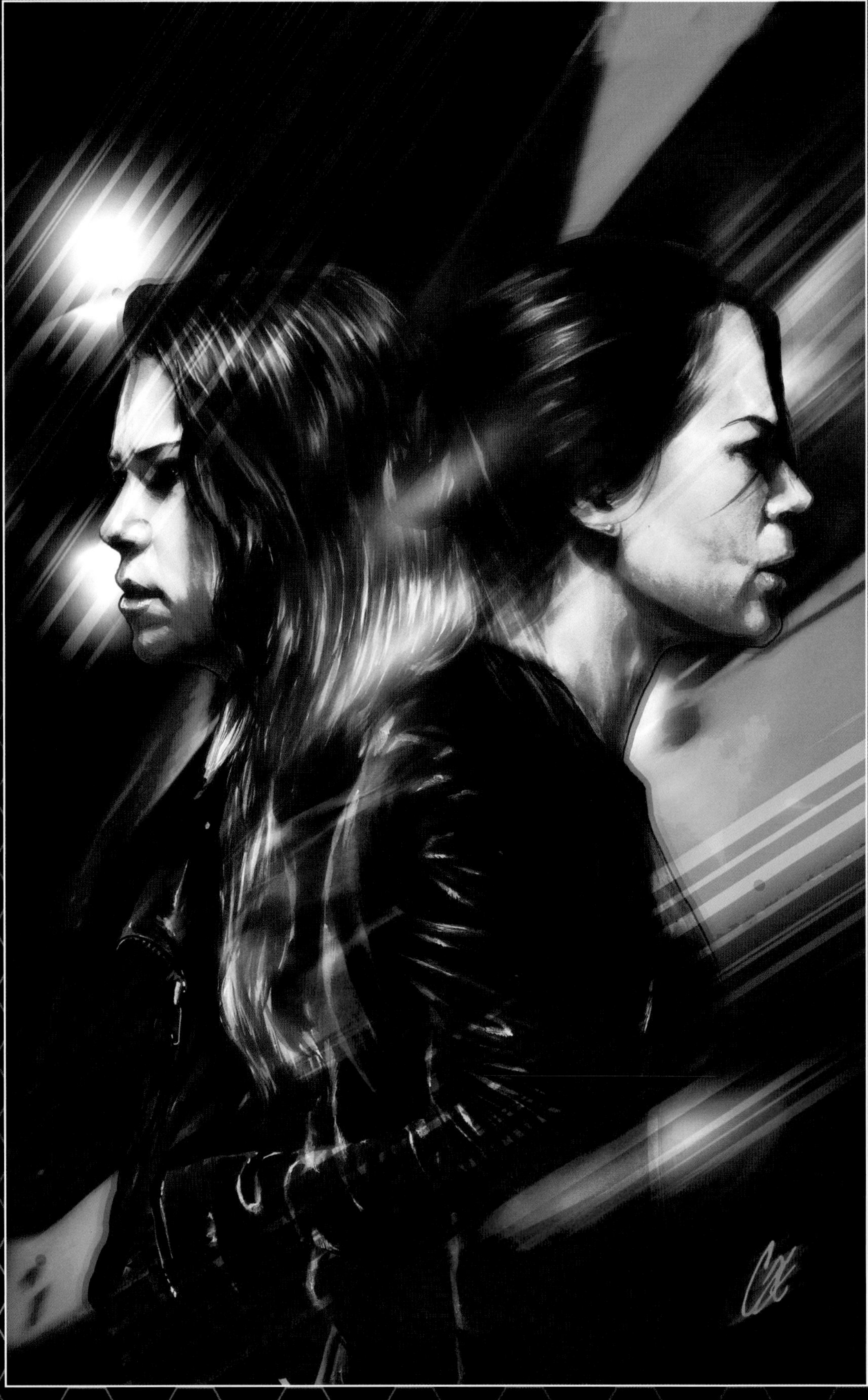

BY **CAT STAGGS**

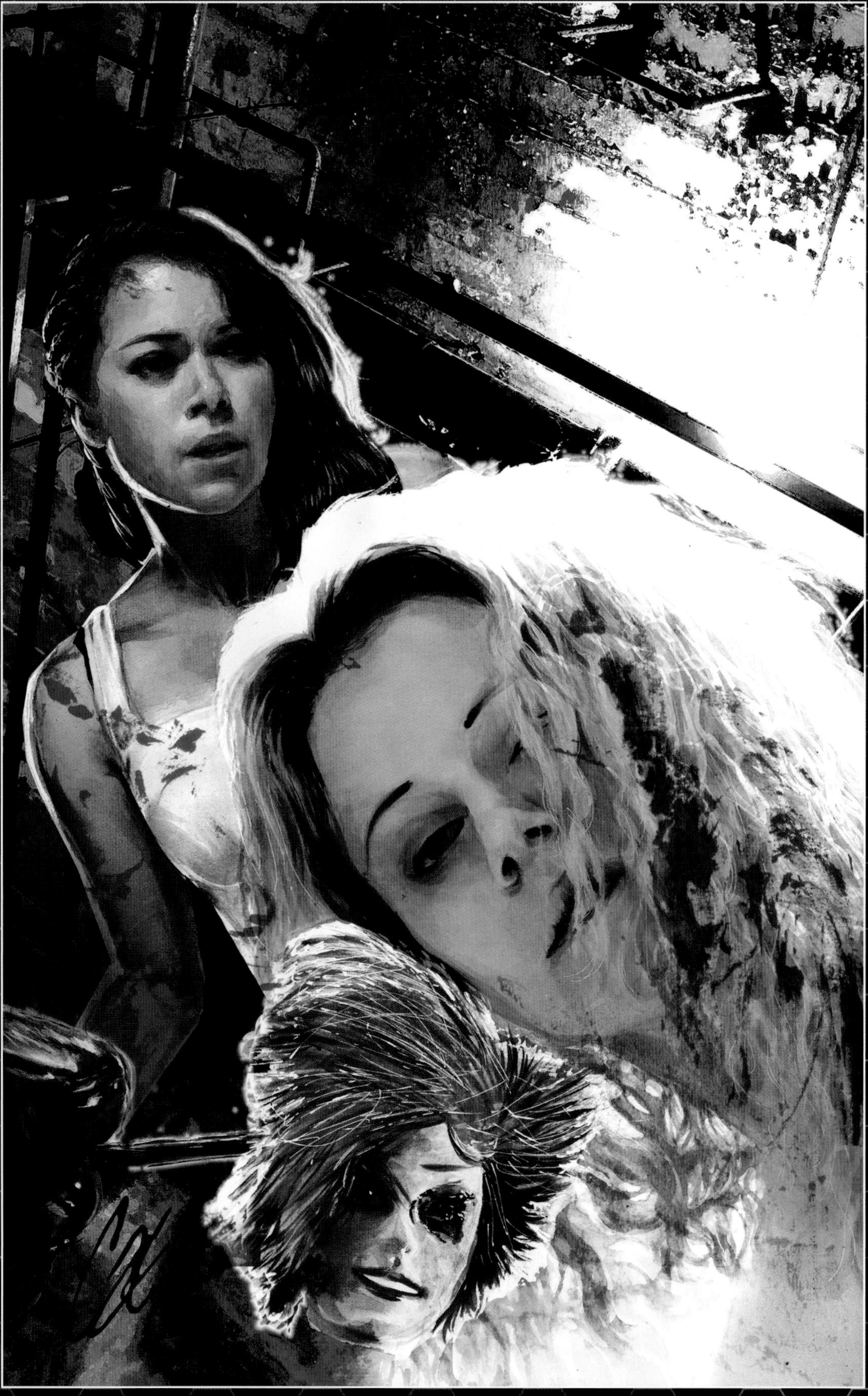

BY **CAT STAGGS**

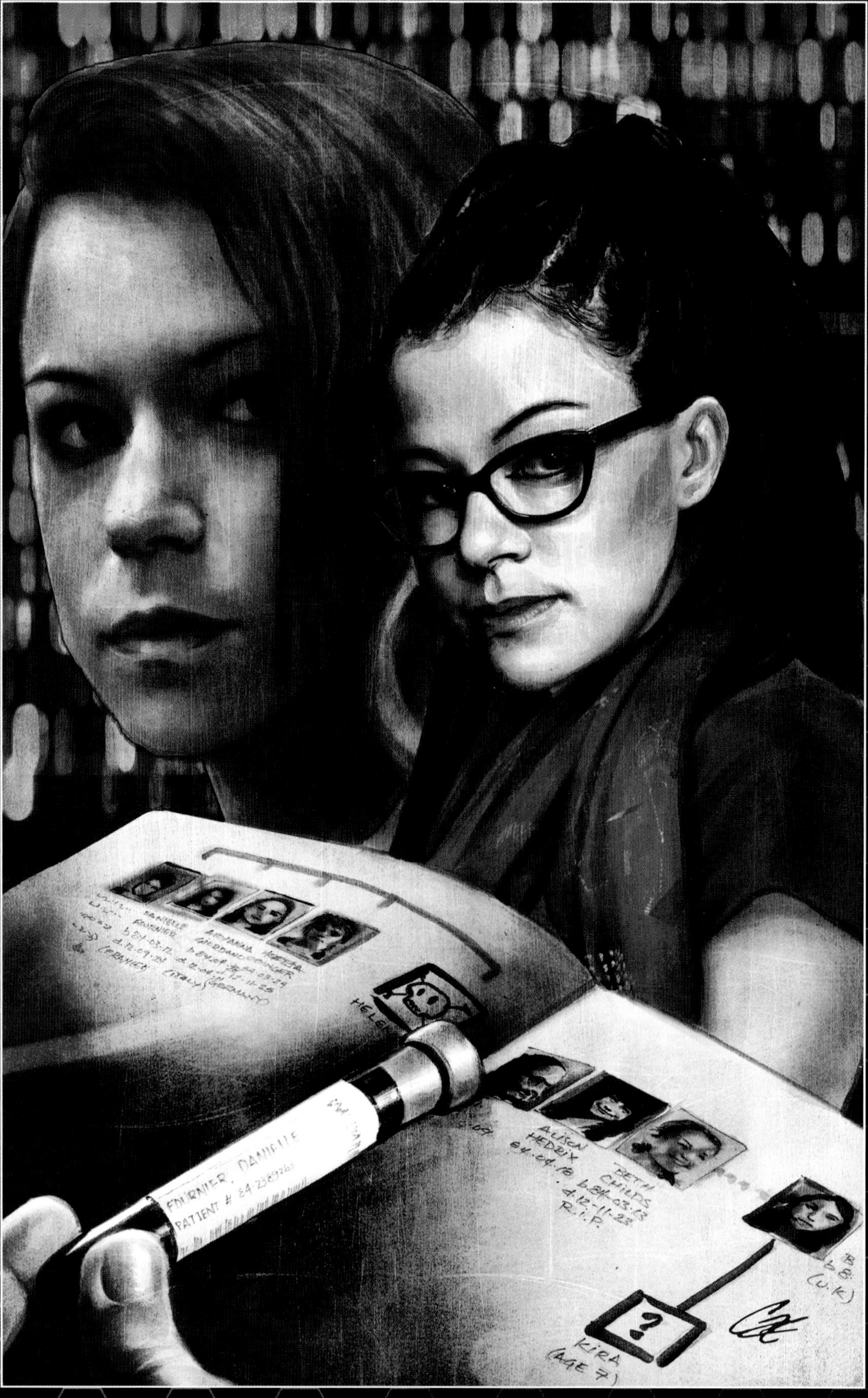
FOURNIER, DANIELLE
BETH
CHILDS
R.I.P.
KIRA
(AGE 7)

BY **CAT STAGGS**

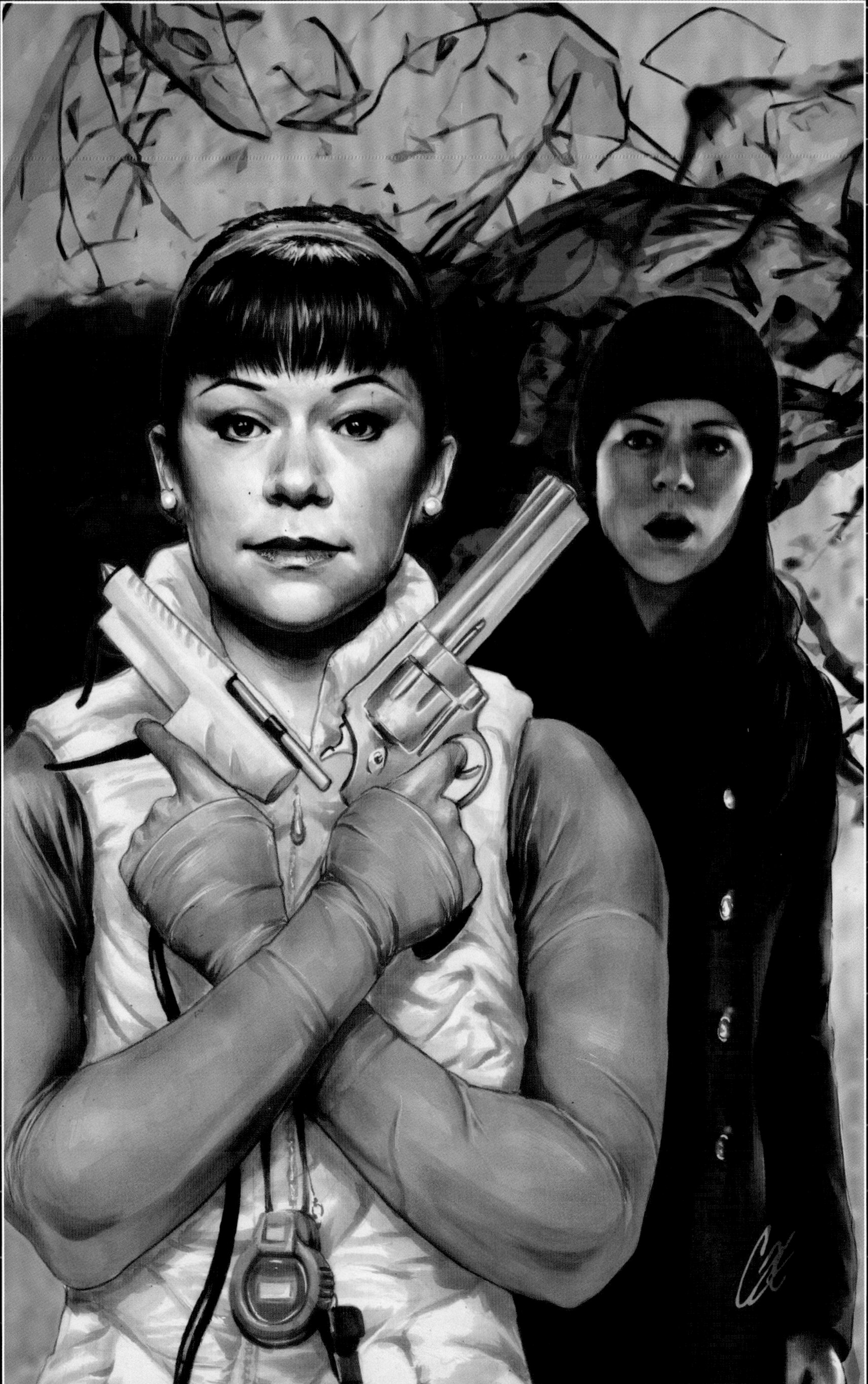

BY **CAT STAGGS**

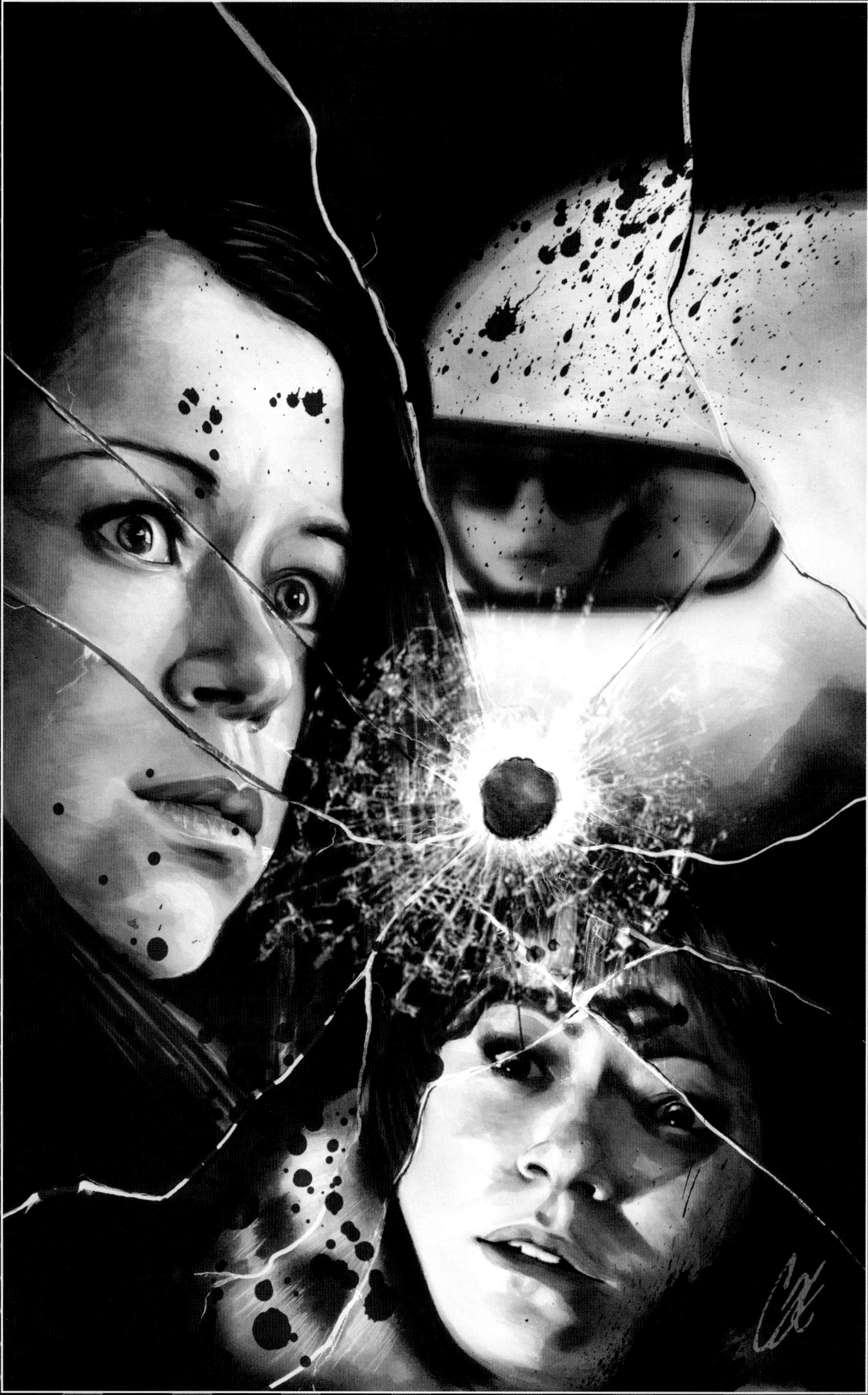

BY **CAT STAGGS**

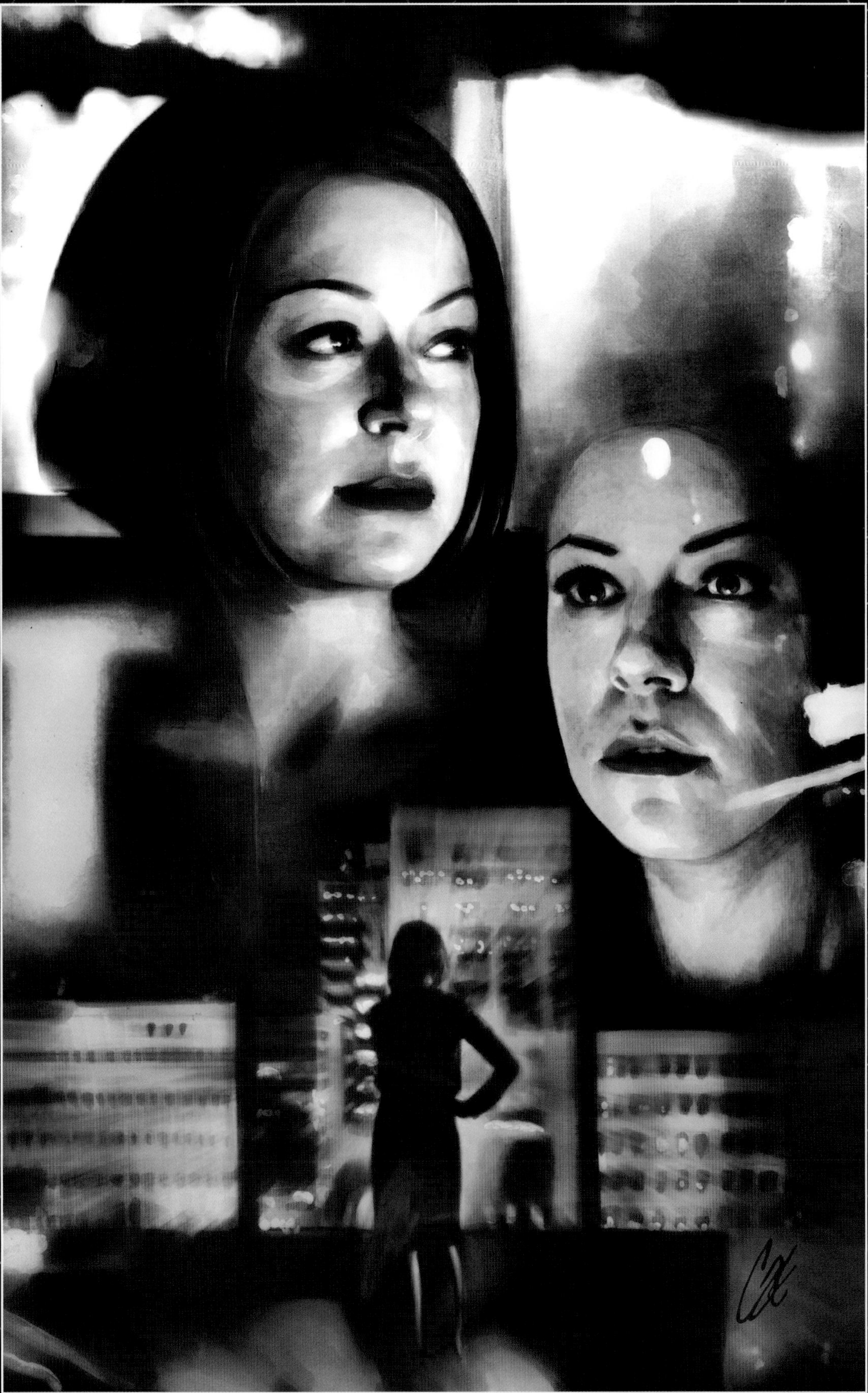

BY **CAT STAGGS**

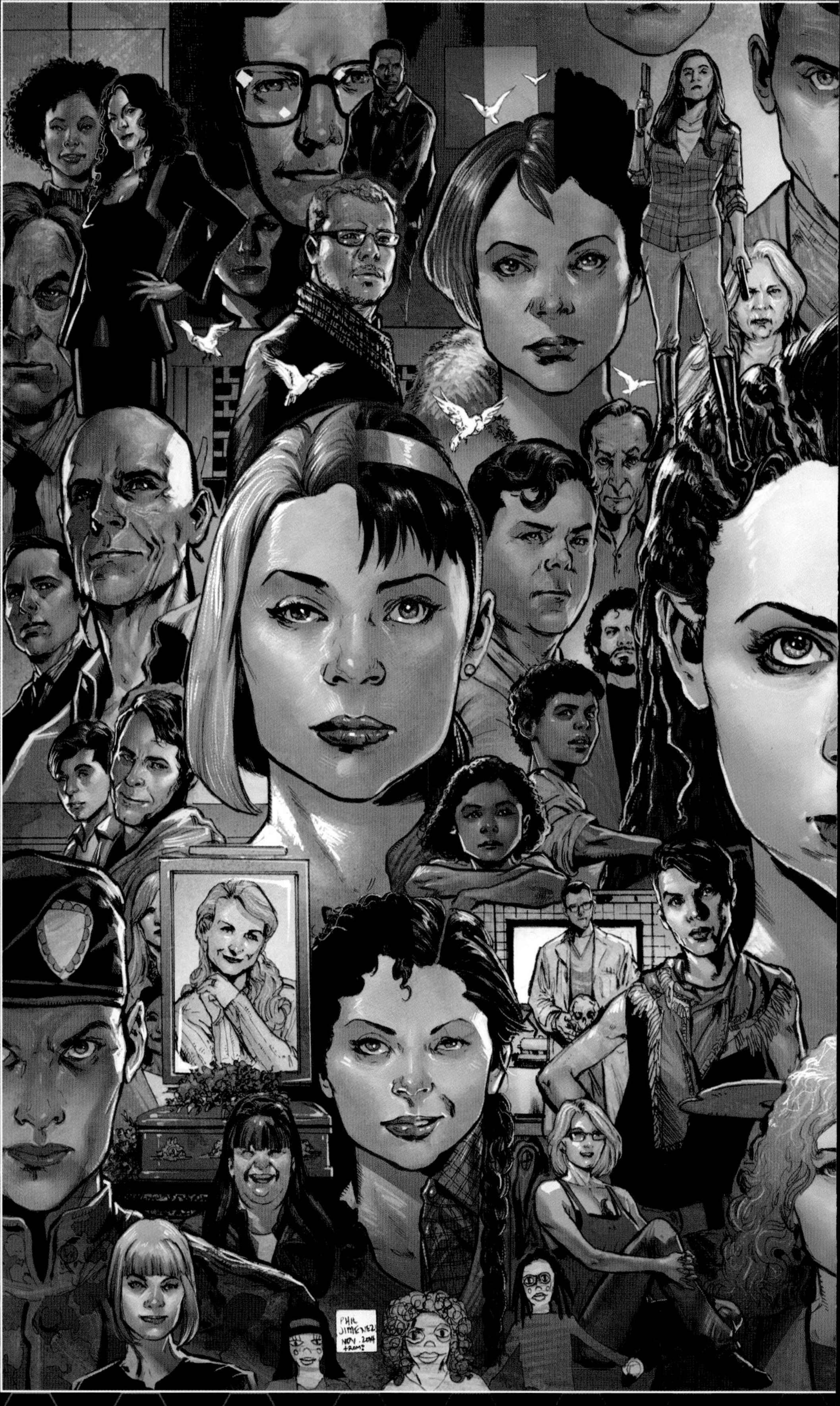
PHIL JIMENEZ

BY **PHIL JIMENEZ** COLORS BY **ROMULO FAJARDO JR.**

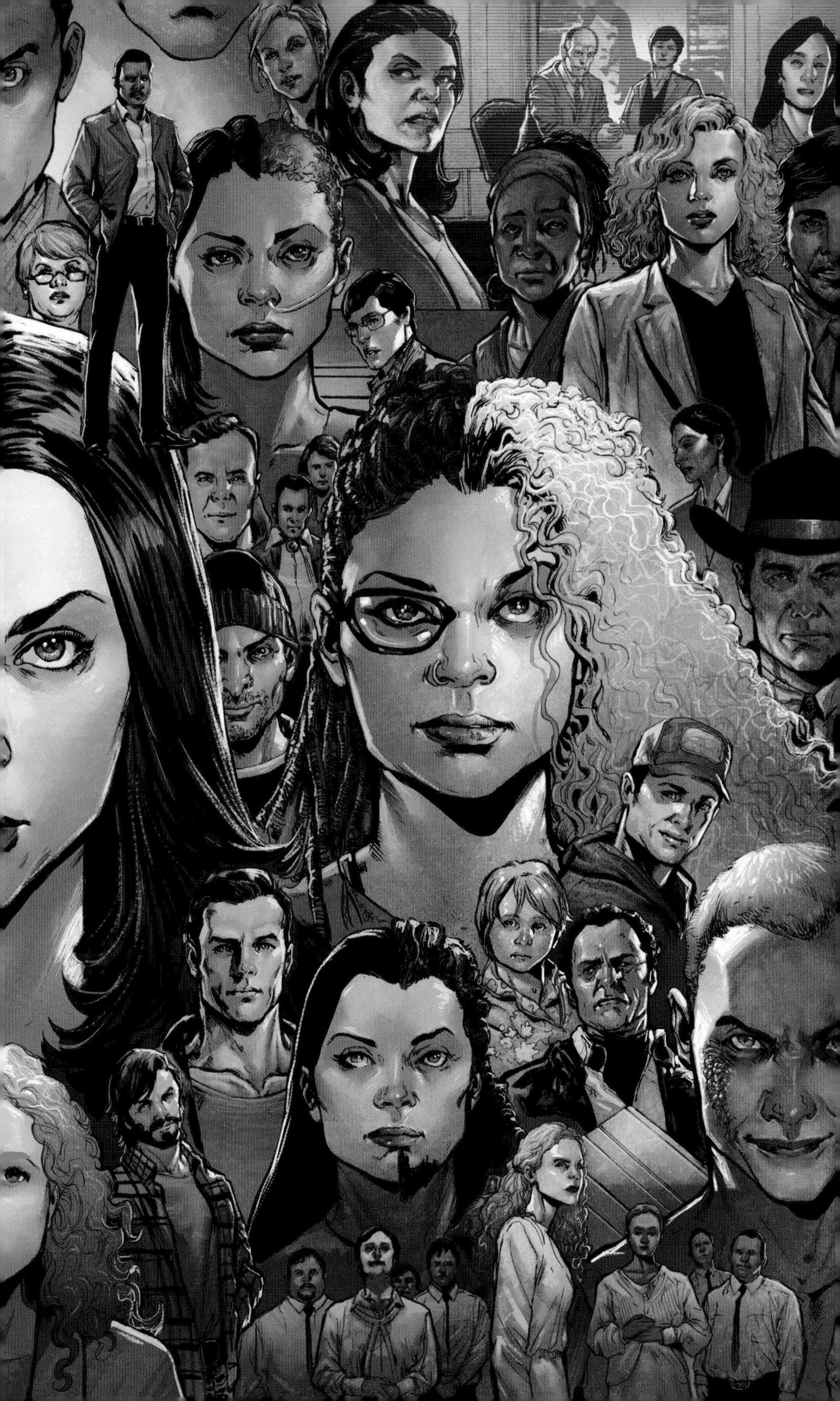

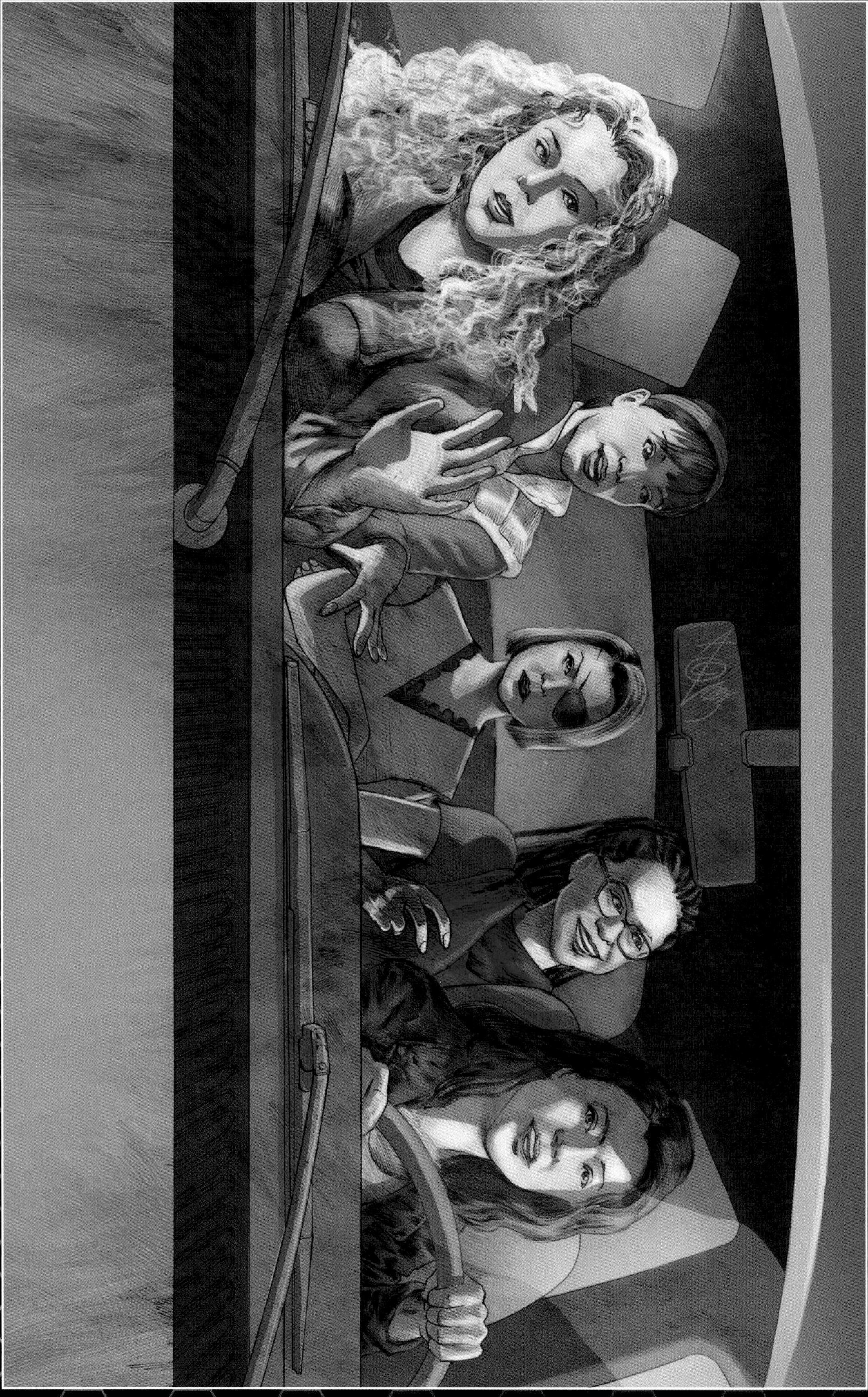

BY **ALAN QUAH**

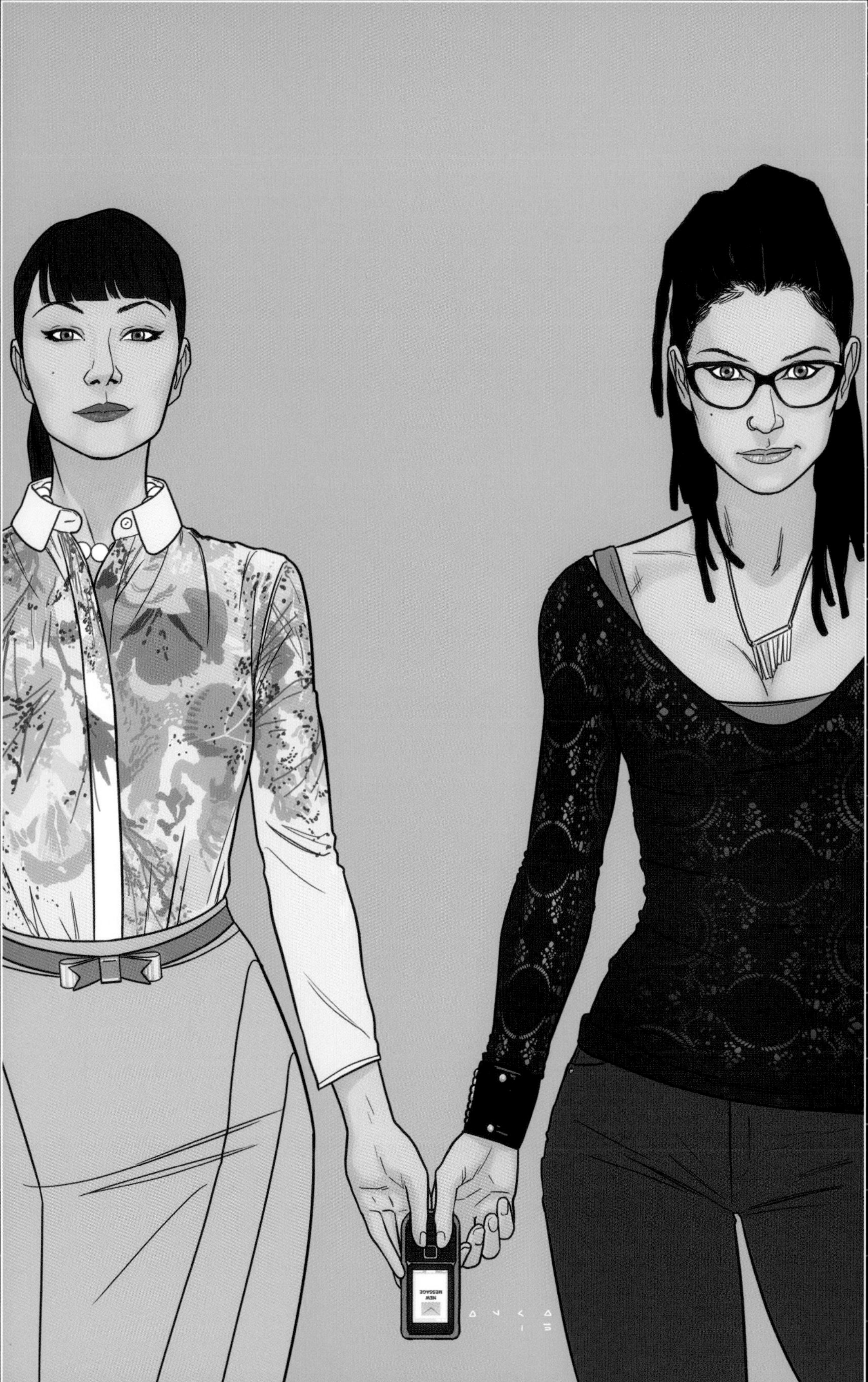
NEW MESSAGE

BY **KRIS ANKA**

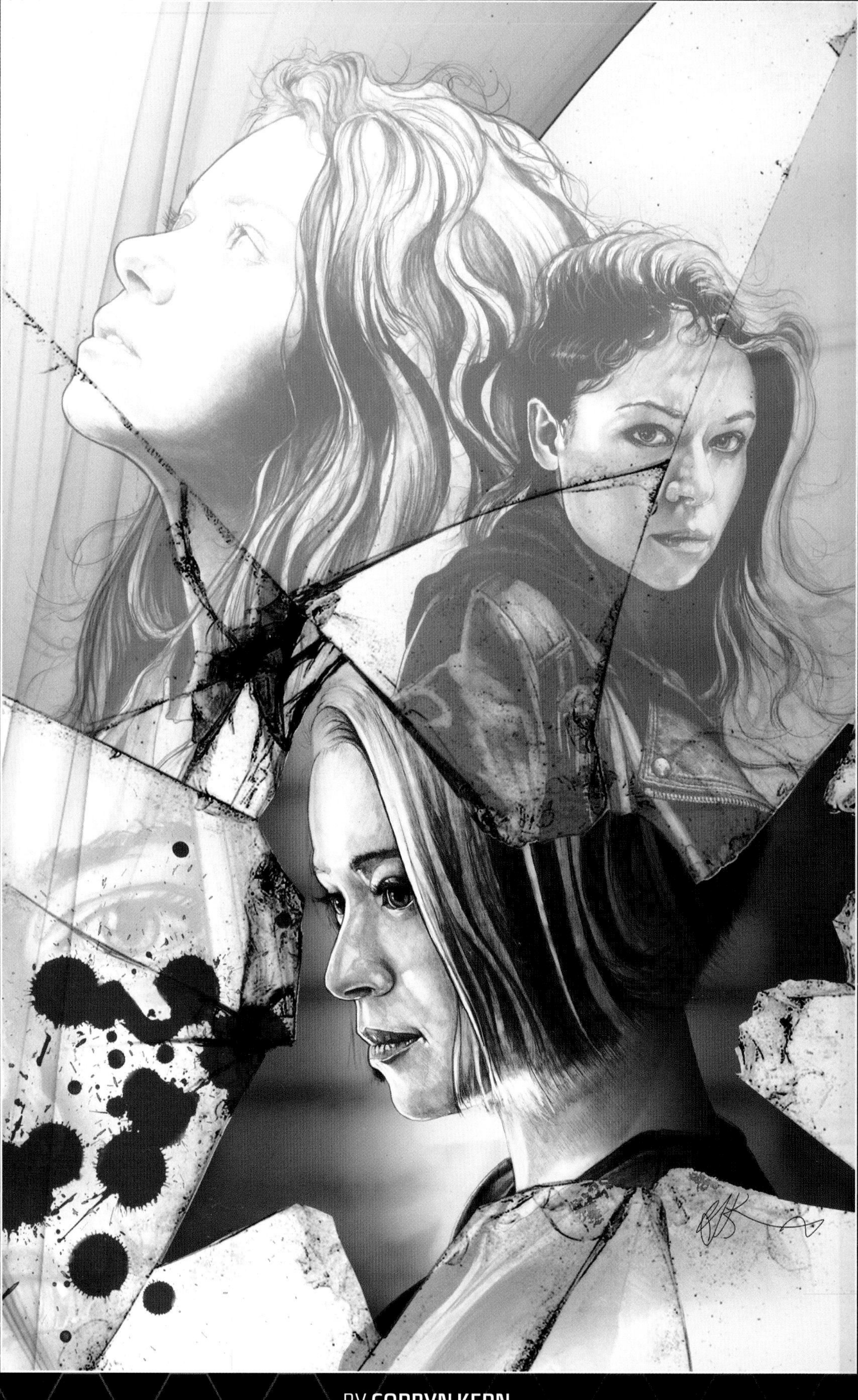

BY CORBYN KERN